THE MAKING OF JOHN LEDYARD

EDWARD G. GRAY

The Making of John Ledyard

EMPIRE AND AMBITION IN THE LIFE OF AN
EARLY AMERICAN TRAVELER

YALE UNIVERSITY PRESS   NEW HAVEN & LONDON

Published with assistance from the Louis Stern Memorial Fund and the
Annie Burr Lewis Fund.

Set in Scala and Scala Sans by Duke & Company, Devon, Pennsylvania.
Printed in the United States of America by Sheridan Books, Ann Arbor, Michigan.

Library of Congress Cataloging-in-Publication Data

Gray, Edward G., 1964–
The making of John Ledyard : empire and ambition in the life of an early American traveler /
Edward G. Gray.
   p.   cm.
Includes bibliographical references and index.
ISBN 978-0-300-11055-5 (alk. paper)

1. Ledyard, John, 1751–1789. 2. Explorers—United States—Biography. 3. Travelers—United States
—Biography. 4. Ledyard, John, 1751–1789—Travel. 5. Ledyard, John, 1751–1789—Friends and
associates. 6. Voyages and travels—History—18th century. 7. United States—Description
and travel. 8. Oceania—Description and travel. 9. Russia—Description and travel. I. Title.
G226.L5G73 2007
910.92—dc22
[B]

                                 2006033476

A catalogue record for this book is available from the British Library.
The paper in this book meets the guidelines for permanence and durability of the Committee
on Production Guidelines for Book Longevity of the Council on Library Resources.

10 9 8 7 6 5 4 3 2 1

For Stacey

It is true, that of all the animals from the polypus to man, the latter is the most happy and the most wretched, dancing through life between these two extremes, he sticks his head among the stars, or his nose in the earth, or suspended by a cobweb in some middle altitude he hangs like a being indigenous to no sphere or unfit for any.

—John Ledyard, *A Journal of Captain Cook's Last Voyage to the Pacific Ocean* (1783)

CONTENTS

ACKNOWLEDGMENTS

THIS BOOK has been a long time in the making and has left me with many scholarly and personal debts. I would first like to acknowledge the institutions that have supported the research and writing. The Huntington Library granted me a Mellon Post-Doctoral Fellowship for the 1998–99 school year that allowed me to begin the project. From that time on, the Florida State University Department of History and the College of Arts and Sciences have provided essential assistance in the form of travel funds and flexible teaching schedules. I would especially like to thank Neil Jumonville, chair of the history department, for his unflagging support and for his enthusiasm for this project. Without Neil's advocacy, the long gestation of this book would have been even longer. Finally, I am grateful to the National Endowment for the Humanities for a Fellowship for University Teachers that allowed me to spend the 2004–05 academic year completing a draft of the book.

Everyone I know (and some I do not) has endured my many and ever-shifting justifications for this project. What they all knew, and what it has taken me some time to recognize, was that a life as extraordinary as John Ledyard's was justification enough. I am especially grateful, on this score, to my F.S.U. colleagues Matt Childs, Mark Cooper, Fritz Davis, Max Friedman, Sally Hadden, Robinson Herrera, Darrin M. McMahon, Joe Richardson, and C. Peter Ripley. When I first began thinking about writing a book on John Ledyard, I received much-needed encouragement from Tom Chaffin, Helen Deutsch, Michael Meranze, Nancy Shoemaker, Tom Slaughter, and Robert Stanton.

For their insightful comments on conference papers and other fragments out of which the book grew, I am grateful to John Brooke, Eric Hinderaker, and Micheal Zuckerman. Eric and Michael, in particular, helped me see the relevance of empire to the story I wanted to tell.

For help with numerous queries and for her assistance when I worked in the Rauner Special Collections Library at Dartmouth College (the principal repository of Ledyard materials), I am grateful to Sarah I. Hartwell. I would also like to thank Kevin McBride, director of research at the Mashantucket Pequot Museum, for answering my questions about dugout canoes. Ann Plane, Dan Smith, and Nina Dayton also very generously answered my obscure queries, and David Byers and Lee Willis took time away from their graduate studies to help me with my research.

I am grateful to the *Journal of the Early Republic* and the University of Pennsylvania Press for permission to reprint portions of my article "Visions of Another Empire: John Ledyard, an American Traveler Across the Russian Empire, 1787–1788," which appeared in *JER* 24:3 (Fall 2004). Portions of the introduction and chapter 4 appeared in *Common-place* 5:2 (January 2005), the interactive journal of early American life, and I am grateful for permission to reproduce that material. The Southold Free Library, Southold, New York; the Rauner Special Collections Library at Dartmouth College; the Houghton Library at Harvard University; the Boston Public Library; the Massachusetts Historical Society; and the New-York Historical Society have all generously allowed me to quote from manuscript materials in their collections.

At Yale University Press, Lara Heimert had enough confidence in me and in John Ledyard to acquire the book. Christopher Rogers, who joined the press just as I completed the first draft, has provided useful editorial guidance, and Ellie Goldberg helpfully shepherded the project through the review and publication process. I also thank Lawrence Kenney, whose expert copyediting has significantly improved the manuscript. The press employed four anonymous reviewers at various stages. All provided immensely helpful criticism, much of which I have tried to address.

Finally, several people read the entire manuscript at a very late stage and offered valuable comments. My mother, Sue Gray, and my friend

James P. Jones assured me that the project was worth the effort and not as far from completion as I thought. Jane Kamensky read the manuscript at an especially sensitive moment and offered a careful and close reading. Insofar as there is any literary grace in this text, it is owing to her superb editorial eye and her example as writer, historian, colleague, and friend. I am deeply in her debt. I also thank Eric Hinderaker, who took time from his busy schedule as a department chair to read and comment on the manuscript.

My children, Tobias and Sophie, have heard much about their father's book and allowed me to rush off to the computer in between piano lessons and backhoe-drawing sessions. For that I thank them. The book is dedicated to the person more deserving of my gratitude than any other. She endured all the ups and downs with me, never wavering in her support and love. It took an act of perseverance worthy of John Ledyard to endure a husband's years of equivocation, self-pity, and self-doubt as he struggled with his latest hobbyhorse. Thank you, Stacey.

A NOTE ON QUOTATIONS

This book relies heavily on the words of John Ledyard, but Ledyard was not a consistent speller, and since the writings of his we do have are mostly transcriptions there is often no way to know what is Ledyard's spelling and what is somebody else's. To simplify matters, and to make the book easier to read, I have thus elected to modernize spelling and punctuation where doing so does not alter meaning.

Introduction

JOHN LEDYARD was ill and haggard. His normally erect frame was bent, making him look much older than he was. On his hands was a series of closely placed reddish brown dots (*tatau*, or "tattoo," as Captain James Cook transcribed the Tahitian word) that resembled a tailor's pattern for cutting fabric. Ledyard had acquired these while sailing with Cook in the South Pacific. He carried a heavy overcoat, boots, and socks made from reindeer hide; a fur cap; and a pair of foxskin gloves lined with rabbit fur. He was penniless, expecting, as he had for most of his days, that friends and acquaintances would provide the essentials of life. Aside from his clothing, his only valuable possession was a travel diary he had kept during the two-year journey he had just completed.

That journey had taken him overland from London to the Far Eastern Russian city of Yakutsk and then back to London—more than ten thousand miles in total. It was a journey Ledyard undertook alone, intending to survive through sheer determination and the goodwill of strangers. It was also an incomplete journey. Ledyard had planned to travel across Europe, Russia, Siberia, and the Russian Far East to the Pacific Ocean and from there to reach the North American continent. He had hoped to then become the first man to traverse the continent, traveling from west to east alone and on foot and relying on his limited knowledge of American Indian languages and customs for his survival. He would collect scientific readings not with instruments and notebooks but with a crudely fashioned sundial and a pointed, stained stick—using the stick to tattoo on his body the coordinates of important landmarks.

Sadly—or perhaps fortunately given the obvious physical peril of such a voyage—the trip was cut short. Suspicious of this foreigner's motives, Russian authorities expelled Ledyard from their dominions before he reached the Pacific Ocean. His return to London in the spring of 1788 was nonetheless a happy occasion. The thirty-seven-year-old American traveler was greeted with news that a group of prominent British gentlemen had formed the Association for Promoting the Discovery of the Interior Parts of Africa. And the association was pleased to employ Ledyard to journey to the headwaters of the Niger River. The traveler would be paid a modest stipend and, if successful, would achieve the kind of celebrity he craved. He would also, he assured his patrons, return to the America in which he was born and attempt once again to traverse its great expanse. "He promises me," wrote Thomas Jefferson, then the American minister to France, "if he escapes through this journey, he will go to Kentucky and endeavour to penetrate Westwardly from thence to the South sea."[1]

He was unable to keep his promise.

A misdiagnosed stomach ailment took him before he ever made it to inner Africa. The honor of making that journey would go to the great Scottish explorer Mungo Park. And the honor of crossing the North American continent would go not to a lone traveler banking on native wit, but to Alexander Mackenzie, the Scottish-born fur trader who led a small party of Indian guides and French Canadian trappers to Canada's Pacific coast in 1793.

This book tells John Ledyard's story. At the center of that story lies the ambition of the man himself. Through a long series of failures—he failed to graduate from Dartmouth College, he failed in bids to enter the Connecticut bar and the Congregational clergy, he failed in business, and his most ambitious journeys ended in failure—Ledyard nonetheless persevered, driven by a burning determination to achieve fame. That determination was not unique to John Ledyard. His generation of Americans, the founding generation, was one consumed with the quest for fame. But in Ledyard's life the quest takes on a distinct shape. Unlike John Adams, Alexander Hamilton, George Washington, and other familiar figures of his age, Ledyard obtained none of the formal distinctions a white man in early America could count on to get ahead—wealth, a college degree, a ministerial post, an officer's commission, or government office. Even as the author of the first book copyrighted in the United States—his account of Cook's final voyage, published in 1783—Ledyard's fortunes improved only slightly. And yet, after his death in 1789, he would come to be among his nation's best-known sons. In part, this was a matter of timing.[2]

The fluid, chaotic 1790s saw Americans struggling to define a new republican greatness. They had their models in the mythic Roman hero Cincinnatus or his modern alter ego, Washington. But in the bitterly partisan public life of the young nation, few escaped the ferocious attacks that lurked in every newspaper and anonymous pamphlet. The architects of the Revolution—Thomas Paine, Jefferson, John Adams, and even Benjamin Franklin—had armies of detractors.

So far as we know, Ledyard had none. To be sure, he has little claim to the importance of the Founders. He signed no important declarations; he drafted no important legal documents; and he had no role in any major military activity. But Ledyard's absence from the major political events of his age helps to explain how it was that he became so well known. He died before the spirit of party enveloped American life, and he spent most of his adulthood abroad, beyond the gaze of equally ambitious, striving competitors. That he spent most of the Revolutionary War years on a widely celebrated voyage of scientific discovery further freed him from the venomous judgments that haunted so many Americans—Loyalist and Patriot—in the immediate aftermath of the Revolution. Ledyard never fought against his neighbors or engaged in any acts of partisan denunciation. His reputation rested on the disinterested pursuit of geographic and philosophical knowledge.

These facts explain Ledyard's posthumous fame. But during his short life he also came to be well known. This was not simply because of his exotic travels, although those did capture the attention of admirers and patrons. It was also the result of his understanding of the fundamental social fact of his age: being somebody in late eighteenth-century America meant being somebody known to the right kind of people. It meant, that is, being admired by the famous and the powerful, people who could help a striving young man make something of himself. Such thinking came to be a kind of religious creed for Ledyard. "It is the good and great I look to," he explained to the British sponsors of his African journey, a group that included prominent politicians and academics. "Fame from them bestowed . . . is closely allied to a well done from God."[3] That Ledyard endured brutal discomfort and much personal peril, only to die an early death, was a testament to just how seriously he took this creed.

Ledyard was also well aware that simple experience in faraway places would never earn him the kind of fame he craved. That is, he was well aware that simply having been to Siberia or Alaska or North Africa would do little for his reputation. The world he lived in was full of people who had been to distant lands as colonists, merchants, servants, slaves, seamen, and so on. What would set Ledyard apart was his capacity to translate that experience into a language familiar to those he sought to impress. As the operative verb here implies, this ability was partly linguistic. Ledyard's use of language was essential to his capacity to lure patrons as powerful and admired as Jefferson and the British naturalist Joseph Banks. Conversation is a difficult thing for historians to recover, but judging from the way others responded to him, Ledyard had a gift for this particular art. Whether aboard the *Resolution* with Cook, in postrevolutionary Philadelphia, or in Jefferson's Paris, Ledyard found his way into the conversations of the elite and the powerful. Language in its written form also has a central place in this story. Ledyard had fully assimilated the relatively modern idea that writing and print lent experience authority. That is, he had fully assimilated one of the central organizing principles of the eighteenth-century republic of letters: information communicated through prose or print—as opposed to some sort of oral performance such as a sermon— was ultimately the most authoritative kind of information. The journals he kept while sailing with Cook and traveling across Siberia reflected this. Ledyard was fully aware that his conversational gifts would inadequately translate experience into factual knowledge. This seems like an obvious point in our own age, when authoritative scientific knowledge generally appears solely in print. But in Ledyard's time the practices of scientific data collection were in their infancy, and the methods of recovering and preserving data from journeys of scientific exploration were even more immature. The central instruments in this process were pen, paper, and a human data collector. Captain Cook, for example, may have been the greatest collector of scientific data of his age. But aside from his skills as a chart maker and navigator, he had no special preparation for assembling

observations on flora, fauna, minerals, peoples, and so on. And yet he
was expected to do so. What gave the data generated by these untrained
scientific observers the authority they had—and that authority was still far
from unquestioned—was its written form. Ledyard's principal writings,
the travel journals he produced, reflect his deference to this imperative.

Ledyard deployed other, less literal languages as well. Most important
among these was the language of clothing. On those occasions when he
did have money he almost always spent it on fine clothing. He recognized
that his access to prominent gentlemen would depend on the perception
that he was a man of refinement and good breeding as much as a man
who had traveled in distant lands. At the same time, on the eve of the
American Revolution, Ledyard was happy to display his contempt for the
luxuries sacrificed in the colonists' rejection of the British Empire by don-
ning simple, homespun garments. In a sense, though, this gesture had the
same function as the acquisition of expensive clothes. It defined Ledyard as
a freeborn, independent gentleman, familiar with the most sophisticated
thinking of the day and fully suited to the company of similar beings.[4]

Running through the story of Ledyard's quest for fame is the story of his
relationship to the defining institution of his age, the British Empire.
In almost every way possible, Ledyard's life was intertwined with this
ubiquitous entity. He was born in the British colony of Connecticut. His
family was dependent on the British West Indies trade. His working life
began aboard a merchant vessel plying the British Atlantic triangle trade.
And his career as traveler and explorer was inseparable from the British
pursuit of empire. Captain Cook's third Pacific expedition would never
have happened had the Admiralty (the agency charged with protecting
Britain's oceanic trade and overseeing all naval expeditions) not sought
easier routes to the rich Pacific basin. And Ledyard's final two undertak-
ings—the attempted crossing of North America and the journey to Africa—
depended partly on the patronage of Britons whose imperial vision was
refracted through the benevolent pursuit of scientific facts.

Ledyard's relation to empire went beyond formal connections to an
actual imperial entity. For him, empire was also a set of attitudes, a frame
of mind, an aesthetic, and a way of relating to distant, foreign worlds.
In his very appearance, Ledyard embodied the cultural back and forth
that defined the early modern imperial enterprise. His body and attire

reflected his travels, but they also reflected his deep aspirations in the Euro-American world to which he always returned. Whenever he could, he used his exotic experience to social advantage, gaining access to elites in Europe and America, elites who defined themselves in part by the sort of armchair cosmopolitanism that came with entertaining a gentleman who had traveled in little-known reaches of the globe. In this sense, empire was for Ledyard quite literally costume. It provided a crucial social currency for a striving eighteenth-century man.[5]

Empire also afforded Ledyard the frame through which he viewed the various peoples and places he went. He could speak with great eloquence about the power and dignity of Tongan chiefs and Maori warriors, for example, but what he said was always inflected with a colonizer's sense of superiority. Ledyard never identified with the people whose clothing he wore or whose languages he studied. He related to them as his social superiors related to him: with a patronizing air of superiority. These were peoples whom he could assist and even admire, but they were in no way his equals. Similarly, when Ledyard gazed upon new landscapes, he could appreciate the distinctive beauty of what he saw. But at the same time, what he saw was often the potential fruit of conquest: the abundant fur-bearing animals of the Pacific Northwest or the amazing nutritive properties of Hawaii's breadfruit trees. When such commodities appeared to be lacking—on Russia's eastern frontier, for instance—he found little about the lands he explored worthy of praise. Distant territories, he clearly believed, were of value for what they could yield to Europeans such as himself.

These beliefs were of more than philosophical significance for Ledyard. They also justified for him a distinct colonial project of his own. Although he is best known as a lone traveler, his solo travels consumed only the last two years of his life. Prior to this, he had spent five years attempting to capitalize on his years as a marine corporal aboard the *Resolution*. While sailing with Cook, he had been astonished by the potential profits of the northwest coast fur trade. Upon returning to the new United States in 1783, he thus embarked on an ambitious project to establish the first trading post in the region. Like so much in Ledyard's life, this scheme ended in failure. But it demonstrates that more than being just a product of empire, John Ledyard struggled to be an agent in empire's growth.

In Ledyard's lifetime, empire as he knew it grew anachronistic and, indeed, was directly attacked by his revolutionary countrymen. But in most of the places Ledyard lived and traveled the rumble of revolution was faint. At times, he eagerly identified himself as a citizen of the new United States and used that putative status in conjunction with his exotic experiences to gain access to European elites. But that identification, it turns out, had little real meaning for Ledyard. He advocated elements of revolutionary ideology—especially its hostility to the staid, corrupt institutions of old Europe and its faith in reason and in the universality of human nature. But he was never a revolutionary. His destiny, as he came to understand it, was too dependent on that old hierarchical, paternalistic way of thinking, unapologetic in its elitism and energized by a prevailing assumption that what was good for a select few, what extended the control and dominance of the wealthiest, most politically connected, was good for all, whether the colonized peoples of the South Pacific or the ordinary seamen who sailed Captain Cook's ships. Although the American revolutionaries attacked this older vision of empire—either in their hostility to the rhetorical condescension implied in the colony–mother country relationship or in their rejection of the political institutions that sustained that relationship—they did not, of course, destroy it. For momentum is a powerful force in history, and at the time of Ledyard's death in early 1789 he still lived in a world dominated by old empire. To understand Ledyard, then, is not to understand him as an apostle of some kind of new revolutionary order. Rather, it is to understand him as a man thoroughly bound to an old imperial order, albeit one at the beginning of its end.

John Ledyard's story is not an easy one to tell. Compared to other, more famous figures from the founding era, he left only a slight imprint on the historical record. His remaining personal correspondence totals a few dozen letters, and his travel journals offer little about his personal experiences.

By gathering testimony about Ledyard from relatives and acquaintances, his first biographer, the nineteenth-century historian and editor Jared Sparks, filled many of the gaps left by Ledyard himself. Subsequent scholars have further illuminated the traveler's life. Sinclair H. Hitchings, former keeper of prints at the Boston Public Library, for example, wrote a carefully researched introduction to Ledyard's *Journal of Captain Cook's Last Voyage to the Pacific Ocean* for an edition published in 1963. Three years later, Stephen D. Watrous, now emeritus professor of history at Sonoma State University, published an edition of the journals and correspondence from Ledyard's travels across the Russian Empire. Watrous's book offers a comprehensive view of Ledyard during a crucial period of his life. Several other modern biographies of Ledyard build on Sparks's work.[6] But there remain substantial gaps in Ledyard's story. There is little, for example, about the period from his birth to his eleventh year, the year in which his father died. The same is true of important later periods of his life, such as his three-month foray into Indian country during his time at Dartmouth College.

These gaps (as well as my particular interpretation of Ledyard) account for the somewhat unorthodox structure of this book. Like most biographies, it follows the chronology of its subject's life. But at points its narrative shifts from a tale of Ledyard's life to an analysis of a specific aspect of his thought or behavior. The longest of these shifts appear in chapters 4 and 9. The first deals with the place of journal keeping aboard British naval vessels, a matter that turns out to have been crucial both to Ledyard's personal ambition and to the greater politics of empire. The second discusses the ways Ledyard reconciled the moral failings of the Russian Empire with his own more hopeful vision of empire. Insofar as Ledyard came to embody the republican values of his revolutionary countrymen, it was a result of this struggle.

CHAPTER I

A Colonial Childhood

JOHN LEDYARD was born in the small port town of Groton in the British colony of Connecticut in the year 1751. It was a happy year in the history of the colony. No major frontier conflict or colonial war raged; the bitter controversy surrounding the Great Awakening, that evangelical surge of the late 1730s and early 1740s, had passed; and the economic and emotional disruptions brought by the French and Indian War were still several years away. This was a happy year for the Ledyard family as well. Aside from witnessing the birth of John, likely heir to the family estate, it saw his parents, Captain John and Abigail Ledyard, enter the path toward prominence and security in this world and the next. The day of their son's baptism at Groton's First Church, Captain John and Abigail formally confessed their own faith in Christ, a gesture that secured for them and their son the spiritual and worldly benefits of membership in the town's oldest church. And finally, it was a year in which the family patriarch, Squire John Ledyard, continued to enjoy the financial benefits of membership in the Connecticut colonial establishment. In the year of his birth, life looked very promising indeed for the youngest John Ledyard.

The events leading up to Ledyard's birth were not quite so promising or happy. His parents had married a little over a year before John was born. This would be unremarkable were it not for the fact that they were first cousins. Elsewhere in the English-speaking world, the desire to keep property in the family fostered a permissive attitude about this sort of intermarriage, but in New England it remained a point of controversy.[1] The Boston jurist and diarist Samuel Sewall had condemned it as a gross violation of the law, whatever its perceived benefits to the family. So opposed had he been that he was willing to endure the opprobrium of his neighbors for refusing to attend the wedding of a "Col. Shrimpton . . . to his wive's sister's daughter, Elisabeth Richardson."[2] It appears that Abigail's parents felt similarly. Her grandfather, the New London farmer and diarist Joshua Hempstead, noted in his diary that Abigail eloped with Captain John "because her parents refused to give her to him to wife." The marriage not only contradicted the wishes of Abigail's parents. It was also contrary to the law. According to Hempstead, the young couple "got a liscense of Doctor Mawason who had Blanks [to dispose of] from the Govr." The couple had obtained a fraudulent marriage license.[3]

It is possible that Abigail's parents had reasons for their disapproval beyond simply the couple's familial ties. Perhaps there was something about Captain John himself, about his character or personality. He may have been a drunkard or simply impious. Or perhaps they were suspicious of the whole Ledyard clan. Relative to Abigail's maternal lineage, the Ledyards were newcomers to the colonies. Their patriarch, Squire John, had arrived from England in 1717, while the patriarch of Abigail's mother's family, the Reverend John Youngs, had established the first English town on Long Island in 1640.[4] Similarly, the Youngs were a family of landowners and farmers; the Ledyards were merchants, sea captains, and lawyers. Perhaps these differences had played themselves out in the marriage of Abigail's aunt, Deborah Youngs. Her husband, Squire John, may simply have been too consumed with his business dealings to make a good spouse, and this may have contributed to Deborah's death several years before her niece married her son. Or perhaps it was a combination of these factors that accounts for the family's disapproval. In any case, the young couple was defiant. In Groton Township, far from Abigail's Long Island family, the newest Ledyards would be welcomed. Squire John would rent the young family a house with some land and a small shop near the town center. There, they would cultivate a small garden and perhaps raise a pig or two. The family's livelihood, however, would come not from this property, but from the sea.[5]

Groton was one of many small commercial hubs, from Portsmouth and Salem in the North to Charleston and Savannah in the South, which dotted the eastern seaboard. Situated on the northern banks of the Thames River and surrounded by steep hills and granite-pocked terrain, the town offered its residents few economic options that did not in some way tie them to the sea.

In Captain John's case, this meant plying the coastwise West Indies trade. That trade carried livestock, horses, timber, dried fish, beef, and other goods south to Barbados, Santo Domingo, St. Kitts, Guadeloupe, Martinique, and other islands and returned to New England with sugar and molasses, the lifeblood of the local rum industry. The West Indies trade linked the fortunes of farmers and distillers in rural Connecticut to those of sugar planters in Jamaica, Barbados, and other Caribbean islands. But for Captain John, the more important links were those connecting him to that community of merchants around the Atlantic littoral whose trading ties constituted the backbone of the British Empire. It was through them that credit flowed to small, provincial towns such as Groton, and it was their political influence in London that kept the British government busy protecting the Atlantic trade.

The coastal trade would never make Captain John wealthy, at least not in comparison to the wealthiest merchants of New England. Lacking a major deepwater port, Connecticut could not accommodate the large-tonnage vessels that plied the most lucrative trade routes in the empire, those between the colonies and Britain and between the colonies and the slave trade centers of West Africa. For the same reason, the colony never attracted the wealthiest, most ambitious merchants and their agents, suppliers of the capital that sustained large-scale seaborne trade. Having limited access to large reserves of credit and capital, merchants and sea captains in Groton and New London and New Haven had few options beyond the much less capital intensive West Indies trade.[6]

Under the best of circumstances, this coastwise trade could bring modest income, perhaps enough to elevate Captain John to the exclusive ranks of the men who, like Squire John, governed the colony. But the risks were enormous. Indeed, less than two years after the birth of his first son, Captain John suffered a devastating loss. Heading south to the West Indies, his ship encountered a violent storm that thrashed rigging and sails and carried away seventeen horses, forty sheep, and assorted other cargo.[7]

In 1757, Captain John suffered another catastrophe. During a south-bound voyage, his ship (perhaps hopefully named), *Greyhound,* was captured by French privateers, who refitted it for raids against British shipping. Leaving his ship behind, Captain Ledyard was able to make his way from French-controlled Martinique to the British island of Antigua. There he was eventually able to recover the vessel. But his losses were immense: in addition to cargo, time, and repair costs, they included substantial fees paid to the British naval officers who helped recover the ship.[8]

These costs would have been difficult to bear under any circumstances, but the financial underpinnings of Captain John's business compounded the problem. Credit from local merchants, farmers, and probably his father allowed him to acquire export cargo; credit allowed him to obtain whatever ownership interest he might have had in the *Greyhound;* and in the event that price fluctuations made it difficult for him to cover the cost of a voyage credit would allow him to sail again. If the price for molasses or sugar was favorable upon his return to New England, a merchant could cover his various debts and even make a modest profit. Over time, enough such voyages could elevate a sea captain from debtor to creditor. But if the tides turned in the other direction, as they did for Captain John, losses could lead to insolvency and even debtor's prison. Captain John never descended to such depths. His family name was enough to reassure creditors. But he did not prosper. For his wife and children, this made life quite precarious. Were Captain John to suffer the fate of so many eighteenth-century seafarers and not return home, they would be left to manage his debts.

This prospect became reality in 1762, eleven years after the birth of John, the future traveler, when not a storm but smallpox took Captain John's life as he sailed toward the Caribbean. Upon her husband's death, Abigail placed his estate before a court of probate. This committee of prominent local men would determine who received what of the sea captain's modest assets. Fortunately for Abigail and her children, Connecticut law was relatively benevolent when it came to probate proceedings. The general practice in the colony was to grant widows one-third of the estate, with any real estate (land and buildings) normally held in trust for the deceased's male heirs. Since Captain John owned no real estate, Abigail mainly acquired household goods such as furniture, linens, tools, cooking utensils, dishware, clothing, and possibly livestock. Her portion of the estate was worth roughly forty-five pounds sterling, a substantial sum, but not enough to sustain the family, which now included John Ledyard's three younger siblings, Thomas, George, and Fanny. To help compensate for her loss, Abigail returned with her children to her hometown of Southold. There she would be the daughter of one of the first families of English Long Island rather than the widow of a modest Connecticut sea captain.[9] Soon after, Abigail married the physician and widower Dr. Micah Moore, and the couple quickly began adding to their family. John's half-sister Abigail was born in 1765; Julia in 1767; and Phoebe in 1769.

Young John would not, however, be around to watch his siblings grow, for he had undertaken his first great journey. Shortly after Captain John's death, Abigail sent her eldest son to live with Squire John in Hartford. Ledyard would spend the better part of a decade in this provincial capital founded by dissident Puritans in 1636.

Hartford's persistence into the middle of the eighteenth century was owing largely to the Connecticut River, an artery that gave the town's small merchant community access to timber, furs, and grain, all produced in the New England hinterland. By the time young John arrived there, Hartford had evolved into a major commercial center, but it was still a frontier town with all the hazards of life on the far periphery of European settlement. The town's local newspaper, the *Connecticut Courant,* was filled with reports of floods, lightning strikes, epidemics, and stray wildlife. Not long after John moved to Hartford, the paper reported that "a large He Bear was discovered in an inclosure, opposite the Treasurer's, and being pursued he took to the Main Street, which he kept till he got to the Lane that turns Eastward, by the South Meeting (notwithstanding his being pelted from every side of the Street, with Stones, Clubs, & C) and was followed into the South Meadow, where he was shot. . . . In the Evening, he was roasted whole, and a large Company sup'd on him."[10]

Far more worrisome for Hartford's residents was the dim, dark welter of conspirators who seemed to loom beyond the town's horizons. For most of its life, Hartford had existed in a perpetual state of fear, gazing North and West to hinterlands populated by hostile native peoples and perfidious French Catholics. The latter proved an unending source of anxiety, even after the peace of 1763 that ended the French and Indian War and transformed New France into the British province of Quebec. British victory simply meant that the British Empire in the American northeast would no longer be a Protestant empire. For New Englanders, there was little comfort in the knowledge that America's French Catholics were now British subjects. It was as if Bonnie Prince Charlie, the long-defeated Catholic pretender to the British throne, continued pursuing his designs from the contested American backcountry. The constant fear of such conspiring forces gave fear mongers and character assassins fertile ground. Hence, in late 1764, when a Mr. S—— arrived in the colony and began attacking the theology of the colony's established church, was it not likely, an anonymous newspaper *Querist* asked, "that he may be an Emissary of the Church of Rome?" Indeed, referring to the itinerant preachers who were constantly passing through the colony, the writer wondered whether "the importing of foreign strange Preachers among us . . . will not soon open a Door wide enough for Admission of some of those Holy Fathers of the Romish Church who compass Sea and Land to make Proselytes?" Given the anxiety Catholicism produced, it is perhaps not surprising that editors of the Hartford paper thought it newsworthy when one Rev. Mr. Vessiere, a former Recollet missionary residing in Quebec "declared himself a Protestant, took the usual Oaths of Allegiance to the King [of England] . . . and subscribed the Declaration against Popery."[11]

For all the hazards of life in this small provincial town, Hartford was the best place on earth for young John Ledyard. There he would be the namesake of one of the town's leading men.

From the day Squire John arrived in the colonies until his death in 1771, he deliberately and shrewdly climbed the colonial social ladder. From an obscure Latin tutor and petty merchant, he rose to become one of Connecticut's most prominent politicians, magistrates, and businessmen. By 1753, he had been elected representative to the colonial assembly from Hartford and continued in that position until 1761. He also served as a justice of the peace in Hartford County from 1754 until his death. During the tumultuous years of the French and Indian War, the colony's governor appointed him to a variety of offices charged with overseeing colonial defense and wartime finances.

In a fashion typical of officeholders in the American colonial government, Squire John parlayed his political and legal power into financial gain. Some of that gain was direct, above-the-board remuneration. As justice of the peace, for instance, he would have received fees for issuing writs and other legal documents. But there were all kinds of other, less direct benefits to working for the government. In helping the colony obtain credit from merchants in New York or London, for instance, Squire John helped himself. That very same credit might be used to purchase supplies for the colonial militia, supplies that Squire John sold. Similarly, when he urged his colleagues in the colonial assembly to dredge parts of the Connecticut River, he did so fully aware that such a project would help him move timber from woodlands he owned in the northwest part of the colony to his sawmill downriver.[12]

The open mingling of political and personal capital was a fact of life in the Ledyards' world, and it could make a man rich. At his death, Squire John's estate was valued at nearly thirty-five hundred pounds, placing him among Hartford's wealthiest 10 percent and among the very wealthiest in the colony. Yet for all his wealth, there was nothing removed or distant about Squire John. He was no dissipated, detached aristocrat but a vigorous and devoted servant of the colony and its business. He was also a man of faith.[13]

Although the uncompromising Calvinism of the colony's founders had long since dissipated—to the consternation of so-called New Lights such as the great Connecticut-born theologian Jonathan Edwards—Connecticut remained a Puritan colony. The vast majority of its churchgoing population continued to worship in Congregational churches, and the colony's governing elite remained overwhelmingly members of the Congregational Church. Squire John was no exception: he was an active member of Hartford's Second Church and a close friend of its pastor, Elnathan Whitman.

That friendship allowed him to draw on Whitman's skills as an educator. Squire John's account book indicates a variety of debits paid to Whitman, including a cash payment for "instructing Johnny Ledyard." Although Hartford did have a grammar school, it appears Squire John determined his grandson would benefit from additional private tutoring—a not-unexpected decision from a man who himself had come to the colonies as a Latin tutor. For men of Squire John's stature, reading and writing Latin and Greek were almost as important as reading, writing, and speaking English. As much as clothing or pedigree, one's familiarity with classical languages was a mark of good breeding, and without it a gentlemanly adulthood, never mind admittance to Yale or the two highest professions, the ministry and the bar, would have been almost impossible.

Benjamin Franklin, whose father had withdrawn him from grammar school after only a year, was so certain of the importance of classical languages that amidst all the trials of establishing a printing business, he found the time to study Latin.[14]

In addition to helping his pupil master the cases and declensions of Latin and Greek, Whitman would have introduced young John to some of the classics in those languages, works he had been required to study during his years as a student at Yale College. Whitman would have memorized passages from Horace, Cicero, and Virgil. He would also have demonstrated some mastery of classical logic and rhetoric through "declamations," or speeches, and twice-weekly debates, often in Latin and sometimes in Greek, Hebrew, or French. All this would have left him well-prepared to tutor John in the classical arts of communication.[15]

Beyond supplementing John's formal schooling, Whitman's instruction also supplemented his extracurricular education. Indeed, few colonists were better equipped to introduce a young man to the moral code of the colony's established leaders. According to that code, things were good as they were, and right-thinking people recognized this. Reflecting this conservative ethos, in a 1745 sermon Whitman urged his congregants to repay the "fatherly affection and tender concern" expressed for them by their leaders. They could best do this through "obedience and submission to those good Rulers, to whom God is pleased to commit the government of this people."[16] In deferring to these "good Rulers," Whitman was suggesting, his congregants affirmed a divinely sanctioned order in which some were meant to lead and others to follow. Whitman revealed a similar conservatism in his attitude toward the itinerant evangelical preachers who began appearing in New England in the 1730s. These preachers—most famous among them, the Anglican George Whitefield—urged their listeners to forge a new and more fervent relationship with Christ. But their preaching style, particularly its reliance on vivid and emotive rhetoric in place of deep biblical exegesis, suggested to many listeners that one needed no special ministerial learning to properly grasp the essence of God's word. The message is a familiar part of modern evangelical Protestantism, but in eighteenth-century America it was new and, in the minds of some, very worrisome.

For Whitman, the crude, enthusiastic words of these new preachers drew people from reasoned and cautious Christianity to a kind of unthinking hysterical religion. "It is well known," he pronounced, that with the new evangelical furor "a strange spirit of giddiness seems to possess the minds of multitudes among us, disposing them to fall in with almost any body, that has either ignorance or confidence enough to pretend that they are immediately led by the spirit."[17] By drawing congregants away from their rightful ministry, Whitman feared, itinerant preachers sowed the seeds of disorder and chaos. Instead of firmly tying their faith to the pillar of Connecticut's established ministry, their followers would founder in a sea of confused and contradictory religious voices. It was, Whitman warned, only a matter of time before this turn from traditional ministerial authority became a turn from established political authority.

For young John Ledyard, Whitman would thus have been a source of affirmation as well as education. He would have affirmed Abigail's choice to send John to Hartford; he would have affirmed Squire John's worth as a colonial leader; and he would have affirmed the values of patience, moderation, and Christian charity that had allowed Abigail and Captain John to enter Groton's First Church. These values would stay with John through his life. The future traveler would have little patience for the satisfactions offered by charismatic preachers or irrational enthusiasms. His would be a faith in knowledge, rationality, nature's majesty, and well-placed affections.

Whitman's calm conservatism must have comforted young John during what was a very difficult adolescence. Not only had his father died, but his family would suffer a series of additional traumas. Soon after John's arrival in Hartford, Squire John began suffering from what would be a long, debilitating series of illnesses. At the same time his fortune suffered from the economic blight affecting the entire colony. In the aftermath of the French and Indian War, new British controls on the West Indian rum trade, a market flooded with surplus goods, and British creditors calling in long-overdue loans wracked the Connecticut economy. As one newspaper put it, "All our money is gone and going to England to pay out debts. . . . Our trade to the *French* and *Spanish* islands, from whence we used to get money is stopped; . . . Husbandry is discouraged, for there is no vent for provisions; Merchants and farmers are breaking, and all things going into confusion." Squire John, who had invested heavily in land, estimated that "the valuable Landed Interest of the Colony is sunk in its value more than 50 p. cent."[18]

Given these troubles, it is no wonder that when news arrived in the spring of 1766 that Parliament had repealed the hated Stamp Tax, the General Assembly declared an official Day of General Rejoicing. The tax was at least one economic insult the colony would no longer have to endure. On that felicitous day, as church bells rang, cannon boomed, and flags flew high, a group of townsmen prepared fireworks in the brick schoolhouse next to the First Church and across the road from the Flagg Tavern. But disaster struck. An accidental fire and ensuing explosion reduced the schoolhouse to a "heap of rubbish." Among the half dozen killed in the disaster was John's uncle, the twenty-six-year-old physician Nathaniel Ledyard.[19]

After such a tragedy, the Ledyard family surely had much need for the reassuring rectitude of Pastor Whitman. But by the beginning of 1767, he himself was so debilitated by illness that he could no longer stand before his congregation. To replace him, the church made the ill-advised choice of William Patten, a Harvard graduate and son-in-law of another prominent Connecticut minister, Eleazar Wheelock. Patten had a drinking problem, and after six years of embarrassing drunkenness he was relieved of his pulpit.[20]

Around the time William Patten began preaching at the Second Church, sixteen-year-old John embarked on his first serious career path. He began studying the law under the direction of his uncle and future guardian, the attorney and a mayor of Hartford, Thomas Seymour.

The career choice was a sensible one, especially given Ledyard's family background. By the middle of the eighteenth century, the colonial bar had begun to resemble the ministry in its elite, closed character. Although there was no formal bar association in colonial Connecticut, courts did license attorneys to make cases before them. The formal licensing process involved little more than an oath of honesty, but in a capital like Hartford the courts demanded additional qualifications, perhaps a basic knowledge of common law, natural law, and civil law. And one obtained these not from any college or law school but from an apprenticeship with a practicing attorney. If an aspiring lawyer apprenticed with as prominent an attorney as Seymour, he could, at best, expect to acquire license to practice law in the colony's courts. At worst, he would have a career drawing up legal documents, a position roughly equivalent to that of a law clerk or an English solicitor. Either way, young John would likely establish a flourishing practice. His family name and his connections to Seymour, Whitman, and others like them would provide a ready constituency should he decide to exchange his new status in the legal profession for political office. John, of course, never took this path, but his legal education, much like his moral education, would have lasting importance.

John would probably have read some of his uncle's law books, but in a typical colonial law office this would not have been a very deep kind of study. Most of the books he would have had access to would have been procedural handbooks designed to instruct laymen on how to make cases in court. A far more significant part of the education would have been John's experience observing Seymour in court and assisting him in the day-to-day management of his office. John's duties would have included copying legal documents or traveling through the countryside by horse and buggy to serve papers. While the work was often mundane, it allowed John to broaden his social network and recognize those qualities that would mark him, through his life, as a gentleman. Above all, he came to see what it was to speak with skill and persuasion. As one late eighteenth-century commentator put it, "The art of speaking in public is better acquired in the practice of law than in any other business."[21] In his discourses before the midshipmen aboard the *Resolution* or at Thomas Jefferson's Paris dinner table, Ledyard would distinguish himself as a passionate and philosophical communicator, a talent he no doubt cultivated during his years as Seymour's apprentice.

In early September 1771, the Ledyard family experienced another blow. After a brief "paralytick disorder," perhaps a stroke, Squire John returned to his maker. The patriarch's demise was not unexpected. He was seventy-one years old and had been battling ill health for nearly a decade. Good Puritan that he was, he was happy to relish mortality in this world as he contemplated Divine reward in the next. "For some time before his death," noted his obituary, "he seemed to have a strange presage upon his mind, that he should not long survive, but always spoke of his departure with that composure, resignation and confidence in divine mercy, as nothing but religion could inspire." Squire John, it seems, knew what a recovered Pastor Whitman would tell his mourning congregation. For a true friend of Christ "Death . . . may be compared to a sweet and refreshing Sleep." It was up to the living, then, to regret the passing of so great and honorable a man. For the colony would not easily replace a politician and jurist who after more than forty years had "behaved with such skill and distinction, that he was able to say, but little before his death, that no judgment of his had ever been reversed by any higher court." This was a clear indication that Squire John had achieved the status of "good Ruler" his friend Whitman had long ago held up as the colonial ideal. When called upon to transact the colony's business, Squire John did "much to his own honor and benefit of the community."[22]

For young John, the loss was a great one. His chief benefactor and role model had left him and had done so at a critical time of life. At nineteen or twenty John would be entering college or committing himself to a profession and his grandfather's connections would have been vitally important to his success.

Squire John did leave his grandson an inheritance of sixty pounds, plus interest, to be distributed when John married or reached maturity. This was a reasonably large sum, roughly equivalent to four or five thousand dollars in the present day. But apparently the probate court did not consider nineteen years full maturity and entrusted Thomas Seymour with control of the money.

In addition to managing John's money, Seymour also managed John's future. And in his capacity as guardian, he determined that John could do better than working as an apprentice in a law office. With John's recent inheritance and the opening of a college in New Hampshire, a promising new path had presented itself.[23]

A week after Squire John's death, the *Connecticut Courant* announced the first commencement at Dartmouth College. It was a grand affair, considering that this class consisted of only four students. New Hampshire's governor as well as members of the colony's General Assembly and the clergy attended. But for a young man with neither the money nor the connections to attend the much larger and more prestigious Yale or Harvard, the smallness of the event would not have diminished its true magnitude. Owing to an innovative financial aid program where graduates would exchange several years' service as Christian missionaries in Indian country for their education, a young man with limited financial resources could now gain access to higher education in New England. It was a momentous development in the life of this particular British province and a momentous development in the life of John Ledyard.[24]

The founder of the college and the man responsible for devising its unique financial methods was Eleazar Wheelock, a friend of the late Squire John's and long a fixture in Connecticut's spiritual life. After graduating from Yale, Wheelock became minister at the Second Church in Lebanon, Connecticut, and quickly acquired a reputation for masterful, rousing sermons. During the Great Awakening, he received requests from Congregational preachers throughout New England to stir their sleeping flocks, and after the awakening died down he turned his attention to education, initially providing the kinds of services Whitman had performed for young Ledyard. Always on the lookout for spiritual lucre, he recognized that his efforts would be better rewarded if he turned to the education of Indians. Wheelock's energies as a preacher served him well in his new endeavor. He was a tireless fundraiser and promoter and by the early 1760s had established Moor's Charity School, named for Colonel Joshua More (the different spellings are likely due to an error by a town clerk who misspelled More's name on a deed granting the school its land), who donated land and buildings near Lebanon for the school. By 1770, some sixty-seven Indian children had passed through the school, and Wheelock, whose fiery sermons had made him the bane of the likes of Squire John and Whitman during the Great Awakening, was now a respected member of the colony's spiritual elite.[25]

When the energetic and deeply pious Wheelock began talking of a new college for training English missionaries, a number of beneficiaries in England took notice, including the college's eventual namesake, president of the Board of Trade (the British government agency that advised the king and the Privy Council about colonial affairs) and noted evangelical the earl of Dartmouth. Dartmouth donated some of his own money to the enterprise and presided over the college's London board of trustees. With such prominent supporters, the college's endowment grew to ten thousand pounds sterling before the first building was built.

Wheelock also garnered the support of Governor John Wentworth of New Hampshire. There was no existing college in the colony, and when Wheelock secured a benefactor as influential as Lord Dartmouth, his newly proposed institution became obviously appealing to the royally appointed governor. In a final, successful effort to lure Wheelock and his trustees, Wentworth secured for the college a substantial land grant in a fertile area along the Connecticut River. He also obtained a charter for the college that allowed it to manage its own affairs with little interference from colonial authorities.[26]

In the spring of 1772, Ledyard left Hartford to attend the new college. As he put it in a letter to his Aunt Betty, written just before he departed, he brought the "qualifications of an humble and contrite heart" and the "impregnable shield of Omnipotence!—Omnipotence my friend!" Such would seem to be the ideal self-image for a man embarking on a career as a Christian missionary—pious and humble, ready to face the hardships of carrying the Gospel to Indian country.[27]

CHAPTER II

On Stage at Dartmouth College

THE FEW DOZEN Dartmouth College students and their tutors must have wondered about John Ledyard when he arrived at the college in April 1772. From the campus, a few rude buildings and recently cleared fields tucked along the Connecticut River, they would have seen a twenty-year-old man approaching in a sulky, a carriage made for carrying one passenger and little else. It was the sort of conveyance a country lawyer might use on his rounds, and perhaps John acquired this one from his uncle. It was also old and rickety, much like the horse by which it was pulled. Nobody had ever seen such a sight in the backwoods of New Hampshire. The roads were too poor and the distances too great for so delicate a vehicle. As Ledyard's first biographer, Jared Sparks, put it, "The journey might have been performed with much more ease and expedition on horseback."[1]

John's audience also would have noticed that the sulky driver himself was dressed in an unusual fashion. Instead of a young gentleman's overcoat, breeches, and stockings, he wore an open-collared shirt and a pair of loose-fitting Turkish-style pants. He appeared more the swashbuckling seafarer than the son of pious New Englanders. The open-collared shirt, in place of the flesh-concealing tunics, waistcoats, and jackets of the typical wellborn young gentleman, suggested sweat and physical exertion. The loose-fitting pants suggested a laboring man's need for mobility, for climbing and straddling.

Then there was the cargo. Ledyard's sulky did not carry what would typically accompany a man traveling to a college founded to prepare Christian missionaries for service among the native peoples of the northeastern woodlands. Ledyard carried no Bible or aids for survival in Indian country such as tools or firearms or wampum beads. What he did carry was the stuff of theater: fabric for making curtains and props for performing classical tragedies. John Ledyard had come to Dartmouth College to perform. He had not come to perform the kind of unscripted displays evident upon his dramatic arrival, but rather to act on a stage.[2]

On several occasions during the months he spent at Dartmouth, Ledyard would perform the most popular tragedy of his age, Joseph Addison's *Cato*. The play is set in Caesar's Rome and dramatizes the struggles of the great politician Cato the Younger as he battled the tyrannical Caesar. Rather than accept defeat and dishonor at the hands of a depraved tyrant, even one so manifestly more powerful than he, Cato commits suicide. The play's message was clear:

> A day, an hour of virtuous liberty
> Is worth a whole eternity of bondage. (II, i)

No price was too great to pay for even a moment of liberty. In the decade that preceded the Revolution, the message had obvious resonance among the aggrieved colonials as they struggled against the mighty British Empire.

From its first performance in the colonies in 1735, *Cato* grew in popularity. Nathaniel Ames, Jr., Harvard class of 1761, saw the play on four occasions and performed in it himself several times. By the time of the Revolution, the play had become veritable scripture. Every phrase seemed to resonate with former colonists as they stood defiantly against Britain. Two of the Revolution's most famous lines, Patrick Henry's "Give me liberty or give me death!" and Nathan Hale's "I regret that I have but one life to give for my country," echo lines in the play. And in the spring of 1778, after a harsh and very costly winter at Valley Forge, General Washington's soldiers even saw a performance of the play, possibly at Washington's behest. There could hardly be a better call to arms for an army about to throw itself into the maw of the world's most powerful military.[3]

John Ledyard would select the cast and direct the Dartmouth production. He would also perform in the play, although he did not choose for himself the role of the great Cato. Nor did he choose to play the other iconic figure, who happened to be George Washington's favorite character, the Numidian prince, Juba. Eternally suffering for his love of the unobtainable daughter of Cato, Juba holds honor above all other virtues:

> Better to die ten thousand deaths,
> Than wound my honor. (I, iv)

Instead, Ledyard's classmate James Wheelock, son of Eleazar, later recalled, Ledyard appeared as the elderly Numidian general, Syphax. Adding a long gray beard to his already theatrical appearance, he recited the lines of the aged tribal warrior and natural-born philosopher.[4] Like the noble savage of the Enlightenment imagination, Syphax revealed virtue and reason born from no cultivation or study, but from nature alone. His was the common sense of the common mind. And unlike the stoic Cato, he never denied his passions. They were part of his nature and thus part of his intelligence. Just as he was slave to no man, so he was no slave to cold reason. His intelligence was born of survival, of flight, of fight, of being the hunter and the hunted. It combined cautious thought with the impulsive dictates of emotion to achieve a state of mind stripped of the anxiety-inducing superfluities of civilization. "What are these wondrous civilizing arts?" Syphax asks the infatuated Juba, blinded by his admiration for Cato's stoic virtue,

> This Roman polish, and this smooth behaviour,
> That render man thus tractable and tame?
> Are they not wholly to disguise our passions,
> To set our looks at variance with our thoughts,
> To check the starts and sallies of the soul,
> And break off all its commerce with the tongue;
> In short, to change us into other creatures
> Than what our nature and the gods designed us? (I, iv)

The civilizing arts, rhetoric and logic, the study of foreign language, the studied oratorical talent, the self-denying philosophy of the Stoics—what are they if not inhibitors of the natural poets and philosophers within every man? What purpose do they serve if not to distance a man from his true self; to render his words cultivated but inauthentic?

Ledyard may have found his true role model in this ancient natural genius. He would be virtuous, he would deny himself superfluous comforts, but he would not do so as a great Roman hero such as Cato might: through carefully cultivated oratorical skill and supreme displays of classical virtue. He would display his good character as nature's hero, as the product of his senses, his emotions, his native intelligence.

In his admiration for this imagined hero of the ancient Roman past, Ledyard would have been like so many other educated colonists on the eve of the Revolution. As they struggled to distinguish themselves from the decadent and corrupt politicians and court cronies who had imposed the Stamp Tax and in 1770 engineered the killing of five colonists in the Boston Massacre, they turned to ancient Rome for role models. John Adams, for example, found one of his models in the great orator and statesman Cicero, a man who did not view government office "as persons do now a days, as a gift, or a farm." Rather, he viewed it "as a public trust, and considered it as a theater, in which the eyes of the world were upon him." The truly virtuous and honorable man, in other words, did not regard public office as an appendage of himself in the way that most people view personal property. He viewed it instead as a charge, to be carried out with a deep commitment to the common good.[5]

In an odd way, Dartmouth College was the ideal place in which to live by the morals of Syphax. Unlike Harvard or Yale or any of the other colonial colleges, it was not a school for aspiring gentlemen, or at least it was not a school for the old provincial gentlemen of the British Empire. At Dartmouth, students studied Latin and some Greek; they learned classical orations; they studied the Bible, much as they would have at any colonial college. But most Dartmouth students did something few Harvard or Yale undergrads did: they worked, and they worked in the fields of the college and in the fields of the Lord. It was one thing to do the kinds of chores lower classmen at other colleges did—run assorted odd errands, stoke a fire, do somebody's laundry, etc.—or to work as a tutor at a local schoolhouse, as Yale and Harvard students often did when in need of money.[6] It was altogether another to do hard manual labor. Work remained, in this revolutionary world of classical republicans, the province of the less educated: small farmers, women, children, servants, slaves, and the generally unfortunate. The male elite simply did not labor.

But at Dartmouth the situation was different. Wheelock believed that whatever he and the missionaries he trained might do for Indian souls would be wasted unless native peoples learned to cultivate the land like Englishmen. The Indians' "universal aversion to cultivate their lands," he explained to the college's trustees, "must unavoidably hasten their destruction, and especially as the English settlements will likely be following close after them."[7] If his missionaries were to create truly self-sustaining communities of Protestant Indians, then they would have to teach their flocks to farm. Dartmouth students, in other words, would have to be prepared to labor for the stomachs as well as the souls of their future converts.

This laboring imperative coexisted awkwardly with economic reality. Few of the colonies' privileged sons would have aspired to live and work in Indian country, let alone on the college's land. And this had been the case for decades. Although the English founded their American colonies partly in the expectation that colonists would work to Christianize and Anglicize their Indian neighbors, few bothered to do so. In pious New England, the several ministers who did accept the mandate found themselves in desperate financial straits. When not protecting their Indian flocks from corrupt fur traders or land-grabbing settlers, they were pleading for financial support from philanthropic Britons. From the middle of the seventeenth century, the work of dedicated missionaries such as John Eliot in Massachusetts and the Mayhew family of Martha's Vineyard attracted only modest support. For most ordained New Englanders, there was little to be gained from ministering to a flock of often impoverished Indians, many of whom spoke no English. By the middle of the eighteenth century, with many young men turning to the bar instead of the ministry, what had been true during the entire colonial era was even more true: there was little hope of finding a devoted corps of missionaries in New England.

For roughly a decade before founding Dartmouth, Wheelock had struggled to remedy this problem. His initial solution was to train native preachers to educate and convert their brethren, and by the early 1760s he had established Moor's Charity School for this purpose.

But those students who survived disease and homesickness bristled at the harsh work regimen Wheelock imposed. As one concerned correspondent told him, word was getting out among the native peoples of New England that he was running more of a workhouse than a schoolhouse. A student named Hezekiah Calvin was leaving for Philadelphia, claiming "you use ye Indians very hard in keeping them to work, and not allowing them a proper privilege." Two girls at the school, Calvin further alleged, had been worked "as if they were your slaves," enjoying no freedoms and earning not a penny for their labor. As if this were not bad enough, Calvin also accused Wheelock of selling the rice, coffee, flour, sugar, and clothes sent by donors for the students' use.[8]

Even Wheelock's most loyal and dedicated Indian students can hardly be viewed as success stories. After concluding his studies, for example, the Mohegan Samson Occom spent twelve years of miserable toil as schoolteacher and lay preacher to the Montauk Indians of Long Island. The impoverished and indebted Montauk could give him nothing for his troubles, and Wheelock did little better. When he was not begging for funds, Occom thus spent his time struggling to feed and clothe his family. He farmed, fished, hunted, and, like so many native peoples living amidst white towns, manufactured wooden spoons, butter churns, gun stocks, ladles, and other goods. The competing burdens of ministering to his flock and feeding his family left Occom deeply in debt and virtually indigent. Ultimately, the few Indian students who retained Wheelock's teachings thus found themselves in a netherworld, having the education of a European and the economic prospects of a dispossessed American Indian. As two commissioners for the Scottish Missionary Society explained in 1796, the product of Indian schools "is neither a white man nor an Indian. . . . Such persons must either entirely renounce their acquired habits [and] resume the savage life; or, if they live among their countrymen, they must be despised, and their death will be unlamented."[9]

Dartmouth represented yet a third way. Instead of relying on Indians or a very few dedicated Englishmen, it would make missionaries out of New Englanders unable to attend Harvard or Yale. As the province expanded and its two oldest colleges receded further and further beyond the financial reach of even relatively prosperous colonists, this latter group grew. In 1777, a year's room, board, and tuition at Yale College was roughly half the total annual income of a skilled craftsman at between sixteen and twenty-four pounds. Wheelock realized that if he offered a diploma in exchange for several years' missionary work, he might be able to exploit the growing market for higher education while addressing the shortage of trained Indian missionaries. One of the consequences of this scheme was that Dartmouth would have little tuition income to cover the costs of educating young men in the northern New England wilderness. But

Wheelock believed that his mission for the school provided an easy solution to this problem. Since these future missionaries would have to model the laboring life for their Indian converts, they needed to learn to labor and there was no better place to do this than the college itself. By working in the fields of the college, students would not only help sustain the institution, they would also further their education.[10]

This work-study system made Dartmouth a strangely egalitarian place. Here were not the sons of the colony's greatest landowners and merchants or the children of famous ministers and prominent attorneys. Here were the sons of country farmers, of Oneida Indians, and of the occasional minister driven by undistinguished reputation to New England's northern frontiers. One could hardly find a place more suited to the revolutionary-era disavowal of luxury and genteel extravagance. Here students would learn their virtue not simply from the classics but also from the actual experience of work. "The College," Wheelock explained to its English trustees, "will stand upon the body of lands designed for cultivation, which situation will be well accommodated to my plan of introducing labor, as the principal or only diversion" and "under the conduct of a prudent and skillful overseer," students would learn "the arts of agriculture without the least impediment to their studies."[11]

Observers were struck by this unique mingling of work and study. In 1774, the New Hampshire pastor and historian Jeremy Belknap recalled the college's saw and grist mills "in which six scholars reside who . . . live a kind of philosophic, laborious life. They maintain themselves by their own labor," and they live in a house "entirely of their own construction" and furnished with furniture that they appeared to have made themselves. A life truer to the classical ethos of Revolutionary America could hardly be found. At Dartmouth, one would find few of the imported consumer goods and superfluous luxuries that circulated through the British Empire and that so many revolutionaries had identified as the cause of a creeping moral lassitude among subjects of the British Crown. Dartmouth students appeared to "resist the temptations of ease and luxury, with which liberty is incompatible." They were the picture of moral goodness and virtue displayed through material austerity, study, and industry. As such, they would be able to resist the designs of those corrupt, self-interested power mongers—those Caesars—who would enslave them as they lavished them with the spoils of empire. As one anonymous patriot warned in a Virginia newspaper in the spring of 1769, "from immorality and excesses we fall into necessity, and this leads us to a servile dependence upon power, and fits us for the chains prepared for us."[12]

In the end, Wheelock was ahead of his times. Fewer New Englanders than he hoped were prepared to support a college that exchanged education for work. Much as he had with Moor's Charity School, he thus spent most of his time raising money and seeking tuition from his few paying students.

However integral work was to Wheelock's scheme, it very clearly had little to do with Ledyard's college plans. He came as one of the college's few paying students, and expected to buy his way out of the hard manual labor expected of the "charity students," as Wheelock called them. The work Ledyard would do would be of a more cerebral, cultivated kind.

That Ledyard was free not to work is reflected in the college's ledgers. These list credits and debits students accrued from the college, usually in the form of goods. They also show credit extended to others on behalf of students—others who may have done work for the student. For Ledyard, there are credited a variety of ordinary items, including room and board, books, candles, firewood, stockings, Irish linen, blankets, nails, and so on. But there is only one entry indicating that Ledyard attempted to repay at least some of this credit as labor. Soon after arriving in Hanover, he was credited for "services in writing." For this he received about six shillings, roughly equivalent to three loads of firewood or about two days of room and board, by far the greatest expense for the paying student. This is the only such entry in the ledger, and not surprisingly it is for the kind of secretarial work Ledyard would have done during his apprenticeship with Seymour; there is nothing about farmwork or other manual labor. When basic work, such as cleaning his clothes, needed to be done, Ledyard paid others to do the chores. In December 1773 there are payments to Wheelock for "washing your breeches 4 times" and "washing your waste coat." The actual work was probably done by one of the young native students whom Wheelock continued to take into his home or by one of his African slaves—he owned as many as seven, although he apparently had only four with him at the time. Whatever the case, it is clear that young Ledyard lived in a world in which manual labor was the province of others. As dedicated as he may have been to Syphaxian virtue, that dedication existed in a kind of awkward middle ground between a disdain for luxury and an elitist sense that some were born to cultivate themselves and some to cultivate the earth.[13]

Dartmouth College, with its spare facilities, its toiling students, and its remote location, might seem the ideal place for Ledyard to craft himself into some sort of homespun, Syphaxian philosopher. Here, admiration for Syphax or Cato or some other imagined paragon of ancient virtue might actually yield a style of life that at least on the surface reflected the values of those figures. The college's very situation, that is, might seem to preclude the consumption and moral lassitude that characterized the more urban and cosmopolitan parts of the empire. But in fact, by the time the college was founded in 1769, a flood of white settlers had begun arriving in the northern Connecticut River valley. Between 1760 and 1776, virtually the entire colony of New Hampshire and most of what would become eastern Vermont (at the time still part of New York) had been surveyed and settled. During these years, nearly twenty thousand migrants traveled north from Massachusetts up the Connecticut River into this former frontier of Puritan New England. And with this migration came the displacement of the native communities and the game they hunted. By the time of Ledyard's arrival at Dartmouth, the lands between the Green Mountains to the west and the White Mountains to the east were still largely woodlands, but they were now distinctly Anglo-American woodlands. Insofar as Ledyard was living according to the new values of a new, revolutionary age, he was doing so in a largely superficial way. His material surroundings remained essentially those of his colonial childhood.[14]

Perhaps for this reason, after about four months at Dartmouth Ledyard left the college for Indian country. He may have traveled north and west to the trading villages that dotted the Lake Champlain basin; or perhaps he went west into Mohawk country. But the college ledger indicates that he did leave since there are no debits or credits in his name from late August 1772 through the first of December of that year. And in the 1820s acquaintances told Jared Sparks that John went to Indian country and that the trip helped him learn Indian languages and customs.[15]

As far as can be known, this trip afforded Ledyard his first sustained contact with native peoples living beyond the formally organized territories of Great Britain. While growing up in Connecticut, Ledyard would have known few Indians. One estimate from 1774 located 5 in Hartford township and fewer than 1,400 in the entire colony of Connecticut. These estimates were, to be sure, low. Intermarriage, particularly between Indians and people of African descent, was common, and white observers often identified the resulting mixed blood families as Negro. Hence, the 101 blacks counted in Hartford township in 1756 probably included a number of "mustees," or persons with mixed Indian-African ancestry. Still, in a township whose total population in 1775 was more than 5,000, the numbers were not large.[16]

For the most part, then, what John Ledyard knew of America's native population before the trip he had learned from the news, from hearsay, or from his encounters with idealized natural characters such as Syphax. Indeed, given Ledyard's affection for Syphax, it seems he embraced the widely held eighteenth-century ideal of the so-called noble savage. According to this view, the untutored children of nature more than the cultivated and refined people of imperial Europe were, much like the great orators of ancient Rome, models of natural virtue and unaffected character. The eventual president of Yale College, Timothy Dwight, also a son of colonial Connecticut and about Ledyard's age, reflected this thinking in an account of his own travels. Speaking of the Indians throughout New England, Dwight noted that "[they] possessed a natural understanding, sagacity, and wit equal to the same attributes in other men." In addition, their passions "were exactly what nature, cherished by regular and unlimited indulgence, made them."[17] There was nothing affected or false about these people. Their passions and their intelligence, much like those of Syphax, bore the untarnished imprint of nature alone. To live among such people was, or so a son of the provinces might have concluded, to live as close to the Numidian warrior as one could in the modern world. But, as would be the case with everything John Ledyard did in his adult life, virtue sat awkwardly alongside personal ambition. There were good practical reasons for a young New Englander to learn to make his way in Indian country, whatever the perceived moral benefits.

Ledyard would have known that since the end of the French and Indian War the frontiers of northern and western New England were no longer really frontiers. They represented no dissipation of British sovereignty, no lurking bands of French-allied Indians drawn into trading networks and military alliances by a gift-giving imperial father. Now, this was all nominal British territory. The fur trade, formerly the lifeblood of New France, was controlled by British subjects. Similarly, the forests and meadows of the region would be settled by British migrants, though the British government struggled to control such settlement. To know the ways of the native inhabitants of the Northeast was thus to be better equipped to trade for goods, land, and souls. For this reason, in the introduction to his *Travels* (1791), the Quaker naturalist William Bartram urged the U.S. government to send "men of ability and virtue, under the authority of the government, as friendly visitors into [Indian] towns: let these men be instructed to learn perfectly their languages, and by a liberal and friendly intimacy become acquainted with their customs and usages, religious and civil; their system of legislation and police, as well as their most ancient and present traditions and history." With all their knowledge, these experts "might assist the legislature of the United States to form and offer to them, a judicious plan for their civilization and union with us."[18] Perhaps a similar spirit drove Ledyard into Indian country. There he would at once cultivate his natural virtue and make himself useful to his country. Able to freely travel between the worlds of native and Anglo-American, he would become a kind of transcultural entrepreneur.

Ledyard stayed in Indian country for a little over three months, hardly enough time to acquire much local knowledge. In terms of language, for instance, he probably learned very little. Jesuit missionaries who spent years living among the peoples of the Great Lakes often struggled to the very end of their missions to master the languages of their Indian flocks. The barriers were enormous. To the nonliterate native peoples of the Northeast, language was a kind ancestral inheritance, to be guarded and protected from outsiders. Hence, missionaries struggled to find committed Indian teachers. And when they succeeded, those teachers often taught trade jargons or pidgins rather than the tongues of their kin. Traders and interpreters or diplomatic go-betweens able to transcend the language barrier had usually spent part of their childhood in Indian country and were often of Indian-white parentage. Their upbringing thus left them with precious and scarce communication skills. But, growing up in provincial Connecticut, the future traveler enjoyed no such advantage.[19]

Ledyard might have acquired some proficiency in the Algonquian tongue spoken by the Western Abenakis, the native people he most likely encountered while at Dartmouth and a group he may have stayed with during his three months away from the college. The Quaker proprietor of Pennsylvania, William Penn, claimed to have mastered the Delawares' tongue within a year. But there is little reason to think that Ledyard was able to work such miracles. His writings show no particular aptitude for Latin or Greek or any of the other languages he may have studied. More probably Ledyard's knowledge of Algonquian was limited to a traveler's understanding of a few useful words and phrases.[20]

Ledyard returned to Dartmouth at the beginning of December 1772. Whatever he had learned in Indian country seems to have manifested itself in a new adventurousness. No longer was it good enough to simply play the part of Syphax. Now he would show his good character and physical strength through acts of courage and a kind of quasi martial spirit. Though hardly the boldest adventure of his life, shortly after arriving back at the college, John led a small group of fellow students on an overnight trek through deep snow, frozen swamps, and dense forest. The journey culminated in the scaling of a small New England summit and a freezing, sleepless night huddled around a campfire. Such an adventure was the perfect way for a young gentleman to display some physical strength and leadership ability in peacetime. Had Ledyard sought to make a similar display four years later, he might have volunteered for the new Continental Army.

Wheelock's son James, who was fourteen at the time of this overnight outing, recalled that his father had supported the trip. As they prepared for missionary work, the old Puritan believed, these young men had to "be inured of some of the fatigues of a savage life." But Wheelock's favorable impressions of this act were overshadowed by one simple fact: John Ledyard was not paying his bills. "[Ledyard] has entered college and been pretty steady, and bids fair to make a good scholar," Wheelock wrote to Thomas Seymour, "but the College lies out of what has been due along for his expences, and [the] needy state of the college is such that I can't do without punctual payment." Ledyard, it seems, had squandered the inheritance that was to pay for his education.[21]

Wheelock was deeply distressed by the whole affair. He had placed his trust in the grandson and son-in-law of his deceased friend and in his view they had abused it. Now, he was forced into the role of debt collector. This, in turn, produced a sad exchange, as President Wheelock and Seymour blamed one another for Ledyard's financial problems. When Wheelock accused the prominent attorney of knowing deception, Seymour in turn accused Wheelock of failing in his role as moral educator. But it was obvious to Wheelock that the failing was ultimately Ledyard's. For all his virtuous displays, he was a young man unable to govern himself and his own selfish inclinations. In Wheelock's mind, Ledyard saw himself as the center of much more than a harmless college production of *Cato*. He saw himself as the center of his own real-life drama, with everyone else in his life a bit player. There was, ultimately, nothing in Ledyard's conduct of the true selflessness exhibited by the classical icon Syphax. Indeed, judging from Wheelock's appraisal, Ledyard's performance of classical virtue was just that, performance. Fundamentally, the Dartmouth president concluded, this was a man driven by base and selfish urges. "Sir," Wheelock explained to Seymour, "had you faithfully done what I expected and joined your ends with mine I don't yet conclude we might not have effected so great a good as the humbling of that youth, and fitting him for usefulness in ye world—but as he secretly got his legacy in to his own hands to waste as his pride and extravagant humor dictated, and all out of my sight and without my knowledge, it was not possible for me to restrain him. My dear man," he concluded, "I think you can blame me for nothing unless for my benevolence to him and his family and my confidence in you."[22]

Had Ledyard been a different kind of man, he might have tried to deflect some of Wheelock's criticism by compensating the college through work, but his righteous insistence on being above mundane toil made this impossible. In the end, he did what many of his classmates did: he left the college. Students were constantly fleeing austere Dartmouth. During its first three years they fled to avoid the summer work regimen, they fled because of homesickness, they fled in search of a more cerebral academic setting, they fled because they could see no point in studying ancient Greek authors, and they fled, one of them explained to Wheelock, "because of the way you treat your men," forcing them "to blow stinky [conch] horns" at mealtime and "eat stinking provisions, kill dogs . . . and many other things scandalous to relate."[23]

Ledyard's mode of departure from Dartmouth was as dramatic and remarkable as his mode of arrival. This time, instead of riding in a sulky, he took to the Connecticut River in a grand fifty-foot dugout canoe. The impression this made as he piloted the craft to the river's banks at Hartford would remain a part of local lore for decades. A cousin, William Seymour, explained to Sparks in 1825, "Nothing had been heard from [Ledyard] for many months, when, early one morning several persons were attracted to the shore of the river by the appearance of a canoe of unusual length coming up the river propelled by a person who was totally concealed by a bear skin drawn close around his neck. The canoe slowly approached the shore, nor was the person with the paddle at the stern recognized by any of the spectators till he leaped upon a rock . . . threw off the bearskin, and greeted his friends in the person, and character of Mr. John Ledyard."[24]

In hindsight, Ledyard's return to Hartford does appear remarkable. But one has to wonder exactly why. Was it remarkable because a man rode in a huge dugout canoe down the Connecticut River? Or was it remarkable because of who that man became? A brief look at the manufacture and use of dugout canoes in colonial New England suggests the latter. These were, it turns out, a common mode of transit. Colonists had acquired the technology from the Indians of southern New England, who had long used the much heavier dugouts (rather than lighter and more maneuverable bark canoes) in large rivers. Timber being abundant, these were relatively inexpensive and simple to make and had been used by colonists to navigate the Connecticut River since the seventeenth century. They were also not unknown near the college. Wheelock wrote of a forty-two-foot craft that was lowered into the river near the college in the fall of 1773. These boats, fashioned from huge pine trunks, remained a staple of American river transport into the nineteenth century. Using a technique learned from the Nez Perce, Lewis and Clark's Corps of Discovery made five of them for their descent to the mouth of the Columbia River.[25]

Furthermore, a dugout canoe would have been the ideal craft for traveling downriver in springtime. The river ice would have melted, and the waters, swollen from spring rains and melted snow, would have easily raced past the shoals and rocks that loomed just beneath the surface in other seasons. Living in Hartford and being familiar with his grandfather's lumber business, Ledyard would have understood the benefits of sailing downriver in springtime. He would have seen lumbermen floating logs down to the sawmills and boatyards near Hartford, and he might even have seen the white pines, some as long as two hundred feet and as much as six feet in diameter, floated downriver from northeastern Massachusetts and southern New Hampshire for shipment to English shipyards. Lacking substantial old-growth forests, the mother country relied largely on the colonies to supply masts for its naval ships. Without these great New England pines, England would have had to rely on much weaker spliced trunks or possibly trees from the less reliable Baltic trade. Ledyard also would have known that to protect the precious timber from falls and rapids, lumbermen had devised systems of levers and wheels to portage the massive logs around these hazards. Those same techniques were used to drag large boats such as Ledyard's around the treacherous falls at Walpole, New Hampshire, Greenfield and East Hampton in Massachusetts, and Enfield in northern Connecticut. With his family connections and a little bit of cash or perhaps some trade cloth or liquor, Ledyard would have had little trouble finding help along the way for portaging a large dugout canoe.[26]

What the episode best reveals, then, is not so much young Ledyard's eccentricity or his future inclinations toward travel. Rather, what it reveals is that for all his righteous gentility and philosophical posturing, Ledyard was ultimately a resourceful young man. He understood the infrastructure of New England and, when necessary, possessed the skill and common sense to use that infrastructure to his advantage.

After returning to Hartford, Ledyard displayed a similar resourcefulness as he went about trying to salvage his reputation. He knew full well that much as the Connecticut River facilitated the movement of commodities, so an individual's reputation facilitated social movement. In a rambling, sometimes incoherent seven-page defense, he challenged Wheelock, accusation by accusation, rather like a mad lawyer. Whatever his financial problems, Ledyard insisted, he remained a man of good character and, as such, a man who would never deliberately defraud anyone. "I now, under the most sacred obligations, bona fide, declare I was *not aware* of it," he wrote of his overdrafts, and "when I saw the letters and account, I was ever after so ashamed of my inadvertency and so justly culpable before you Sir that I could not compose myself to come before you & answer for my misconduct." He had never intended to insult so prominent a man as Wheelock and assured his late grandfather's friend that he would make good on his debts, "as my life was concerned and at stake—this I declare was the honest purpose of my heart and to make your reparation still is."

Ledyard's burden went beyond simply making good on his debts. Wheelock had questioned his character in writing, and the young man feared this would reverberate for generations. "What do you think Dr. Wheelock," he asked, "the effect of this . . . would have upon a child or a grand child of mine (or anyone so much concerned) was he to come across it in Mr Seymour's file hereafter—you surely are very sensible Sir that they should think I was one of the most openly vile far spent volunteers of hell." What Ledyard ultimately sought was some sort of formal, written acknowledgment from Wheelock that he had merely erred in his judgment, that he was neither prideful nor extravagant, and that his financial troubles were simply matters of misfortune, reflecting nothing about his true character. The acknowledgment never came.[27]

From forward actor, Ledyard had descended to humiliated debtor. An acquaintance told Wheelock that he had "seen John Ledyard but once," in Hartford, and "he seems to avoid all company and conversation."[28]

Having dropped out of college and abandoned his legal career, Ledyard turned to the only real profession that remained open to him, the ministry. But his entrée here would be sharply constrained by the bitter feud with Wheelock. Without the famous preacher's recommendation, Ledyard would have to look far and wide to find a minister willing to embrace him as a student. To assist him with this project, he turned to two of Connecticut's most progressive preachers. The Reverend Joseph Bellamy and the early antislavery activist Reverend Levi Hart were what the son of the great Connecticut theologian Jonathan Edwards, Jonathan Jr., referred to as Edwardeans. The term was a reference to their theological forefather, for like Edwards Sr., these ministers called for a return to an authentic Calvinism born of a sincere, reverential love of God.[29]

Bellamy and Hart urged Ledyard to pursue a suitable teacher in eastern Long Island, a region beyond Wheelock's primary sphere of influence. But Ledyard's search for a minister with whom to apprentice turned out to be fruitless. About all the Long Island ministers would offer was confirmation that his current troubles were the result of a soiled reputation. The trip taught him, he later recalled, "that the sufferings I met with, and the contemptuous ideas the people where I was born and educated had of me, were nothing strange, but reflected honor on me" because "a prophet is hardly accepted in his own country." Emboldened by this conclusion and by twelve days' "feasting" in the library of one minister, Ledyard returned to Connecticut. He carried new letters of introduction from Long Island, including one from Samuel Buell, a prominent Easthampton revivalist and admirer of Samson Occom. But these did little for Ledyard; his reputation had apparently preceded him. A man unable to make good on his debts to so prominent a figure as Eleazar Wheelock was not a promising candidate for the Connecticut clergy.[30]

With his options dwindling, this twenty-two-year-old son of one of Connecticut's leading families found himself face to face with a problem he had managed to evade for his entire life. Having little means and a tarnished reputation, he would have to work to survive. It must have been a jarring blow. Despite all his efforts to maintain an existence consistent with his elevated self-image, Ledyard now faced the cruel truth that he had little more than a body with which to labor. Sometime in late 1773 or early 1774, as New England remained embroiled in controversy over the hated tea tax, Ledyard thus returned to Groton, where his father's name was still familiar among merchants and sea captains.

It was the logical course for a man whose professional aspirations had come to nothing and whose financial resources had all but disappeared. If Ledyard had preserved his inheritance, he might have been able to purchase a farm. But by the eve of the Revolution, even this would have been very difficult. There was little farmable land remaining in Connecticut, and, indeed, younger sons of landowning families had been leaving southern New England for several decades, heading south and west to New Jersey and Pennsylvania or north into western New Hampshire and New York. Emigration was not an option, however, for someone who had neither money nor family to supplement his labor. If Ledyard's situation had grown truly desperate, he might have found employment as a wage laborer, working alongside indentured servants or slaves as a farmhand or stevedore. But his reputation remained sufficiently intact to enable him to acquire a perhaps less degrading form of employment as a common sailor.

Although the colonies were embroiled in a bitter debate over just what their relationship to the mother country would be, that debate had done little to shake the rhythms of maritime life. Ships still came and went from Groton and New London, and young men in New England's coastal towns continued to find in the sea their source of well-being. Much of Connecticut's maritime activity centered on the coastal trade and transport that moved goods from the colonial hinterland to the larger ports of

New York and Boston. But the West Indies trade and a less substantial, though no less important, trade to southern Europe remained essential components of the region's mercantile economy.

Ledyard's first voyage would be aboard a New London vessel plying this European trade. These ships carried Connecticut flour, dried fish, timber, and rum to markets in Gibraltar, Cádiz, and North Africa. In return, colonial merchants gained access to some of those very luxuries—wine, spices, and Turkish carpets—that to many revolutionaries indicated colonials' excess dependence on the spoils of empire. But they also acquired more vital commodities, including salt for preserving meat and, most important, currency in the form of Spanish coins and British bills of credit. The credit could be redeemed for valuable British manufactured goods.[31]

Just how Ledyard earned his pay on the voyage is unknown. As an inexperienced seaman, he would normally have begun work as a regular deckhand, heaving and hauling lines and tackle and bearing other menial burdens. But given his superior sense of self, it seems unlikely he would have entered the maritime trades at this low level. For the most part, such work would have been reserved for boys, the youngest mariners (usually in their mid or late teens), or perhaps servants and slaves. Older and better connected crew members, such as Ledyard, might apprentice with captains to learn the fine points of navigation and the business of trade. As Sparks understood it, he signed on as a common seaman "but was treated by the captain rather as a friend and associate, than as one of the ordinary crew." This would be Ledyard's way: charm, intelligence, and good character would free him from true labor.[32]

This first voyage took Ledyard to the British controlled port at Gibraltar. The journey lifted his spirits. Freed from the social struggles at home, he now contemplated the fascinations of the world beyond. To his cousin Isaac, with whom he had spent his Hartford adolescence, he wrote, "We had a rough passage of forty days but fully compensated when we arrived at the great, the curious Rock of Gibraltar: a description of which tho it may afford you satisfaction, exceeds the most romantic genius." The wonders of the world beyond seem to have drawn the young man to yet another career. He briefly joined the British army garrison stationed at Gibraltar, but the military did not protect him from his obligation to his employer and returned him to his captain's custody. Something, though, had happened to Ledyard. If his poverty and reputation kept him from higher callings at home, they would now do no such thing. In fact, they would be assets for a man who would make his way as a traveler, unburdened by family and property. "Although the past has long since wasted the means I had," he explained to Isaac, "now the body becomes a substitute for cash and pays my traveling charges."[33]

After returning to New London, Ledyard went to sea again, this time aboard a New York vessel bound for Falmouth, England. As he had in Gibraltar, he abandoned the ship and made his way to Bristol in search of wealthy relatives. Not finding these, he was arrested for vagrancy and offered the choice of either shipping off to the convict colony at British Guinea or enlisting in the army. He chose the army.[34]

The choice may have initially seemed preferable to life in a penal colony but soon presented the novice soldier with its own problems. In the spring of 1775, a band of local militiamen in the Massachusetts towns of Lexington and Concord rebuffed an assault by several hundred redcoats. This stunning colonial victory made it almost certain that the American Ledyard would be asked to raise arms against his countrymen, something he later claimed he refused to do. By a rare stroke of good fortune, though, he was given a reprieve and allowed to join the (not yet Royal) marines. These seaborne soldiers resided in barracks or aboard sailing vessels, and since the events in Massachusetts still seemed to be an isolated affair involving a crowd of riotous New Englanders, Ledyard and his superiors had little reason to think the marines would soon be heading to America. As the scope of the war grew, however, many of them would end up in the colonies.

After he transferred to the marine barracks at Plymouth, another stroke of good fortune came Ledyard's way. In July 1776, Captain James Cook and his ships the *Discovery* and the *Resolution* prepared to set sail for the Pacific. The purpose of the voyage was to locate the mother lode of eighteenth-century oceanic exploration: the Northwest Passage, a widely hoped for waterway through the upper reaches of North America that would allow easier passage from the Atlantic to the rich trading centers of the Pacific Rim. Like many British naval expeditions, this one would sail with a complement of marines. Ledyard was to be one of them, freeing himself "forever," he later wrote, "from coming to America as her enemy."[35]

John Ledyard was twenty-four years old when he set sail with Cook. He was unmarried and had no father or grandfather, he had no estate, and beyond his college stage performances he had done little to distinguish himself. His professional life had been a failure and his short military career completely unremarkable. But now he would have his chance. Here, sailing the Pacific, his debts would be a distant memory. Who his grandfather was, what church young John had attended, whether or not he had entered Yale College or graduated from Dartmouth—all of this was of no consequence now. His success, perhaps even his survival, would depend on his ability to master the codes of conduct and sociability of the British navy.

CHAPTER III

Serving Captain Cook with Honor

THE *Resolution* would be Ledyard's principal home for the next four years. This former North Sea coal-hauling vessel was not a particularly large or grand ship. At 462 tons, it would have ranked among the smaller vessels in the navy, and its crew of 112 officers, sailors, and marines was modest in number (larger ships routinely sailed with crews double or triple that size). But what it lacked in stature, it made up for in other ways. Having already been around the world with Cook, the *Resolution* had proven itself ideally suited for voyages of discovery. Its broad, shallow hull allowed it to carry sufficient provisions to sustain a crew for many months at sea. The flat bottom design also allowed the ship to maintain a very shallow draught, a vitally important quality for a ship sailing uncharted coastal waters. Vessels with deeper draughts were faster but would more easily run aground.[1]

If Ledyard's seaborne home had passed the test of circumnavigation, his commander had now done so twice. By the time Ledyard sailed with him, Cook had already charted the eastern coast of Australia and had established that the great southern continent was no continent at all. On his first voyage aboard the *Resolution* (1772–75), Cook had circumnavigated the globe in high southern latitudes, rising above even the Antarctic Circle, to prove that Australia was not the northern tip of some great southern land mass. This third voyage would be Cook's longest yet. It would take the *Resolution* and her consort ship, the somewhat smaller *Discovery*, south

The *Resolution*, sketched in pencil by John Webber, the expedition's official artist. British Library. Add. MS 17277.1.

to the Cape of Good Hope and then east through the Indian Ocean, below Australia to New Zealand. From there, the ships would sail north to America's northwest coast, Alaska, and the Bering Sea. They would be the first European vessels known to have encountered the Hawaiian Islands, and they would successfully carry their crews along the treacherous and virtually uncharted northwest coast of the American continent.

Even for a man from the colonies, a man familiar with non-European peoples, a man accustomed to the deprivations of frontier life and the hardships of life at sea, this was to be an extraordinary journey. Ledyard would be at sea for more than four years and away from home and family for nearly six.

While this journey is the best documented of Cook's three great voyages, and perhaps even one of the best documented in the history of exploration, the record of Ledyard's activities is slim. Even Ledyard's own account of these years offers little about the author himself. The book, *A Journal of Captain Cook's Last Voyage to the Pacific Ocean,* appeared in 1783 and was drawn from the journals Ledyard kept during the course of the voyage. Its concerns are scientific and ethnographic, and for the most part its form reflects this. Chronological entries describe the movements of the *Resolution* and the *Discovery,* the landscapes and peoples encountered, and the commands of Cook. Mercifully, the endless weather reports and lists of coordinates that fill other logbooks and journals from the voyage are few, but still, Ledyard's account is in most ways an exemplar of the genre: a spare, factual accounting of the voyage, interspersed with several artful essays on Pacific Islanders, the breadfruit tree, and other objects of scientific interest. Still these offer few clues about how John Ledyard spent his years sailing with Cook, about how he whiled away the months at sea, about how he was viewed by Cook and the others with whom he sailed, or about how he endured these years away from friends, family, and homeland.

Other accounts of the voyage are similarly spare in their offerings about Ledyard. And those that say anything at all add little to what Cook himself wrote. In a brief entry for Thursday, October 8, 1778—more than two years into the voyage—Cook described an encounter with two Aleutian Islanders off the coast of Unalaska, a large island toward the eastern end of the Aleutian chain. After seven disappointing months sailing up the treacherous American northwest coast, then along the Alaskan coast and north into the Bering Sea (none of which yielded the sought-after Northwest Passage), Cook had found sheltered anchorage near the island to repair the *Resolution*'s leaky hull. This would take several weeks. During that time, Cook would do as he had been instructed to do on all such stops. He would gather data about his natural surroundings and any humans with whom he came into contact. The two Aleut visitors presented him with an opportunity to do the latter. But they also presented Cook with an additional opportunity. In addition to an insatiable appetite for tobacco (for which they traded ever-larger amounts of dried fish), the

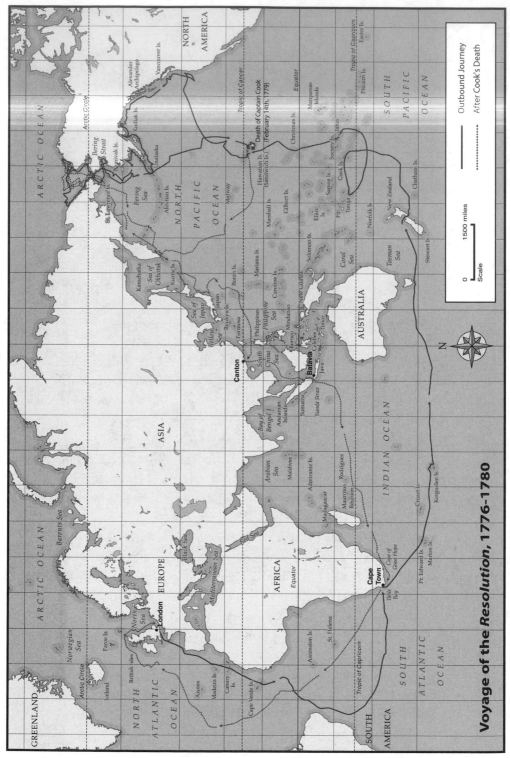

Voyage of the Resolution, 1776-1780

Outbound Journey

After Cook's Death

Scale

0   1500 miles

N

By Mapcraft.

Aleuts brought a strange gift: a rye loaf filled with seasoned salmon and a note in Russian which "none of us could read." Unbeknownst to Cook, the document was a receipt for furs paid to Russian traders as royal tribute. These local natives were simply demonstrating to this European that they had already filled their tribute quota. But Cook assumed the natives were merely messengers bearing an invitation to a Russian camp somewhere on the island.

In response to this supposed European overture, the captain sent several bottles of rum, wine, and port. He also made plans for diplomatic contact with the Russians. Exactly how to do this proved a delicate problem. Cook could have sent an armed unit, but the men would have proceeded slowly and might have compromised the peaceful purpose of the mission. The alternative was to send a single unarmed representative who, if lost, would not have significantly reduced the ship's manpower. Given the risks, Ledyard explained, "it seemed extremely hard to single out an individual and command him to go upon such [an] expedition, and it was therefore thought proper to send a volunteer, or none." Ledyard came forward, and Cook assured him "that he was happy I had undertaken the rout as he was conscious I should persevere, and after giving me some instructions how to proceed he wished me well." Cook's own journal says little about this episode, other than that his chosen emissary was "an intelligent man."[2]

While these few words seem paltry, compared to Cook's comments about other marines and enlisted men, they were voluminous. For the most part "the people," as Cook referred to his crew, received no individual recognition in his journals unless they had died or had somehow failed in their duties. Indeed, quite like any military commander, Cook made it his business to view his men as a single organic whole, the better to insulate himself from emotional ties that might cloud his judgment.

Ledyard's own description of these events, his crowning moment aboard the *Resolution*, is more detailed. It offers a view of a far fringe of European colonialism. But it is also the only section of Ledyard's book in which the author is the central character.

Ledyard's journey began on foot, in the company of the two natives who had initially approached Cook. The three traveled some fifteen miles into the interior of the nearly eighty-mile-long island, traversing its mountainous and largely treeless Aleutian landscape. In early October,

A Unalaskan man, engraved after a sketch by John Webber.
From James Cook, *A Voyage to the Pacific Ocean*, 2d ed.
London, 1785. Courtesy of Strozier Library Special
Collections, Florida State University.

the journey would have been cool and damp and the travelers would
probably have walked for a time through the dense fog that sweeps back
and forth across these northern islands. After a night in a native village,
where the islanders appeared totally indifferent to their visitor's presence, further confirmation of the routine contact with Europeans, John
and his guides traveled on for another day, the American's feet painfully
swollen from the trudge across the wet Aleutian terrain. That evening,
Ledyard's guides carried him across a small bay in the cargo hold of a
two-man kayak. This configuration meant that Ledyard had to lie on the
bottom of the canoe under the skin top, "wholly excluded from seeing the
way I went" and totally lacking "the power of extricating myself upon any
emergency." After traveling in this manner and then proceeding on foot

The Unalaskan waterfront, engraved after a sketch by John Webber. From James Cook, *A Voyage to the Pacific Ocean*, 2d ed. London, 1785. Courtesy of Strozier Library Special Collections, Florida State University.

in the company of his native guides, Ledyard finally arrived at the Russian camp.

It was a great relief to find the "fair and comely" Europeans Cook had believed to inhabit the island. The Russians had been expecting their visitor and prepared for him a dry suit of European-style clothes and a meal that included boiled whale and rye bread, all of which Ledyard welcomed. Ledyard repaid the hospitality with tobacco and the bottles of rum, wine, and port his commander had given him. After a comfortable night's sleep in a warm bed of animal furs, Ledyard joined his hosts for that familiar Russian ritual, the steam bath. He found the crude hut that housed the bath "hot and suffocating" and was disoriented by the need to disrobe in the presence of other naked men and their native Kamchatkan servants. The whole ritual of scrubbing oneself in the steam-filled room while being splashed alternately with hot and cold water left Ledyard feeling queasy and lightheaded. The morning meal of dried and smoked meats only made his condition worse, as it "produced a composition of smells very offensive at nine or ten in the morning." But ever aware of his duties, Ledyard concealed his discomfort and forced himself to eat some smoked salmon. For "hospitality is a virtue peculiar to man, and the obligation is as great to receive as to confer."

Ledyard was taken to a Russian fur-trading camp in the cargo hold of a two-person kayak similar to the one pictured here. Engraved after a sketch by John Webber. From James Cook, *A Voyage to the Pacific Ocean,* 2d ed. London, 1785. Courtesy of Strozier Library Special Collections, Florida State University.

Cook had told his envoy that if he failed to return after two weeks, he would be left on the island. Ledyard was thus eager to return to his ship, but a snowstorm made travel difficult, and he was forced to spend an additional day in the Russian camp. This afforded him time to reflect on his surroundings. What he saw was a village of some thirty grass-roofed huts inhabited by about thirty Russians, seventy native Kamchatkans whom the Russians had carried to Unalaska as servants and hunters, and a small group of Native Aleuts who had converted to Russian Orthodoxy.[3]

The following day, Ledyard and three Russians returned to the *Resolution.* Ledyard had conducted himself, at least according to his own account, in perfect accord with Cook's orders. Yet there is nothing in Ledyard's book or in Cook's journal to suggest that Cook felt any need to recognize the American marine's service. There is no testimony anywhere in the expedition's records about Ledyard's conduct, about the physical suffering he endured, about the diplomatic skill he exhibited, or about his acuity as an observer of exotic peoples and places. The lowly marine was a subordinate, competently carrying out orders. And perhaps the best way to say this was to say nothing at all.

The navy's documentary record of the voyage offers little more about Ledyard's time aboard the *Resolution*. In the pay book for the ship, Ledyard's name appears in a list of twenty marines. But the entry indicates little about him. This was true in general of the marines. The navy apparently felt no particular need to preserve data about these enlisted soldiers. Columns for describing appearance, place of birth, and reason for enlistment are blank. Columns entitled "Time of Discharge" and "Whither or for what Reason" are also largely blank, excluding notations about one man lost at sea and four killed in the melee that took Cook's life. Otherwise, the pay book enumerates charges against the marines' pay, including ones for clothing, for tobacco, for venereal disease treatments (which Ledyard received on two separate occasions), and for dead men's clothes.

There is one distinguishing feature in the entry for Ledyard. On September 23, 1780, just before the expedition's end, Marine Sergeant Samuel Gibson died, and the acting commander, John Gore, promoted Ledyard to fill his post. This gave Ledyard the highest noncommissioned rank in the marines. That day the *Discovery* and the *Resolution* lay anchored off the port of Stromness on the northern Scottish island of Orkney, having been blown from their course toward England a month earlier. Apparently Gore, the American first lieutenant aboard the *Resolution* who had taken command after the death of Captain Charles Clerke (who had himself succeeded the deceased Cook) saw fit to reward his fellow countryman for good service. But as promotions go, this one was of little real consequence. The ships were in friendly waters and less than two weeks from the Deptford naval yards near London, the voyage's terminus.

Concerning Ledyard's treatment for venereal disease, the documents indicate nothing about the severity or the specific nature of his case, nor do they say anything about its particular type; no distinction was made between gonorrhea, syphilis, and other sexually transmitted diseases. The documents do reveal that 66 out of the full complement of 112 crew members were treated at least once, and the rate of infection was certainly much higher since men were treated only when they had visible lesions. Also, there was more than ample reason for sailors to conceal their cases. The treatment itself, which involved ingesting straight mercury,

Ledyard appears fourth in this list of marines from the *Resolution*'s paybook. Beneath his name is a small notation recording his promotion to sergeant, and to the right are columns indicating charges for venereal treatments, clothes, bedding, and tobacco. National Archives, United Kingdom, ADM 34/651.

produced a host of unpleasant symptoms, including black secretions from the salivary glands. For such discomfort, the men were charged fifteen shillings against their already meager pay.[4]

There is no way to know where Ledyard became infected, but as a veteran of the merchant marine and the British military he had ample opportunity for exposure. Every major port of the Atlantic had its complement of prostitutes, many of whom had been infected. Given his later behavior—Ledyard mentions a liaison with a Parisian prostitute—it is possible he acquired the disease in New York, Gibraltar, Plymouth, or some other port he visited. It is also possible he was infected while with Cook. By the great navigator's third voyage to the South Pacific, venereal disease had grown common among the Maori of New Zealand and the Tahitians. Cook had struggled to limit the spread of the disease by barring local women from his ships, maintaining shipboard cleanliness, and inspecting the men's genitals. But these measures seemed to do little to stop the epidemic. One problem, which Cook eventually recognized, was that he and his surgeons had wrongly assumed the diseases were contagious only when visible sores were present.[5]

Ledyard says nothing about his own sexual activities during the course of the voyage, and what he says about the sexual conquests of the other men suggests that he was philosophical about the whole business. The costs, in terms of disease and misunderstanding, were great, but men's sexual appetite would "like hunger pervade stone walls." There was little to be done, in other words, to contain the passions. They were stronger than any man. And if, as was his habit in other aspects of his life, Ledyard had been inclined to succumb to his own passions, the opportunities for sating his sexual appetite abounded. For the price of a few nails or glass beads, or even no price at all, he could have consorted with native women in New Zealand, Tahiti, the Tongan Islands, North America, or the Hawaiian Islands (named the Sandwich Islands by Cook in tribute to the Earl of Sandwich, First Lord of the Admiralty). On their initial encounter with the Hawaiian islanders in late January 1778, local women appeared to throw themselves at the Englishmen. "The young women," surgeon's mate David Samwell wrote, "used all their arts to entice our people into their Houses," and when the men resisted in deference to Cook's orders, the women "endeavoured to force them and were so importunate that they absolutely would take no denial."[6]

Sex in Hawaii, at least on the voyagers' first visit there, would not have led to venereal disease, since it had been hitherto unknown in the islands. But when Cook returned the following year, the scourge had already taken hold. Ledyard's treatment for venereals, though, had come before this visit, so he evidently acquired the disease somewhere else. Perhaps the most important point is simply that Ledyard allowed himself to be treated at all. We might take this as a sign of his determination to play by the rules, to conceal nothing from his superiors, and to endure routine physical suffering in deference to their wishes.[7]

Ledyard the soldier, then, would appear a far way from Ledyard the troubled adolescent. There was none of that insolence, that rebellious spirit, that antiauthoritarianism of his ill-fated college years. But tempting as it is to see in Ledyard's life some kind of revolution in behavior and values, the continuities are as striking as the changes. The most revealing of these is simply Ledyard's determination to distinguish himself as a man of good character. In a world in which a man who could convincingly act the part was no actor at all, Ledyard's early interests in the theater and the pulpit served him well. As stages for unveiling admirable young gentlemen, the confined wooden worlds of the *Resolution* and the *Discovery* could hardly be surpassed.

When it came to achieving distinction, the marines offered certain benefits. Although most viewed them as beneath common seafarers in the naval hierarchy, there was no confusing able-bodied seamen with these "sea soldiers." As one observer remarked, "No two races of men, I had well nigh said two animals, differ from one another more completely than" marines and seamen.[8]

The differences began with clothes. There was no mistaking a marine's red coat, white waistcoat, and breeches for a seaman's long trousers and short jacket—the latter fashioned for climbing aloft. The marines' red coat pointed to a far more fundamental fact. Aboard a sailing vessel, the marines were landsmen. Their functions were in no way essential to the actual sailing of a vessel. Every commander knew this; hence, we can assume that when Cook asked for volunteers to go ashore at Unalaska, he was really asking for a marine to step forward. The loss of a skilled sailor was a price he would have been unwilling to pay for this sort of diplomatic gesture.

What marines did do further accentuated their distinctiveness. For the most part, they had four functions: they enforced shipboard discipline; they added to the firepower of a naval vessel; they served as boarding parties; and they defended landing parties and beach encampments. They also provided unskilled labor for cleaning decks and infested cargo holds or for pulling lines, hauling sails, and turning the capstan to raise anchor.

As a corporal, Ledyard enjoyed somewhat higher status than a lowly private. He would have led marching drills and landing parties, and he might even have messed with the other noncommissioned officers. Further, as an educated twenty-four year old, he was not typical of the peasant boys, felons, and vagabonds who tended to populate this branch of the enlisted military. Of course all this implies that the naval bureaucracy was able to distinguish between the skilled and the unskilled, the experienced and the inexperienced. In fact, with corruption and bribery rampant, particularly in the recruitment process, such fine distinctions were rarely made. Cook seems to have been more involved than others in manning his ships, but still, bad information, limited manpower, and a corrupt naval bureaucracy no doubt made the process immensely cumbersome and frustrating.[9]

In some ways, then, it was fortunate for Cook that by whatever circuitous path Ledyard found his way aboard the *Resolution*. At the very least, he was not simply the untutored teenage son of a peasant farmer, but rather an educated, literate man, familiar with oceanic travel, somewhat accustomed to interacting with indigenous peoples, and eager to win the approval of his superiors.

This was the very sense of himself Ledyard sought to convey, and it is apparent in his only real discussion of his conduct as a soldier. This after-the-fact discussion appears in the one section of Ledyard's book critical of Cook, suggesting that he thought his American audience would appreciate a favorable picture of one of their own alongside a not-so-favorable image of one of Britain's greatest men. Nonetheless, it does offer a glimpse of Ledyard's conduct as a soldier and of his chief ambition in that role: that he appear honorable, disciplined, and duty-bound. It also suggests that as a marine on a voyage of discovery, those qualities were about the highest attributes Ledyard could hope to display. Achieving anything more, particularly true military valor, would have been all but impossible, even for the most remarkable marine.

◆ ◆ ◆

In January 1779, Cook brought his ships into Kealakekua Bay, one quarter of a mile from the shore of the island of Hawaii. For most of the previous six weeks he had inexplicably cruised several miles off the island's coast, to the infinite consternation of his sex-starved, land-starved, and just plain starved crew. During this time, Cook had also supplied the crew with sugarcane beer, a drink made from diluted rum, in place of the usual grog. He had hoped to save the grog for the cold months the expedition would again spend in the far North Pacific.

The crew found the beer disappointing and had no sense of why, a short sail from this land of plenty, they were forced to endure such rations. They apparently resorted to a measure that had never been taken on a ship under Cook's command: a formal letter of protest. To Cook, the whole affair provoked a sort of sentiment he rarely expressed, but a sentiment all too familiar in a stratified English society. As Cook understood it, as much as a man might do for the welfare of his social inferiors, their lack of education and refinement would always leave them fearful of change and innovation. Such was the great obstacle of eighteenth-century liberal-minded philanthropy. The people simply did not know what was in their own best interest. "Every innovation whatever, tho ever so much to their advantage is sure to meet with the highest disapprobation from Seaman," Cook complained. "Few men have introduced into their Ships more novelties in the way of victuals and drink than I have done; indeed few men have had the same opportunity or been driven to the same necessity." And yet, despite the manifest value of these efforts in preventing suffering, "the turbulent crew alleged it was injurious to their healths."[10]

The underlying source of the conflict—Cook's extremely slow and deliberate approach to the island of Hawaii—remains something of a mystery. Cook himself said little about his reasoning, but scraps of testimony are suggestive. The voyagers' first visit had shown that Hawaiians would eagerly trade with the Europeans immediately after landfall, but as the novelty of English trade goods declined, the number of Hawaiians willing to barter vegetables, fruits, meat, and labor declined as well. Hence, perhaps Cook delayed landfall to keep trading terms as favorable as possible. Also, the longer the ships were anchored near shore, the more opportunities there were for desertion, for the spread of disease, and for the theft of valuable arms and equipment (the latter was a problem that had plagued the voyagers in their previous encounter with Hawaiians and other societies of the South Pacific and American northwest coast). On shorter visits these problems could be managed. But Cook expected to spend the entire winter in Hawaii, preparing his crew and vessels for a final thrust north through the Bering Strait into the Arctic Ocean.[11]

Was the delay a miscalculation? Was the great man's judgment beginning to falter? The question might never have been raised had not Cook been killed on February 14 amidst a chaotic clash involving some of his own men and an angry crowd of Hawaiians. With the luxury of hindsight, the delayed landfall seems insensitive, and when viewed alongside some of Cook's other actions immediately before his death, including the uncharacteristically insensitive desecration of a Hawaiian temple site, a pattern suggests itself. This is how Ledyard saw all the events of those two months. They were an interconnected series of bad choices that inevitably culminated in tragedy.

What Ledyard himself did during these weeks cruising the waters off the islands is unknown. But once the men went ashore, he spent most of his time as sentry at the expedition's camp and observatory, watching carpenters, an astronomer, and their various helpers toil in the warm Hawaiian sun. The Europeans had set up the camp in a sweet potato field between the beach and a large religious monument, or *heiau*. Cook and his officers were aware of the potential hazards of housing a group of mostly ordinary Englishmen near so sensitive a religious shrine. To insure a respectful attitude, the commerce at the camp, human and otherwise, was kept to a minimum. The quiet scene apparently afforded Ledyard time to befriend a priest who lived nearby. We can imagine Ledyard filling his time, conversing by signs and gestures with this man Kunneava, perhaps inquiring about Hawaiian custom or language or religion. Ledyard's duties, one must conclude, allowed much time for the vast inefficiencies of cross-cultural communication.[12]

Soon, however, the thin thread of peace began to unravel. Eleven days before Cook's death, he had sent a group of men ashore to retrieve the *Resolution*'s rudder after repairs by the ships' carpenters. The simple errand provoked a small crisis when the men clashed with the Hawaiians who were helping them. The incident began when master's mate Henry Roberts did to some of the Hawaiians what he would have done to any hands who appeared to slack: he struck them. As a large crowd of Hawaiians began gathering, Ledyard acted:

Though I plainly foresaw these things and was conscious that they originated chiefly from our imprudence as well as the propensity among the natives to envy, . . . I could not justify a passive conduct, and therefore acquainted the commanding officer at the tents of the disturbance, requesting that I might put the guard under arms, and at least make a show of resentment to which he acquiesced and came out of his tent to appease the fray in person, and it was a pity that so much softness, humanity and goodness should have been so roughly dealt with as he was, for they pelted him and the file of men with him with stones back to the encampment. This, however, did not provoke him to fire among them, and after laughingly saying, they were a set of sad rogues and were spoiled he retired again to his observatory.[13]

The marine guards, as Ledyard's actions suggest, were more peacekeepers than policemen; more intermediaries than law enforcers. Part of this was a function of circumstances, part of military protocol. Like any enlisted man, Ledyard had limited latitude to act on his own. The best he could do was seek permission from his superiors, and what that permission granted was not the free use of force so much as the freedom to display force. To open fire on the rebellious rabble was simply not an option. It might have provoked war and would certainly have defied the entire peaceful ethos of the expedition. Still, Ledyard's action says something about the symbolic function of the marines.

Their uniforms, their marching and drilling, even the muskets they carried—of questionable use in the confined quarters of a ship under mutiny—were all symbols of power. In an environment in which those symbols were confused and uncertain—gentlemen officers with their uniforms, skills, and talents and, above all, their multitude of ranks; the officers' servants, the cook, the surgeon, the carpenters, the astronomer, and other landsmen; professional seafarers with their own confusing grades, hierarchies, and allegiances; and native peoples whose conceptions of spiritual and political power revealed themselves in ways totally alien to Cook and his men—the marines provided one readily identifiable symbol of military authority. But as actual fighting soldiers, little could be expected of them.

The one occasion on which the marines faced actual combat was perhaps indicative of their fighting ability. The occasion was that fateful day in February. After several tumultuous weeks on the island of Hawaii, the ships raised anchor and sailed for the island of Maui, but foul weather and a damaged foremast on the *Resolution* forced them to return to the area of their earlier anchorage in Hawaii's Kealakekua Bay. As they reentered the bay, the throngs of Hawaiians who had greeted them a month earlier were nowhere to be seen. This was a bad omen. The following week witnessed a series of skirmishes, thefts, and disruptive punishments (especially of one Hawaiian who received forty lashes for theft). The anxiety and stress brought on by all this disorder convinced Cook that a show of force was needed. After some Hawaiians took one of the *Discovery*'s boats, Cook went ashore accompanied by nine marines and their commander, Lieutenant Molesworth Philips.

The captain planned to capture his friend, Chief Kalei 'opu 'u, and ransom him for the boat. He apparently concluded that marines bearing muskets would be show of force enough to convince the Hawaiians, despite their vast numerical advantage, to give up the chief without a fight. It was not. After coming ashore, Cook and his armed men found themselves engulfed by an enraged crowd, and rather than give the command to fire (which would have been suicidal), Cook led a slow, deliberate retreat. This short walk devolved into open combat after an obviously confused Cook fired at a man who he thought was threatening him with a dagger; amidst the ensuing clash, Cook was killed. While he and his escorts were able to get off one shot, the bumbling marines could not reload and fled back to their boats, losing four of their own along the way. The whole affair was a perfect testament to the largely symbolic power of this force. To William Bligh, master aboard the *Resolution,* the marines failed completely to provide the protection their commander needed: they simply "fired and ran which occasioned all that followed for had they fixed their bayonets & not run, so frightened as they were, they might have drove all before them." The judgment is perhaps a bit harsh given that the Hawaiians so enormously outnumbered the British force. But still, the circumstances surrounding Cook's death suggest that these men were ill prepared for even a hasty retreat.[14]

Although he never really clarifies this point in his own account, Ledyard had not been one of the marines to accompany Cook ashore. While the celebrated sea captain was clashing with the Islanders, Ledyard was guarding a camp on the other side of the bay.[15]

Ledyard's marine uniform may have suggested a certain amount of symbolic power, but his actual status on the ship was low. He shared a rung on the shipboard hierarchy with assorted landsmen and teenaged midshipmen. This must have been a very difficult position for a man hailing from the highest social strata of his province. Having squandered his inheritance and the social capital that came with his name, he was left to climb his way up from the low rungs of the British military. But it would not have been a lonely position. Ledyard was one among a group of striving men from the British provinces. With so widely admired a commander as Cook, these Pacific voyages were coveted assignments for young officers and enlisted men. A recommendation letter from Cook, they all knew, carried immense weight when it came time for the Admiralty to distribute commissions.

Ledyard's provincial origins would also have done little to set him apart. Cook's voyages drew crew members from across the empire. While most of the crew hailed from England, of the 182 men aboard the two ships, eleven were Scots, seven Irish, and seven Americans. The Americans included John Gore, first lieutenant on the *Resolution* and a veteran of two previous Pacific expeditions. There was also the Pennsylvania-born boatswain on the ship, William Erwin, and two seamen, the Bermudan Thomas Roberts and George Stewart of Charleston. It is significant that the only member of this group Ledyard appears to have befriended was Gore, a skilled navigator and an established member of the naval officer corps.[16]

Gore was much older than Ledyard, perhaps as many as twenty years (his exact age is unknown), but the two men appear to have had a genuine rapport. Together they had hunted wild fowl near the entrance to Alaska's Prince William Sound, and Ledyard claimed that Gore had recommended him for the trip across Unalaska. This "intimate friend," as Ledyard described him, had begun his naval career during the Seven Years War and had served as third and then second lieutenant aboard the *Endeavour*, the ship Cook sailed on his inaugural Pacific voyage. Gore had also slowly and deliberately risen through the officers' ranks, finally taking command of *Discovery* after its commander, Charles Clerke, took charge of the deceased Cook's *Resolution*. Much like Cook's story, Gore's was one of merit and

John Webber painted *The Death of Captain Cook* in England between 1781 and 1783. This widely reproduced image did much to ennoble Cook in the British imagination. He stands in the foreground, arm raised in a cease-fire gesture moments before being stabbed. To the left, fleeing pell-mell, are the marines, overwhelmed and lacking the calm nobility of their ill-fated commander. The Dixson Galleries, State Library of New South Wales.

patronage rather than privilege. It would have been an appealing story for Ledyard, whose birthright carried no particular weight in the Royal Navy.

Still, Gore and Ledyard were, in some sense, an odd pair: second in command aboard one of His Majesty's vessels befriending a lowly marine corporal. The relationship may have had something to do with the two men's origins, but little is known about exactly where Gore was from. Some sources say Virginia, but this has never been confirmed. More likely, Gore simply came to see in Ledyard an appealing personality who was also a dutiful member of the ship's company. At the end of the expedition, after Gore had taken full command of the voyage, he recommended Ledyard for an officer's commission. His recommendation is perhaps the best indication of how he viewed the younger man. "Ledyard," he wrote Lord Sandwich, "is a Young active Man [who] hath done Good service on our late Circumnavigating Voyage, and Is one who from Education and abilities is (I think) Properly Qualified and justly merits a higher Rank Than That which he holds at present."[17]

If this friendship is any indication, Ledyard's education and his gentlemanly comportment served him well. In Gore he had a powerful patron, at least while at sea. But if he was truly to distinguish himself, he had to set his sights higher and garner the attention of Cook himself. For ultimately, if the voyage was to help Ledyard recover some of the social capital he had squandered, it would have to yield an endorsement from Captain Cook. Never in his life had Ledyard been around a figure of such stature; never in his life, that is, did he have access to so powerful a potential patron. But there is little indication the two had any significant interaction. Still, one has to assume that Cook was an important presence for Ledyard, as he no doubt was for all aspiring men on the voyage. For Cook lacked the qualities that would ordinarily entitle a man to the kind of esteem he came to enjoy. He was the son of a poor farm laborer, and his early sailing career began in the very undistinguished North Sea coal trade aboard a vessel much like the *Resolution*. A unique aptitude for navigation and some good fortune had earned him a commission in the navy. But upward mobility in British society was never simply the result of luck and aptitude. At some point in every ordinary person's rise, a patron intervened. And Cook was no exception. Hugh Palliser, a naval captain whom Cook had served during the Seven Years War and who rose up the naval hierarchy to become

Captain John Gore painted by John Webber, 1780. National
Library of Australia.

an admiral and comptroller of the navy, was responsible for Cook's first
command. He had recommended the veteran seafarer to the Admiralty as
it was planning its 1768 expedition to the Pacific. We can assume that Ledyard, along with all the midshipmen and other young gentlemen aboard
the *Resolution* and the *Discovery*, saw in Cook a similar potential patron. By
the time they sailed with him, he had become a figure whose reputation
was almost unimpeachable, a figure, that is, whose word carried much
weight in the naval bureaucracy.

What Ledyard would have seen in Cook was a stern and somewhat
distant figure, a man who emerged from his cabin fully attired in his
captain's uniform, cleaner and perhaps clearer-eyed than the rest of the
crew. He would also have been the picture of *sangfroid,* a man who stoi-
cally endured the pressures his duties brought upon him.

It is not difficult to imagine just how intense those pressures were. Cook's orders sent him to uncharted waters, in search of unknown trans-continental waterways; they required him to keep a scrupulous accounting of his progress; and they called for detailed records of any discoveries of potential scientific interest. While carrying out these orders, Cook was to maintain friendly relations with numerous peoples with whom neither he nor most anyone else on board his ships could speak. All the while, he carried the burden borne by all naval commanders: preserving order and discipline among his raw, mostly young crew.

The difficulties of life at sea merely added to a commander's stress. As Samuel Johnson famously remarked, "No man will be a sailor, who has contrivance enough to get himself into a jail; for being in a ship is being in a jail, with the chance of being drowned."[18] And in some sense Johnson was right, especially regarding ordinary seamen. The men were confined, badly fed, and constantly under the surveillance of officers and marines. But unlike prisoners, sailors possessed something scarce and valuable: a trade. The ship's mission as well as the safety and survival of the entire crew depended on the labor of these seaborne workingmen. And every commander knew that the lash alone was not enough to secure that labor. The men expected the sailor's usual rations of beer, grog, salted or pickled meats, and hard biscuits as well as some freedom to trade with, have sex with, and otherwise interact with people ashore. But these ex-pectations could not be allowed to compromise the purpose of the voyage. It was Cook's obligation to find a way between two often countervailing mandates: that of "the people" and that of the Admiralty.

By his third voyage, Cook had indeed distinguished himself as one of the British navy's most skilled commanders. He was a remarkably precise and systematic navigator and also had earned a reputation for being among the navy's best coastal surveyors. But even more, Cook had shown an uncanny ability to keep his men safe and alive, suggesting that under his command, contrary to Johnson's generalization, one was actu-ally safer at sea than on land. As Cook's biographer J. C. Beaglehole has observed, in contrast to most ordinary people in Georgian Britain, Cook's crews might "reflect that, while they would undergo discomfort, as long as they were with Cook their lives would be reasonably safe."[19]

Compared to the appalling casualty rates common on other naval ships, Cook's record was truly astonishing. On his first two Pacific voyages, totaling six years at sea. Cook lost only one man to disease while at sea. On his last and longest voyage, he lost five men to disease, and three of these had been sick when the ships sailed from England. Had it not been for the catastrophic exposure to malaria and dysentery while at the Dutch port of Batavia (now Jakarta) on the final leg of his first voyage—which ended up costing twenty-nine lives—Cook's record would be even more remarkable. The numbers are especially striking given that longer voyages were most vulnerable to scurvy (caused by a vitamin C deficiency) and malnutrition.

The problem was not limited to the months at sea. Making matters worse, as a way of guarding against desertion, commanders routinely confined men to their ships for weeks before setting sail. The consequences of this practice were particularly gruesome on the celebrated Commodore George Anson's ships. Anson's voyage, which began in 1740, was to involve six navy ships on a round-the-world search for the elusive Spanish treasure galleon that carried American silver from Acapulco to Manila. After months of delays at the Spithead anchorage near Portsmouth, Anson's crew were prime candidates for disease, and within six months of being at sea, they began to fall victim to cases of scurvy. Eventually the squadron was so badly afflicted with this and related ailments that the ships were, in effect, left to sail themselves. Those who recovered from this first bout faced further ravages as the ships set out to make the Pacific crossing. In the end, hundreds of Anson's men perished.[20]

Incredibly, on Cook's three Pacific voyages, totaling nearly a decade at sea, not a single crewman died of scurvy or malnutrition. The achievement was entirely owing to Cook's relentless determination to maintain the health and well-being of his crew, a determination manifest not so much in any innovative treatments as in more general measures for maintaining health. He routinely inspected his men's hands for cleanliness, penalizing those with dirty ones by limiting grog rations; and similarly punished sailors who resisted his demand that whenever possible they consume fresh meats, fruits, and vegetables. The tensions these efforts produced must have been oddly comforting to this son of a day laborer. Here he was, struggling with the main problem of every patriarch: serving the people, even when their passions would dictate a contrary path.[21]

It must have also been comforting to know that his peers among Britain's scientific and maritime elite saw fit to celebrate Cook's concern for his crew's health. Indeed, it was perhaps this hard-won humanitarianism more than any other of his achievements that earned Cook almost universal admiration among his contemporaries. In one memorial to the great navigator, James King, second lieutenant aboard the *Resolution*, reminded his readers that "the method which [Cook] discovered, and so successfully pursued, of preserving the health of seamen, forms a new era in navigation, and will transmit his name to future ages, amongst the friends of mankind." The absence of the usual death and prolonged suffering that had for centuries plagued oceanic navigation prompted another of his memorializers to observe that Cook possessed what was perhaps the chief distinction of a great man of the age. He was brave and unflinching but at the same time capable of the noblest acts of humanity. To combine strength and stoicism with "all the tenderness which was requisite to diffuse benevolence amongst untutored minds" was to achieve the epitome of eighteenth-century manhood. Indeed, that Cook ultimately "fell a sacrifice to that nobleness of spirit" would only confirm for posterity the flawlessness of his character. "Mild, just but exact in discipline," another wrote, "he was a father to his people, who were attached to him from affection, and obedient from confidence."[22]

That peculiar fatherly combination of courage and empathy, strength and compassion, and decisiveness without arbitrariness was something Ledyard strove to emulate but never really achieved. To be empathic, at least in the eighteenth-century sense of making a lesser being's life better, one had to have power over somebody—over one's spouse, one's children, one's crew, one's servants. Ledyard never achieved any of this. But his reputation aboard the *Resolution* suggests a carefully honed strategy for compensating for that absence.

That strategy is suggested, first, by Cook's characterization of Ledyard when he selected him to be the envoy at Unalaska as "an intelligent man."[23] It is significant that among the others whom Cook described in this way was Tupaia, the Tahitian priest and navigator who joined Cook's first expedition as interpreter and translator and who was supposed to return to England under the care of Joseph Banks, the expedition's young aristocratic naturalist. Banks had urged Cook to let Tupaia join the expedition, and, as Cook explained, "we found him to be a very intelligent person and to know more of the Geography of the Islands situated in these seas, their produce and the religion laws and customs of the inhabitants then any one we had met with." When Banks suggested that Cook take Tupaia aboard as guide and interpreter, Cook resisted, fearing that he lacked the means to support and care for Tupaia. In obliging fashion, though, Banks agreed to adopt Tupaia, although as described by Banks that adoptee sounds more like a pet. "I do not know why I may not keep him as a curiosity," he noted in his journal, "as some of my neighbors do lions & tigers at a larger expense than he will probably ever put me to." Unfortunately, Tupaia did not survive the voyage, falling to disease at Batavia along with so many of his British shipmates.[24]

If we can take this common attribution of "intelligent" to link Ledyard and Tupaia, we might draw from it the suggestion that, like that of an uneducated islander, Ledyard's mind reflected not so much interactions with highly educated tutors or professors or gentlemen associates as a kind of native intelligence, an intelligence that suggested natural, innate talent. And although eighteenth-century gentlemen were endlessly obsessed with examples of primitive intelligence—the parade of non-European peoples to European courts, the reams of poetry, doggerel, and philosophical disquisition celebrating the natural intelligence of uncultivated minds—that obsession was not born of a sense of affinity. It was akin to a parent's amusement at the insights of a child. There was little sense that untutored natural or primitive intelligence alone, however remarkable its displays, equipped a man to make his way in the world. For this, he needed socialization, he needed entrée to the circles of like-minded, liberally educated men.

For an aristocrat like Banks or an esteemed navigator like Cook, such naturally intelligent men must have had a kind of affirming, totemic function. In return for paternal affection, they provided loyalty and deference, two commodities often in scarce supply on a naval vessel.

Besides elite gentlemen themselves, the ordinary seamen who sailed these vessels were about the closest thing the eighteenth century had to a self-conscious class. Like Britain's gentlemen elite, they wore distinctive clothing; they spoke in distinctive ways; they had their own morals and rules of conduct. And, above all, they very much viewed themselves as a distinct social stratum, defined by their particular skill but also by their fellowship with other seamen—men who, like the gentlemanly social elite of the age, existed in a suprapolitical, transnational realm. Irish, Scots, blacks, whites, Spaniards, Portuguese, New Yorkers, Jamaicans—their origins were diverse. But aboard ships, they were all seafaring laborers. It was the sense of fellowship that characterized these men, and the recognition among commanders that those bonds of fellowship were stronger than the naval command structure, that left the Royal Navy with the obligation of policing its own, that is, of employing marines to maintain order on a ship whose skilled crew members had no particular allegiance to Britain or its commissioned representatives.[25]

Amidst the tensions and uncertainties of life at sea, then, figures like Ledyard and Tupaia must have been reassuring. Their allegiance to social superiors was, at least on the surface, unquestioning. Ledyard, set apart from the ordinary men on board by his privileged background and eager for a patron's recognition; Tupaia, the Polynesian priest whose native status meant little in the wooden world of the ship and who was totally dependent on Banks and Cook for his well-being. In a sense, that is, what these two men had in common was their dependence on superiors, dependence born of aspiration and necessity. And that dependence, we can assume, afforded the ship's gentlemen a valued reminder of an ideal world of patrons and deferential, grateful clients.

Ledyard, of course, wanted to be more than simply a comforting presence to his social superiors. He wanted to be somebody known for talents worthy of their deepest admiration. To obtain this, he turned to the written word, the one tool with which he believed he could truly distinguish himself.

CHAPTER IV

Seeking Distinction with the Pen Aboard the *Resolution*

IN A CHRONICLE OF North Pacific exploration published in 1819, the *Discovery*'s former first lieutenant James Burney, brother of the novelist Fanny, recalled that sometime after Cook's death, John Ledyard petitioned his superiors for appointment as official historian of the voyage. Burney explained that in pursuit of this office, late in the voyage Ledyard presented Captain Charles Clerke with "a specimen, which described the manners of the Society islanders, and the kind of life led by our people while among them."

Writing the official account of the voyage, especially after Cook's death, was no minor responsibility. The job would have given its holder substantial influence over Cook's legacy and over the professional futures of most others on the voyage. It would also have entitled him to a share of the substantial income the published account would generate. Not surprisingly, then, Ledyard's aspirations were not unique. As Burney noted, Ledyard "was not aware how many candidates he would have had to contend with, if the office to which he aspired had been vacant; perhaps not with fewer than with every one in the two ships who kept journals."[1] Ledyard, in other words, was not alone among the literate journal keepers on this voyage; nor was he alone among those who would have wanted to create its official history. Indeed, there was something of a little Grub Street aboard these vessels: aspiring men like Ledyard scribbling in their journals while looking for some way to distinguish themselves with their pens.[2]

Most of these journal writers were commissioned officers and mid-shipmen, but there were also warrant officers, supernumeraries, and ordinary seamen in the group. Among them, for example, were Master's Mate Henry Roberts, seaman William Charlton, the surgeon John Law, and the ploughboy turned ship's astronomer, William Bayly. In total, nearly thirty journals and logs remain from the voyage, but it is almost certain that many more such documents have been lost. They likely suffered the same unknown fate as the writings of William Bligh, master aboard the *Resolution*. Bligh would have been responsible for daily entries in the ship's log and, as was common practice, would almost certainly have kept a running journal, narrating the ship's daily progress. But none of these writings are known to exist. Similarly, Ledyard's own journal, which was the basis for his published journal, is lost.[3]

Motives for keeping personal journals (as opposed to the more factual ship's logs) were no doubt as diverse as the journal keepers themselves. For some, it may have simply been a way to counter the boredom of weeks at sea. For others, it may have served a scientific interest. But for the officers and those who aspired to join their ranks, the journals had an almost legal or contractual function. The Admiralty would review them all at journey's end, making them a crucial record of performance, a fact that produced one of the voyage's most remarkable documents. As the ships prepared to make the final return passage from Macao to England, the crews learned that the Revolutionary War had broken out and that any ships sailing the Atlantic faced grave danger from French and American warships. The possibility that battle or capture could erase the record of the previous three and a half years' achievement was simply too much for First Lieutenant James Burney to face. Burney, who had first sailed in 1760 as a ten-year-old captain's servant, was obviously hoping to continue his steady climb up the naval ladder. To preserve the vital record of his and his shipmates' service, he copied his entire journal in tiny script—some three and a half years' worth of entries—on sheets of Chinese rice paper and folded the whole into an easily concealed 3½-inch bundle. A note on the document's paper wrapper explained that he had taken this action so that, "if bereft of our other journals there might be one saved for the Admiralty."[4]

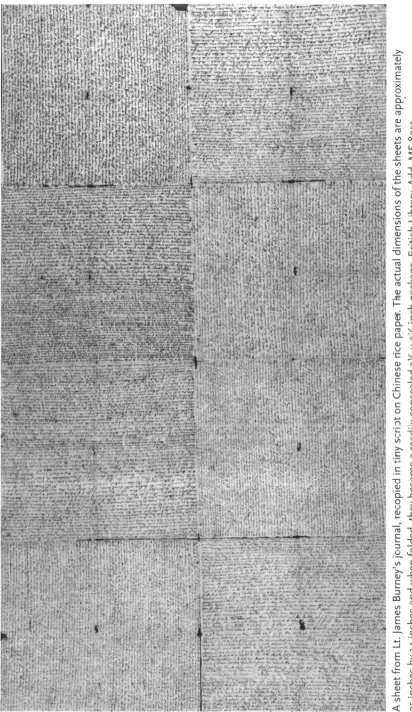

A sheet from Lt. James Burney's journal, recopied in tiny script on Chinese rice paper. The actual dimensions of the sheets are approximately 25 inches by 14 inches and when folded, they became a readily concealed 3½ × 3½ inch package. British Library. Add. MS 8955.

The need to demonstrate officers' rigorous and faithful execution of orders is difficult to grasp without a sense of just how detailed and particular those orders could be. Aside from directions regarding where and when he was to sail, Cook's orders contained detailed instructions regarding the data he was to collect. For any land he discovered, he was "very carefully to observe the true situation of such places, both in Latitude and Longitude; the Variation of the [compass] needle; Bearings of Headlands; Heights, Direction, and Course of the Tydes and Currents; Depths and Soundings of the Sea; Shoals, Rocks, & c.; and also to survey, make Charts, and take views of, such Bays, Harbours, and different parts of the Coast, and to make such Notations thereon, as may be useful either to Navigation or Commerce." He was also to carefully describe any new plant or animal species; he was to keep detailed ethnographic notes on Native peoples, focusing particularly on their "genius, temper, disposition, and number"; and finally, he was to observe and describe topography, soil type, and any mineral deposits. To the British state, the importance of these data is clear: all of it served the colonizing interests of a country increasingly aware of the strategic importance of the Pacific basin. But for Cook and his officers, its value was more personal. There was, in their world, no distinction between record keeping or data collection and the carrying out of one's duties. Only with the former could there be indisputable evidence of the latter.[5]

It was one thing to keep records of the voyage and its discoveries; altogether another to produce inaccurate or divergent accounts. The latter could be as damaging to officers' reputations as a failure to execute orders. In their quest for accuracy and consistency, journal writers thus endlessly inserted, redrafted, revised, and refined their observations. The drafts of Cook's own journals are punctuated with corrections, erasures, insertions, and blank spaces, the latter points he intended to return to with more accurate coordinates, bearings, or place-names.[6] The quest for a uniformly accurate record of the voyage must also explain the repetitiveness of the more than two dozen logs and journals remaining from the voyage. Indeed, so redundant are many of the journals and so close is their wording that one has to conclude that in order to maintain consistency, the writers copied from each other or just read their journals aloud with the understanding that shipmates would offer correction and elaboration.[7] Such was the practice of one journal keeper whom Herman Melville recalled in his semifictional tale of the antebellum American navy, *White Jacket: or, The World in a Man-of-War* (1850). That writer would "frequently read passages of his book to an admiring circle of the more refined sailors." The sailors "vied with each other in procuring interesting items, to be incorporated into additional chapters." In this case, however, the public readings had an undesired effect, at least as far as the officers were concerned. As the journal "contained reflections somewhat derogatory to the dignity of the officers, the volume was seized by the master-at-arms, armed with a warrant from the Captain."[8]

For any officer who might question the value of well-tended, redundant accounts of a voyage and its discoveries, the well-known fate of the navy captain Christopher Middleton was a cautionary tale. In 1741, the former Hudson's Bay Company captain was commissioned to lead two ships on a search for a water route to the Pacific thought to empty into Hudson's Bay. A year later, Middleton and his haggard, depleted crew returned to London with little to show for their labors other than malnutrition, scurvy, and frostbite. The whole business was basically a fruitless disaster. Being a typical duty-bound officer, Middleton duly presented the Admiralty with the charts and journal he had maintained during the voyage. None of these documents suggested the sought-after Northwest Passage, yet after poring over Middleton's journal Arthur Dobbs, the Irish member of Parliament who initially sponsored the voyage, declared that Middleton had falsified his journals, concealing the fact that he actually had found the passage. As the historian Glyn Williams has written, Dobbs's assertion was "breathtaking in its implication that Dobbs from his desk in Dublin could discern straits and channels in Hudson Bay that had somehow escaped Middleton's notice."[9]

The affair was devastating for Middleton. In questioning the data, Dobbs was questioning Middleton's very character. "He has no mercy on any Man's Reputation," the humiliated sea captain wrote, "and the person who contradicts him, is sure to have his good Name, more valuable than Life, inhumanly stabbed."[10] The Admiralty eventually determined that Dobbs's accusations were without merit, but the damage had been done. Middleton spent the next few years struggling in vain to salvage his reputation. In the affair's sad culmination, he was forced to appeal directly to Dobbs, his powerful antagonist, but his reputation never recovered. After a brief command aboard an obscure sloop, Middleton was to spend the final twenty-two years of his life on the navy's undistinguished "half-pay list," a pension program for retired officers.[11]

When viewed amidst the poaching and posturing, the greed and careerism that accompanied them, it is a wonder that anything at all of lasting scientific value came to light from these exploratory voyages. It is also a wonder that anybody's reputation survived them.

Cook, Ledyard, and all the other literate men aboard the *Discovery* and the *Resolution* knew this. In the end, it would be an authoritative, unimpeachable record of their journey that would protect them from those many and often contrary interests for whom the truth would be a bitter pill.

While a crew member could distinguish himself by joining the ranks of those who kept logs and journals, this was not the only vehicle for writing one's way into the literate class aboard the *Resolution*. The other was a weekly newspaper or handwritten circular members of the crew produced. None of these are known to have survived, but judging from later examples, they were valued more for entertainment than information. Their content included miscellaneous doggerel, riddles, diverting stories, philosophical essays, and possibly drawings and cartoons. In the only known reference to them, Burney describes them as the result of a widespread "literary ambition and disposition to authorship" among the men. "When the paper in either ship was ready for delivery," he explained, "a signal was made, and when answered by a similar signal from the other ship, Captain Cook, if the weather was fine, would good-naturedly let a boat be hoisted out to make the exchange, and he was always glad to read our paper, but never favoured our editors with the contribution of a paragraph."

Ledyard, however, did contribute to the circulars, but what he wrote did little for his reputation. Although "no one . . . doubted that his feelings were in accord with expression," Burney recalled that readers thought his ideas were "too sentimental, and his language too florid." While these qualities may have been harmless in a diverting ship's paper, they were precisely the sorts of things to be avoided in any authoritative, factual accounting of the voyage.[12]

Although Ledyard's original journal has been lost, the version he eventually published offers ample evidence of the kind of writing he had apparently been known for. One emblematic passage concerns a high point for Ledyard during the weeks of the voyagers' fateful second visit to the Hawaiian Islands. He had been assigned to an unarmed party sent to explore the island of Hawaii's interior. To date, this was Ledyard's first and only experience in an actual overland expedition; it also marked the first of what would be a string of failed exploratory journeys for Ledyard. The expedition, which included several Hawaiian guides, the gardener David Nelson, the gunner on the *Resolution,* Robert Anderson, the *Discovery*'s American-born gunner's mate Simeon Woodruff, and George Vancouver, then a young midshipman on the *Discovery,* set out to reach the great snowy peak of Mauna Loa, one of two volcanic peaks that rise above the island. After five days and a hopeless struggle to penetrate the dense Hawaiian forest encircling the steep sides of the volcano, the men returned to Kealakekua. Ledyard's is the only substantial account of the excursion by any of the participants, and like so much in his journal, the account says little about his actual conduct.

What it does say is fully consistent with Burney's characterization. Consider, for example, Ledyard's description of the breadfruit trees that grew around the temperate base of Mauna Loa. This strange tree, whose fruit, when cooked, resembles something between a potato and a loaf of bread, was to be a prized food source among mariners traveling in the South Pacific in the nineteenth century. The tree is also well known for its role in the life of William Bligh. In a scheme devised by Joseph Banks, Bligh would set out on the ill-fated *Bounty* to transport breadfruit saplings from the South Pacific to the West Indies. There the fruit was to be used to feed African slaves.

For Ledyard, though, the utility of the tree barely did justice to its actual meaning. The tree, in his view, was nothing less than the nectar of paradise; it was this apparently endless, indestructible food source that freed the people of the South Pacific from want and hard labor. To England's sons, immortalized by poets for their endless labors in the fields of wheat and corn, he pronounced, "What are thy fields but the sad testimony of toil, and when thy feeble plants hath passed the thousand dangers that attend its progress to a state of perfection in the field, what is it then? . . . Here is neither toil or care, man stretcheth forth his hand and eateth without parsimony or anticipated want."[13] This was Ledyard's way. A tree was not just a tree: it was the fount of an entire civilization. Such sentimental philosophizing might have played well among Dartmouth undergraduates, but to the young officers of the British navy it suggested an undisciplined mind.

With all the scribbling and literary posturing taking place aboard the *Resolution* and the *Discovery*, one wonders whether Ledyard was initially drawn to the expedition as a means of achieving literary celebrity. Perhaps when presented with the opportunity to sail with Cook, he saw potential income from a published firsthand account of the voyage. Accounts of exploratory expeditions were hugely popular, and accounts of Cook's, especially so. John Hawkesworth, the Admiralty's chosen editor of the published version of Cook's journals from his first voyage, earned £6,000 for his efforts, a vast sum by the standards of the era. For the first two volumes of his enormously popular *History of England*, David Hume received a mere £1,940, and the similarly revered William Robertson earned £3,400 for his three-volume *Charles V*, published in 1769. By 1785, Hawkesworth's volumes had gone through three English editions, a New York edition, and French and German editions.

The popularity of the work is also evident in the records of lending libraries. These institutions, some private businesses, some clubs requiring payment of a subscription fee, allowed aspiring gentlemen the benefit of the kinds of grand libraries formerly available only to Britain's leisured elite. The Liverpool library, the oldest of England's subscription libraries, had a membership consisting of professionals, tradesmen, and merchants—aspiring men who recognized the social benefits of reading but who lacked the material resources to acquire their own substantial libraries. Among the most popular works in these libraries were histories and travel narratives, and Hawkesworth's volumes figured prominently in this group. Between 1773 and 1784, members of the Bristol library borrowed the volumes 201 times, making the work among the institution's ten most popular.[14]

Ledyard may have thus joined the expedition in hopes of being the Hawkesworth of the third voyage. His petition to write the official account suggests as much. But it also suggests how naïve he was about the literary politics of exploration. Not only was he unaware that his prose was thought to be too poetic and sentimental, but he was also unaware of the elaborate and complex process by which the official accounts came into being.

Whoever would prepare the authoritative account of the voyage would not be an unknown marine corporal whose reputation as a writer came from scribblings in a shipboard newspaper. It would be a person with some literary reputation in London (something which, of course, Cook himself also lacked) and, more important, a person with connections to the Admiralty, the custodian of Cook's journals. To distill Cook's journals into the official account of his first voyage, prominent friends, including the celebrated composer and musicologist (and the father of Fanny and James) Dr. Charles Burney and the actor David Garrick, had recommended the well-known essayist and editor John Hawkesworth to Lord Sandwich.[15] And while the published version of Cook's journals from his second voyage was more the result of Cook's own labors, he was substantially assisted in preparing them for the public by John Douglas, an Anglican cleric with a reputation for literary skill and honesty and a list of prominent patrons including Lord Sandwich. The latter, of course, had recruited Douglas to assist Cook. Sandwich also turned to Douglas to edit the posthumous journals of Cook's last voyage. Hawkesworth and Douglas were minor literary celebrities, Ledyard a literary unknown. That he even thought he could fill the much lesser role of shipboard chronicler in the aftermath of Cook's death is an indication that Ledyard's reputation for fanciful thinking was deserved. It is also perhaps an indication of his provinciality. A youth spent in the American provinces may have made Ledyard sensitive to the wonders of nature, but it left him naïve about the literary economy of the metropolitan navy. Here, what mattered was not a capacity to write evocatively of breadfruit groves, but rather a capacity to transparently recount what it was the voyagers themselves actually saw and did.[16]

There is one other way in which personal ambition and writing may have converged when Ledyard sailed with Cook. He may have intended to publish an unofficial account of the voyage. Whatever aspirations he might have had in this regard, the reality was that it would be difficult to do and, as Ledyard discovered, virtually impossible to do profitably. The chief obstacle to the publication of unofficial accounts was simply the imperative of secrecy with which the expedition was undertaken. The last thing the government wanted was for Cook's findings to fall into the hands of its imperial rivals. Britain was not the only European country with designs in the Pacific. Both Spain and Russia were seeking to extend and protect their claims there, and France had maintained designs on the South Pacific since Louis Antoine de Bougainville's circumnavigation between 1766 and 1769. Furthermore, one of the incentives for a skilled navigator like Cook to undertake these extremely hazardous journeys was the celebrity and income generated by publication of the journals. A raft of contradictory unofficial accounts would only raise questions among the public about the veracity of Cook's own account.

To control the flow of information, the Admiralty ordered Cook to confiscate all shipboard logs and journals and to "seal them up for our inspection, and enjoyning them, and the whole Crew, not to divulge where they have been until they shall have permission so to do."[17] James King, who had taken command of *Discovery* during the last leg of the journey, recounted his efforts to carry out these orders in December 1779, just after the ships anchored off Macao, en route to England. The account offers a concise description of the literary politics of the entire business of exploration. It was clear to King, for example, that the men would not eagerly abandon their personal writings to the naval bureaucracy. "The execution of these orders," he noted, "seemed to require some delicacy, as well as firmness. I could not be ignorant, the greatest part of our offi-cers, and several of the seamen had amused themselves with writing accounts of our proceedings for their own private satisfaction, or that of their friends, which they might be unwilling, in their present form, to have submitted to the inspection of strangers." They would have, that is, been disinclined to have their rough prose and potentially compromising thoughts reviewed by anonymous superiors at the Admiralty. Nonethe-less, King was convinced that such concerns had to be subordinate to the larger issue addressed by the Admiralty's orders. The various shipboard writings, "either from carelessness or design, might fall into the hands of printers, and give rise to spurious and imperfect accounts of the voyage, to the discredit of our labors, and perhaps to the prejudice of officers, who, though innocent, might be suspected of having been authors of such publications."[18]

Middleton's case must not have been far from King's mind. Every crew member was a potential source for scraps of information, from fully realized journals to fragmentary notes; from coastal charts to sketches of unknown lands and people. And any of these could lead to controversy and damaged reputations.[19]

Not surprisingly, the Admiralty's orders, no matter how faithfully car-ried out, were not entirely effective, and this had been the case for all of

Cook's voyages. A little over two months after the end of the first voyage, the anonymous *Journal of a Voyage round the World* appeared, probably written by the New York–born midshipman James Magra. And the number of substantial accounts preceding Cook's official account simply grew with the conclusions of the second and third voyages, the former yielding two and the latter three, including Ledyard's.[20]

Still, this hardly represents a stampede, and of these accounts, none did much for its author. From the final expedition, the first was written by Second Lieutenant John Rickman, although, in an effort to protect the author from retribution, it was originally published anonymously. Another was written by the surgeon's mate William Ellis, a man so desperate for money that he was willing to sacrifice any future naval career by putting his name to the unauthorized account. Indeed, there is no evidence that either Rickman or Ellis enjoyed more than a brief cash infusion for their risky publishing enterprises. And finally, Ledyard published his own account only after deserting and fleeing to his home in the newly independent United States. For him, there was nothing to lose. But neither, as it turned out, was there much to gain: the book did little for Ledyard's long-term financial well-being. The war-ravaged United States was evidently not the place to publish an account of a British expedition to the Pacific.

The point is simply that whatever Ledyard's ambitions, writing would ultimately do little to help him achieve them. He would have to find other ways to distinguish himself.[21]

When Cook ordered the *Resolution* and the *Discovery* to raise anchor and sail from Plymouth Sound on July 12, 1776, neither he nor his American crew members nor anybody else in Britain yet knew that the American colonies had formally declared their independence from Great Britain. They knew that some sort of rebellion was happening in the colonies; they knew that the British government had been sending naval vessels and army regiments to quell that rebellion; but they had no sense that these events would lead to a hugely costly war. Indeed, Cook would never know that many of the men he commanded would be returning to England only to put to sea again, headed for battle in the Caribbean and along the Atlantic coast of North America.

The first news the voyagers received of developments in America came at the beginning of December 1779, as the ships began preparing to return to England. What the crew took from this was not so much that the empire they had always known was in peril, but that Britain was at war with its French enemy. While anchored off Macao, Midshipman George Gilbert noted, "We heard of the war with France which was a very unexpected event to us; as in general we were of opinion that the Rebellion in America would have been quelled long before that time."[22] This was ominous news. France was a much more formidable opponent than a ragtag band of renegade colonists, and the only European power with a navy that could challenge British seaborne supremacy.

What Ledyard thought about these developments is unknown. But nothing suggests that the news brought warm feeling toward his native land or that it aroused some latent revolutionary sentiment. If anything, the record suggests he only grew closer to Britain and the Royal Navy.

Less than a year after he safely returned the *Resolution* and the *Discovery* to the Deptford Naval Yards on October 6, 1780, Gore recommended Ledyard for an officer's commission. Included with his letter of recommendation was Ledyard's own petition for the promotion. This document reveals none of Ledyard's early rebelliousness and individualism. Instead it presents him as a man struggling to play by the rules of the highly stratified, patronage-driven world he inhabited:

> May it please your Lordship
> The dignity of your situation and the obscurity of my own very much circumscribe me, as well as my apprehensions of Assuming a merit that few in my situation would perhaps aspire to. Yet, when I reflect that I can appeal to the testimonies of such as have done honour to our Navy, to the World, and to your Lordships patronage, the propriety of an apology seems to disappear and I flatter myself justified in looking upon your Lordship for a reward for my past and an encouragement for my future services.

Although Cook was not alive to testify to his good service, Ledyard continued, the commander's journal would make clear his esteem for Ledyard and his willingness to entrust the lowly marine with "very honorable commands." Further, Ledyard insisted that his was not the petition of just any marine. It was the plea of a worthy gentleman, cast adrift by the uncontrollable winds of history. "I am a native of North America, of a

A captain of the Marines. Hand-colored print after a drawing
by Thomas Rowlandson, 1799. © National Maritime
Museum, London.

good Family and once had considerable connections there," he explained,
"until the rupture with England in 1775 when I abandoned all and entered
the Army here."[23]

Were it not for the "rupture with England," this wellborn American
would have no need to grovel for another Briton's favor. For he would have
been able to employ family connections to achieve a station better suited
to his abilities and character. But now this was impossible. Because of circumstances beyond his control, he had no option but to address the great
Lord Sandwich and request recognition for a good Briton's good service.
Such a man as himself, he seemed to say to Lord Sandwich, ought not pay
for the irresponsible conduct of his countrymen. He remained a good and
loyal servant of the British Crown and, as such, entitled to its favor.

Ledyard's reasoning fell on deaf ears. The commission never came. His four years' service earned him little money and left him languishing in the lower ranks of the British military. Had he been more candid, more of the independent, natural-born intellect he believed himself to be, he might have revealed this frustration. He might even have penned lines such as these by Midshipman Gilbert: "Thus ended a long, tedious, and disagreeable voyage, of four years, and three months, . . . Finis."[24]

CHAPTER V

Following the Revolution Home

A LITTLE OVER A YEAR after returning to England aboard the *Resolution*, Ledyard found himself sent to sea once again. This time he would leave England not as part of a benevolent expedition of discovery but rather as a member of a fighting force. And he would be asked to do what he had hoped never to do: raise arms against his American countrymen. For his ship was sent to America to cruise Long Island Sound in search of American privateers and blockade runners.

Ledyard arrived in the former colonies in October 1781, just before his thirtieth birthday and the same month of the catastrophic British defeat at Yorktown, Virginia. Though it would be nearly two years before a formal peace was settled, the surrender of Lord Cornwallis on October 17 effectively ended any hope of British victory. Not only did Ledyard find himself having to raise arms against his countrymen, but he now found himself having to do so for a lost cause. As if this were not bad enough, he arrived in America to discover that he was part of a force responsible for some of the Ledyard family's darkest days. The British military had not been kind to the Ledyards of Connecticut.

On September 6, 1781, Benedict Arnold, the onetime patriot turned Loyalist general, led a devastating attack on New London and Groton. The assault was part of a British campaign to disrupt supply lines and draw patriot forces northward, away from strongholds in Virginia. In the assault, Arnold's men burned a dozen ships and much of the two towns. They also took Fort Griswold, built on a bluff above Groton to defend against enemy forces approaching from the Thames River below.

One hundred twenty volunteers under the command of Ledyard's Uncle William had defended the fort against eight hundred British regulars for almost an hour while awaiting reinforcements from the surrounding countryside. These never came, and the redcoats overran the fort and killed William, father of seven, with the very sword he had presented in surrender. Ledyard's cousin Youngs was also killed, and his cousin William Seymour was seriously wounded. In the end, the patriots suffered some seventy dead and nearly everyone else wounded. The British showed no more regard for the patriot wounded than they had for the surrendering Ledyard and his men. "Soon after the surrender of the Fort," the *Connecticut Gazette* reported, the British troops "loaded a wagon with our wounded men . . . , and set the wagon off from the top of the hill [on which the fort is situated], which is long and very steep. The wagon went a considerable distance with great force, till it was suddenly stopped by a tree; the shock was so great to those faint and bleeding men, that some of them died instantly."

Others in the Ledyard family were also drawn into the mayhem. John's younger sister Fanny, who had been visiting from Southold, helped tend the wounded and came to be called "the angel of Groton" for her good deeds. She performed her services in the home of Ebenezer Avery, who along with nine of his relatives had also been killed that day.

The defeat at Fort Griswold was a symptom of broader problems. Local authorities had been struggling for some time to raise a larger force to defend the fort but with no real success. And when presented with the opportunity to help defend Groton and New London, volunteers from the countryside proved reluctant to engage the enemy. After more than six years of sacrifice, the citizens of coastal Connecticut, it seems, were beginning to tire of the war. They had no idea that in just over a month the British would be defeated at Yorktown.[1]

From a British frigate in the waters of Huntington Bay, Long Island, Ledyard wrote his grieving cousin Isaac, whose brother Youngs had been killed in the massacre. The letter was the first he is known to have written since sailing for England on the eve of the war, seven years earlier. And it is one of the few occasions on which John Ledyard was at a loss for words. It was also an occasion for him to remind Isaac that although he himself had not suffered the trials of war and revolution, fortune had not been kind to him. "After my seven years absence, after the various revolutions in the political affairs of America—my own extraordinary fate and the present situation of my dear dear friends—believe me I know not what to write or what I ought write. My heart I send you—my whole heart . . . could I embrace thee, thou best of friends, I should forget even my own misfortunes." Ledyard may not have paid the price of patriotism, he was telling Isaac, but he had paid a dear price. From his forced enlistment in the British military to his current service, he too had been the victim of fate and ill fortune.[2]

The assertion seems disingenuous in light of Ledyard's pursuit of higher military office. But his subsequent actions lend it at least a tincture of sincerity. Facing a stalled military career in a force that had inflicted so much suffering on his family, Ledyard not surprisingly deserted. Sometime in 1782 he obtained a shore pass and traveled to his mother's house in Southold. His stepfather, Micah, had died in 1776, leaving Abigail a widow once again. To make ends meet, she had turned her house into a tavern and had been taking in boarders. Like others on eastern Long Island, Abigail became a dedicated patriot and during the course of the war harbored British deserters. Her son's visit was brief. He chose to flee further inland, away from British shore patrols, to the relative peace of Hartford. There he would undertake another journey, this one of a more lofty, cerebral sort. He would write a travel book.[3]

Picture the author toiling before an oil lamp, scratching a quill pen across rough parchment day after day in the drafty confines of a wood-frame colonial house. Those ponderous hours yield a book fashioned from the author's experience. As a travel book, it is a book of facts and observations, organized chronologically, dates functioning like factual anchors for the wondrous and fantastic sites described beneath them.

The writer of such a book is more translator than inventing author. His burden is to make his experience available to his readers in the most persuasive, vivid, and authoritative possible fashion. He does this by crafting a narrative that limits his own presence in the work. Much like the writer of a shipboard journal or log, the writer of the published travel

A
JOURNAL
OF
Captain COOK's
LAST
VOYAGE
TO THE
Pacific Ocean,
AND IN QUEST OF A
North-West Paffage,
BETWEEN
ASIA & AMERICA;
Performed in the Years 1776, 1777, 1778, and
1779.
Illuftrated with a CHART, fhewing the Tracts of
the Ships employed in this Expedition.

Faithfully narrated from the original MS. of
Mr. JOHN LEDYARD.

HARTFORD:
Printed and fold by NATHANIEL PATTEN,
a few Rods North of the Court-Houfe,
M,D,CC,LXXXIII.

Title page, John Ledyard's *A Journal of Captain Cook's Last Voyage*. Hartford, 1783. Courtesy, American Antiquarian Society.

journal must build his narrative on a range of conventions. It must be chronological, it must accord with other accounts, and it must relate occurrences and facts in an unencumbered, unembellished fashion. As one reviewer wrote favorably of a similar account, a voyage must be "narrated in such a plain unaffected style that there can not be the least doubt of its authenticity."[4]

If Ledyard's shipboard writing is any indication, "plain, unaffected" prose was not something at which he excelled. Perhaps this deficit explains his relative failure as an author. Only one contemporary edition of his book was ever published, while Second Lieutenant John Rickman's unofficial account reached four editions by 1785. Cook's own published journals from the voyage went through four editions (one of which was French) in less than two years after initially appearing in 1784. Perhaps Ledyard's sentimental and florid writing simply raised too many questions about the truthfulness of his account.

But there were other reasons for readers to question the reliability of Ledyard's journal. For one thing, although the book retains a diurnal form, the question arises, how did Ledyard recall the dates of events several years after they happened? It is possible he disregarded Admiralty orders and retained his original journal, but this seems unlikely. He was too much the aspiring officer to defy so important an order. What seems far more likely is that he drew on the journal of another voyager for his basic time line.

The one such journal that would have been available to him was Rickman's nearly identically titled *Journal of Captain Cook's Last Voyage to the Pacific Ocean,* first printed in London in 1781. The most obvious indication that Ledyard used the book is simply that the last thirty pages of the two books are identical. Ledyard may have obtained a copy of Rickman's book before leaving for America, or perhaps he was able to use a copy belonging to an officer aboard one of the vessels on which he served. It is also possible that a copy had made its way to Hartford. At least one copy had circulated in the United States, allowing a Philadelphia printer to publish an American edition in 1783.[5]

It must be said that in an era known for rampant plagiarism, Ledyard's borrowing was relatively minor. For one thing, the portion of the book he copied covers the voyage's final year, a largely uneventful period during which the ships made their way back to Britain. In addition, much like authors of any philosophical or historical tract, Ledyard drew freely on other works as well, especially John Hawkesworth's edition of the journals from Cook's first voyage. He made little effort to conceal that borrowing, sometimes even reproducing whole sentences of Hawkesworth's. Finally, it is not known where Rickman obtained his own original account. During the final year of the Pacific voyage, he served with Ledyard aboard the *Resolution,* and it is entirely possible that the two drew on one another's shipboard journals. What Rickman published, that is, may have been a collaborative work to begin with.[6]

In the end, the real failing of Ledyard's book was not its unoriginal content, but rather its original content. For most of the book is unquestionably Ledyard's. And, as we have seen, it reveals his signature mingling of speculative natural history with romantic prose. The most emblematic and extensive sections of the book thus concern Ledyard's own explorations—the journey across Unalaska and the trek up Mauna Loa. But most telling is the book's ethnological content. Throughout all his later writings, Ledyard would reveal a preoccupation with the distant past of non-European peoples. The book represents his first lengthy meditation on the subject.

Ledyard's interest in the history of human societies was characteristic of Enlightenment era ethnography. Virtually every intellectual of the age who wrote about human history, from Adam Smith to Jean-Jacques Rousseau, from Thomas Jefferson to Princeton University president Samuel Stanhope Smith, sought answers to one fundamental question: could the proposition enshrined in such liberal documents as the American Declaration of Independence, that all men are created equal, be empirically proven? For Americans, the question had significance that went beyond the merely philosophical. If all human beings could somehow be shown to emanate from the same ancestors, then their natures had to be fundamentally the same. And if this was the case, the revolutionary experiment in America rested on an actual natural law rather than on the vain hope of idealistic philosophers, as the nation's monarchical critics contended. Only if human nature was fundamentally uniform could people be truly self-governing because only then could there be such things as universal natural law. Insofar as John Ledyard was committed to the cause for which his relatives died, he was committed as a theorist of human history and firm advocate for the view that human beings the world over are fundamentally the same, originally created by the same God and sharing a common early history.[7]

Consider first John's treatment of Tahitian religion. What most struck him was simply its nebulousness. There seemed to be no system or ordering principle. Individual priests could make of it what they would—an abhorrent situation for a good Protestant. Because the Tahitians had no Bible or other sacred text, there was no authority above the priest's, leaving the various rites with no apparent rationale. Their religious customs, Ledyard explained, "are simple, detached, individual and various; they seem to be fragments of many different theories." But the latter point was most telling. As Ledyard interpreted them, these were not the isolated customs of isolated, distinct people, but rather the fragments of ancestral rituals shared by peoples the world over.

One custom, especially revealing in this regard, was Tahitian circumcision. Cook had earlier suggested that the practice had a hygienic purpose, but Ledyard doubted this, believing instead it had a ceremonial function and was probably even inherited from one of Israel's lost tribes. "The particular form of the incision," he claimed, "is not so different from that now used among the Jews." The only meaningful difference in the procedure is that the Jews "have the finest instruments to perform the ceremony and the Otaheitean [as eighteenth-century writers referred to Tahitians] has only an oyster shell." But the Tahitian "member" is no less "a delicate, a nervous and sensible member." The different methods of circumcision, that is, did not reflect any physical differences among the practitioners. History and biology both suggested a connection between these Pacific Islanders and the ancient peoples of the Near East.[8]

Even cannibalism, in Ledyard's lexicon, could be understood in terms of universal religious practices. For Ledyard, it very clearly evolved—or really devolved—from human sacrifice, something Jews and Christians had also practiced. "The circumstances of Abraham's intended sacrifice of Isaac to which he was injoined by the Deity," or the story of Jephtha, who, "it is said, . . . sacrificed his daughter as a burnt-offering to the God who had been propitious to him in war" amply proved the point. Some form of sacrifice, in other words, was universal in early human societies. It stood to reason, then, that "the custom of eating human flesh," which "pervades much the greatest part of the habitable earth," began with the "custom of sacrificing human flesh." The "favored Israelites," in other words, were little better than the world's uncivilized peoples. For they "were perpetually deviating into schisms and cabals and frequently into downright idolatry, and all the vanity of superstition and unbridled nonsense from the imbecility of human policy when uninfluenced by heavenly wisdom and jurisprudence." Would it have been so absurd, Ledyard was asking, for them to make the jump from sacrificial offering to cannibalism?[9]

Much like Tahitian religion, Tahitian government was not simply Tahitian. It resembled, Ledyard explained, "the early state of every government, which in an unimproved and unrefined state, is ever a kind of feudal system of subordination: Securing licentious liberty to a few, and a dependent servility to the rest." The Tahitian system was composed of four estates or "orders," the first being the great chiefs; next come regional chiefs, and the third order "are those who occupy and improve certain portions of land in each district, for which he is accountable to the chief of the district: He is a kind of tenant." After these tenant farmers comes the fourth order, "who labor and cultivate the land and do other services under the tenant." The whole system seemed remarkably like Europe's feudal order of kings, lords, freeholders, and tenants.[10]

In his description of the Maori, the indigenous people of New Zealand, Ledyard focused less on institutions than on character. But here, too, his comparative reference points are the ancient ancestors of the Occident. In terms of their physical power, their highly cultivated emotional sensitivity, and their intelligence, the natives of New Zealand were the picture of Syphaxian virtue: "When a [Maori warrior] stands forth and brandishes his spear the subsequent idea is (and nature makes the confession) there stands a man." These were fighters who could not be dismissed as mere savages. "It is," Ledyard explained, "their native courage, their great personal prowess, their irreversible intrepidity, and determined fixed perseverance that is productive of those obstinate attacks we have found among them when we have appealed to the decisions of war." These were not cowardly, skulking fighters; they were noble warriors in the greatest ancient tradition, strong, virtuous, and manly. Syphax could hardly be more vividly evoked.[11]

Among the Tongan Islanders, Ledyard found similar grounds for praise. After a display of their wrestling and boxing skills, he could not help but be struck by the emotional equilibrium the athletes maintained, even in defeat. "I never saw any of them choleric, envious, malicious or revengeful," he noted, "but preserving their tempers, or being less irascible than we generally are, [they] quit the stage with the same good nature with which they entered it." In the end, "the best general idea I can convey of their attitudes in this exercise is to compare them with those of the ancient gladiators of Rome which they much resemble."[12]

Ledyard reserved his highest praise for the Tongan chiefs Polahow and Phenow. These men were powerful and revered, and the reason for this was not crude politics or the force of arms. These were simply admirable men. This was especially the case with Phenow, who "was one of the most graceful men I ever saw in the Pacific Ocean":

> He was about 5 feet 11 inches high, fleshy but not fat, and com-
> pletely formed : He was open and free in his disposition, full
> of vivacity, enterprising and bold, expert in all the acquirements
> of his country, particularly in their art of navigation, over which
> he presided, and what is esteemed among them as a necessary
> ingredient in a great character was possessed of uncommon
> strength and agility; he was besides extremely handsome, he
> had a large prominent eye full of fire and great expression, an
> aquiline nose and a well formed face : His hair which was long,
> hung after the manner of the country in thick bushy ringlets
> over his shoulders; With all these accomplishments he was ex-
> tremely popular among the people, and the idol of the fair, hav-
> ing himself one of the most beautiful brunettes for a wife that
> the hands of nature ever finished, but during our stay he was
> seldom with her or with us, his active soul was ever on the
> wing, and in his canoe which sailed exceedingly swift [.] He
> would in twenty-four hours surround the whole group of
> islands, and almost visit them individually.[13]

Phenow and his people seemed to grasp the basic truth of John Ledyard's world that looking the part was the first step toward nobility. Every right-thinking man would admire the Tongan chief's combination of grace and stature.

When it came to grasping the deeper animating forces of human-ity, Ledyard again turned to the universalizing enlightenment formula that shaped his ethnography. For all his physical presence, Phenow still struggled with self-control. For even he engaged in theft, his people's most troubling habit. But this too could be attributed to universal human nature, involuntary impulses that did not eclipse the essential goodness of this natural nobleman. "How often, Phenow, have I felt for thee, the embarrassments of these involuntary offences against [us]," and yet, Led-yard had to acknowledge, those offenses would be no offense at all were it not for the Europeans' "theory of moral virtue," at the center of which was the idea of property. Much like Rousseau, Ledyard here seems to be suggesting that in its most primitive form, society has no need for the superficial encumbrances of property or law. For, in the end, the so-called civilized are "more savage themselves with all their improvements than thou wert without a single one of them." With all their weaponry, with all their alluring baubles, with their uniforms and rigid conventions, what gave the Europeans the right to judge this noble Tongan a thief? It is hard not to think that Ledyard was here reflecting on his own latent frustrations with the navy and the British Empire. The traditions and customs of that chivalric society had misjudged him just as it misjudged Phenow.[14]

Ledyard's celebration of the Pacific Islanders' essential humanity sits awkwardly with his treatment of one aspect of Hawaiian culture—sodomy. He devoted only a page to the subject, but felt obliged to "inform the world of a custom among [the Hawaiian Islanders] contrary to nature, and odious to a delicate mind, yet as such a remarkable incident in the history of a new discovered people." The practice appeared to be limited to chiefs and their male concubines, or *aikane*, potent political agents who often mediated between the British and local leaders. "Though we had no right to attack or ever to disapprove of customs in general that differed from our own," Ledyard concluded, "this one so apparently infringed and insulted the first and strangest dictate of nature, and we had . . . so strong a prejudice against it, that the first instance we saw of it we condemned." What seems to have affected Ledyard more than even the sex was the total inversion of familiar gender roles: "By a shocking inversion of the laws of nature," the chiefs "bestow all those affections upon [their *aikane*] that were intended for the other sex." The striking thing here is not that Ledyard, the child of New England Puritans, disapproved of sodomy. It is that he said virtually nothing about the rampant displays of heterosexuality that were also so obvious a part of Hawaiian cosmology. Apparently sex in whatever form, so long as it was heterosexual, was sufficiently normal to warrant no comment.[15]

If in terms of ethnological content, Ledyard's book generally bears his mark, in terms of political content the connection is not so clear. Early in its life, commentators viewed the journal as hostile to Cook and, by extension, anti-British. "The train of events at the Sandwich Islands [as noted earlier, Cook had named the Hawaiian Islands after Lord Sandwich], which led to the death of Captain Cook," Jared Sparks observed, "is narrated by Ledyard in a manner more consistent and natural than appears in any other account of it." And what Ledyard's story revealed was the rash behavior of the ships' officers "and of Cook particularly." This, to Sparks's mind, "was the primary cause" of Cook's death and "was kept out of sight by the authorized narrators." Only an American deserter could afford to be so candid.[16]

Sparks based his assessment on a single paragraph in which Ledyard accused Cook of permitting his men to seize as firewood a fence surrounding a sacred site, or *heiau*. As Ledyard tells the story, Hawaiian leaders were justly shocked "to behold the fence that enclosed the mansions of their noble ancestors, and the images of their gods torn to pieces by a handful of rude strangers." Responding to the chiefs' outrage, according to Ledyard, Cook disdainfully offered the Hawaiians some hatchets as compensation. "It was a very unequal price if the honest chiefs would have accepted the bribe," Ledyard concluded "and Cook offered it only to evade the imputation of taking their property without payment."[17]

To the nineteenth-century American missionary Hiram Bingham, Ledyard's account of the *heiau* incident showed Cook's very British disregard for the Hawaiians' rights, "both civil and religious," and explained how it was that the commander of a benevolent voyage of discovery could "awaken . . . resentment and hostility" that would culminate in his death. Ledyard's story also explained why Protestant missionaries were having so much trouble indoctrinating these Pacific islanders. Instead of patiently leading them away from their pagan beliefs, Cook actually discouraged conversion by allowing himself to become their god Lono. For Bingham, this audacious act was proof of Cook's inability to act on behalf of any but the British.[18]

To more recent commentators as well, Ledyard's book has an anti-Cook, pro-American bias. In his definitive 1967 edition of Cook's journals, J. C. Beaglehole condemned Ledyard's account as that of "a patriotic and free-born American" who "did not omit to slip in a few episodes discreditable to the British." Another twentieth-century biographer of Cook, taking offense at Ledyard's portrayal of the great man, dismissed the young marine's account entirely: "Knowing little or nothing of the facts of the matter, Ledyard came to unwarranted conclusions." As recently as 1995, the American anthropologist Marshall Sahlins also acknowledged in an otherwise favorable treatment that Ledyard "is not the most reliable of the Cook chroniclers."[19]

Running through all of these judgments is one basic question: is there something distinctly American about Ledyard's account, something that explains either his bias or his unique candor? Put differently, is this published journal in some cryptic way a patriotic tract? To be sure, there are several instances in which Ledyard questions Cook's leadership. One involves the desecration of the *heiau*. Others highlight the "severity [with] which [Cook] sometimes" punished natives for minor transgressions.[20] In one case, Cook imprisoned a group of local chiefs to secure the return of two deserters in the Society Islands. According to Rickman, Cook held a king and several young princes, threatening them with death if his men were not returned. "This might seem hard usage," Rickman explained, "yet it had its effect, and without this steady resolute proceeding the deserters would never have been recovered." Observing the distress this tactic caused the natives, Ledyard noted, "I would not have been the author of such grief for two deserters." This kind of second-guessing is hardly damning condemnation.[21]

By far Ledyard's sharpest remarks come as the voyagers returned to the Hawaiian Islands in late 1778. "It was immediately and very naturally supposed," Ledyard explained, "that Cook's first object now would be to find a harbour, where our weather-beaten ships might be repaired, and our fatigued crews receive the rewards due to their perseverance and toil through so great a piece of navigation as we had performed the last nine or ten months." But, as we have seen, Cook delayed landfall. In his assessment Ledyard sided with the "people." What in Cook's eyes had been a mutinous threat was justified, Ledyard explained, "as it appeared very manifest that Cook's conduct was wholly influenced by motives of interest, to which he was evidently sacrificing not only the ships, but the healths and happiness of the brave men, who were weaving the laurel that was hereafter to adorn his brows."[22]

It makes sense to view these complaints in light of the revolutionary environment in which they were made. Ledyard's book appeared in 1783, the year the Treaty of Paris officially ended Anglo-American hostilities. A book about a British expedition written by an American would naturally emphasize the very qualities that led to independence: corruption and neglect. Much like King George III and his ministers, so the reasoning might have gone, Cook allowed his own quest for power and personal gain to cloud his judgment. Instead of providing that patient, fatherly care expected of a great patriarch, he resorted to petty retribution. For such behavior, Cook lost his life, King George III, his empire.

The problem with this reading is that, first of all, Ledyard was not alone in his criticism of Cook's conduct. The Englishman Rickman's account, printed in London, hardly offered a flattering portrait of Cook, especially his disciplinary practices. From this published journal, we learn that one Tongan Islander was "punished with seventy two lashes, for only stealing a knife, another with thirty six for endeavoring to carry off two or three drinking glasses; . . . but what was still more cruel, a man for attempting to carry off an axe, was ordered to have his arm cut to the bone." "It is not to be wondered, that after such wanton acts of cruelty," the islanders took every opportunity to be "vexatious." In terms very similar to Ledyard's, this author seemed to be saying that Cook's methods would only stimulate the very theft and annoyance he was determined to counter. A British audience, it would appear, was no less likely than an American one to learn of Cook's bad behavior.[23]

In addition to the ecumenical nature of anti-Cook sentiment, another factor casts doubt on a patriotic reading of Ledyard's book. His treatment of Cook was not wholly negative. Cook, he wrote, was a navigator of "consummate accuracy," and although his punishment was often harsh, it was also at times justified. Observing the ravages left by venereal disease in the Hawaiian Islands, Ledyard applauded Cook for using every measure to prevent such horrors. Had he known that those measures were being violated, Ledyard noted approvingly, he would have punished the violators "in the severest manner."[24]

In January 1783, the governor and General Assembly of Connecticut accepted John Ledyard's petition for a copyright on his new book and adopted the "Act for the encouragement of Literature and Genius." Aside from being the first truly American copyright law, the act would be a bold acknowledgment that "it is perfectly agreeable to principles of natural equity and justice, that every author should be secured in receiving the profits that may arise from the sale of his works, and such security may encourage men of learning and genius to publish their writings; which may do honor to their country, and service to mankind."[25]

Never before had Ledyard truly owned the product of his labor. But now the government of Connecticut conferred on him just that privilege. "There is nothing which so generally strikes the imagination, and engages the affections of mankind, as the right of property," wrote the British jurist William Blackstone. For the right of property is "that sole and despotic dominion which one man claims and exercises over the eternal things of the world, in total exclusion of the right of any other individual in the universe."[26] To this point in his thirty-one years, Ledyard had never had sole or despotic dominion" over anything or anyone. Now, he truly did own something—if only briefly.

Shortly after obtaining his copyright, Ledyard sold it to the Hartford printer Nathaniel Patten. The transaction would prove to be very costly to Ledyard, but in the years immediately after the Revolution it was likely the only way for an unknown author to get published.

Printing a complete book in the United States so soon after the war was no simple matter. Paper, ink, and especially type were all in short supply. Before the Revolution, most of these materials had been imported from Britain. During the course of the war the supply fell to a trickle, forcing printers to rely on poorer quality paper and worn out typeface. Even after the war, the added wear and tear on limited type, the still costly paper and ink, and the investment in a little-known author would have all entailed significant financial risk for Patten. The Connecticut law gave a printer a new way to control this risk. By maintaining exclusive rights to Ledyard's book for a period of fourteen years, it improved Patten's chances of recovering his costs.[27]

Before this law was enacted, a typical colonial American printer would have controlled such risk by soliciting prepublication subscriptions. In place of a single great patron (there were few colonists who alone could afford to underwrite the publication of books) or a large concentrated population of book-buying gentlemen (such as existed in London), a book's cost would be borne by a series of patrons, whose names were acknowledged in subscribers' lists printed at the beginning of the work. That was the strategy of the New York publisher James Rivington, who reprinted a pirated version of Hawkesworth's edition of Cook's first journals in New York in 1774. Rivington solicited subscriptions with the promise that advance purchase of this multivolume work would encourage the development of domestic industry and help maintain a favorable balance of trade for the American colonies. Purchasing such a book, in other words, would be the patriotic thing for a gentleman to do because it would stimulate the colonial printing industry. Without copyright protection, though, Rivington risked the same piracy he himself had committed.[28]

Beyond this, we tend to assume that copyright represents society's endorsement of a given author; it is a privilege, as the Connecticut statute suggested, granted to deserving citizens in recognition of their service to their nation. There is little in the statute's language, or really in any of the other revolutionary-era justifications for copyright, to suggest it was intended to protect printers and booksellers. And yet, if Ledyard's book is any indication, this is precisely the way it functioned. To strengthen the relatively weak legal basis for copyright, London booksellers had long applied an informal principle that effectively made copyright perpetual. When a Scottish bookseller began disregarding this long-standing practice in his London shop by publishing works copyrighted by other booksellers, Samuel Johnson condemned the man, explaining approvingly that "it has always been understood by the trade, that he who buys the copy-right of a book from the author, obtains a perpetual property."[29]

Nothing suggests that Ledyard saw anything unjust about the fate of his own copyright. Perhaps this was because his world was still not one of individuals with special legal rights but of patrons, and clients. The best indication of this social reality was the petition he submitted to acquire his copyright. Although the resulting law was applied generally, Ledyard's original intention was that the legislature pass a law particularly applicable to his case. Hence, the document emphasized that although general good might come out of a copyright, the true value would be in its benefit to the petitioner himself: "Your memorialist having lost his pecuniary assistance by his abrupt departure from the British is thereby incapacitated to move in a circle he could wish without the assistance of friends and the patronage and recommendations of the government under which he was born and whose favour and esteem he hopes he has never forfeited: he therefore proposes as a matter of consideration to your Excellency and Council that he may be introduced into some immediate employment wherein he may as well be useful to his country as himself." That employment was, of course, the preparation of his journal for publication. By granting his request, these authorities would enable Ledyard to be a productive, fully employed member of society. He would be an author, an author whose work had obvious value in a region dependent on oceanic trade. A history of Cook's last voyage, Ledyard concluded, "may be essentially usefull to America in general but particularly to the northern States by opening a most valuable trade across the North Pacific Ocean to China and the East Indies." There is no sense of inalienable right in all this. Neither is there any sense that the copyright would do anything for its author other than provide him with basic employment.[30]

Whatever its promise as a means of employment, Ledyard's copyright did very little for him. In a matter of months the money he had made from the sale of the copyright would be gone.

Sparks later wrote that Ledyard sold the manuscript and its copyright to Patten for twenty guineas, the equivalent of twenty-one pounds sterling. If the story is correct, then for the first time in his life Ledyard found himself among the solvent few. Guineas were gold coins, named for the West African colony from which seventeenth-century British merchants obtained the gold. In a postwar American economy in which inflation was still rampant and in which paper money had ever-falling value, actual money was king, and Ledyard would have been able to do things he had never before been able to. In modern American money, these twenty guineas would amount to roughly one thousand dollars.[31] With that sum Ledyard could buy any number of consumer goods, and it would appear that that is exactly what he did. In January 1783, he wrote to Isaac that he was "happy as a Bee," for he had "three pairs of Breeches, Three Waist-coats, Six Pairs of Stockings, Two Coats, and a half a dozen ruffled shirts."[32]

For the first time since his Dartmouth days Ledyard enjoyed the luxury of having multiple suits of clothes. It was also the first time since those days that he could actually dress the part of the gentleman he aspired to be. Now that independence had been achieved, there was no need for any Syphaxian austerity. Wearing fine clothes no longer meant one was buying the goods that sustained an oppressive British Empire; now it meant one was patronizing the merchants who would create a new American empire. Nor would Ledyard have to resort to the tar-stained garb of the common seafarer or the tattered redcoat of the British soldier. He had earned the right to be a gentleman, refined and dignified in dress. With his new clothes, some money in his pocket, his reputation untarnished by wartime partisanship, Ledyard traveled to Philadelphia sometime in the late winter of 1783. There, amidst the bustle of entrepreneurial artisans and haggling merchants, he believed he would find new employment, employment that would sustain him on the path toward gentlemanly well-being.

But the city, its merchants hobbled by seven years of British blockades and wartime financial chaos, lacked employment for the well-traveled author. Within several months of his arrival, Ledyard's resources had

The *Resolution* and *Discovery* at Ship Cove, Nootka Sound. Drawing by John Webber, 1778. © National Maritime Museum, London.

dwindled, and once again he turned to the merchant marine. But this time his timing was very poor. Writing in May 1783, he told Isaac that the ships in port were all foreign vessels needing no additional hands. The morning he arrived at the docks, "fourteen [American] sailors went out to the northward," presumably heading to New York in search of employment, but many others remained, "strolling the docks of this city" in a hopeless search for work. A frustrated Ledyard returned to his rented room "and went up and counted my cash—and turned it over—and looked at it, shook it [in] my hand—recounted and found" a miscellaneous collection of largely worthless coins and bills. In the end, all poor Ledyard could do was implore Isaac to send him "by the first conveyance some Cash."[33]

Amidst despair, Ledyard's fortunes would turn once again. He would find support for a bold scheme to exploit a rich new commercial resource. The plan, it seems, had been on his mind for some time. In his book, he had written of the incredible wealth of fur-bearing mammals to be found around Nootka Sound on Vancouver Island's Pacific coast: "They have foxes, sables, hares, marmosets, ermines, weazles, bears, wolves, deer, moose, dogs, otters, beavers, and a species of weazel called the glutton." Cook's men discovered that the skins of these animals could be purchased from native hunters for very little. They could then be sold for the equivalent of as much as thirty guineas in Canton or Macao. "Neither did we purchase a quarter part of the beaver and other fur skins we might have done and most certainly should have done," Ledyard remembered with regret, "had we known of meeting the opportunity of disposing of them to such an astonishing profit."[34]

The commercial possibilities of North America's Pacific coast were thus nearly unlimited. Those exotic goods, particularly Chinese tea and porcelain, that occasionally made it to North America, usually via Britain, could now be obtained for the price of a few sea otter skins. And the fur trade, which by the late eighteenth century had slowed to a trickle in eastern North America, could become once again a viable American business. Much as it had been for France and Britain and Holland in the seventeenth century, it would be the economic engine of a new American imperial project. There, on North America's Pacific coast, empire would assert itself once again, now unencumbered by the tired trade routes of the crowded Atlantic and governed by a new breed of American empire builder.

CHAPTER VI

From Author to Fur Trader

SOMETIME DURING THE LATE spring of 1783 the struggling Ledyard met Robert Morris, a Philadelphia merchant, former member of the Continental Congress, and superintendent of finance for the United States. The controversial Morris was perhaps the most influential financier in the new country, having amassed Philadelphia's largest fortune. In the early years of the Revolutionary War, he used his political connections and a web of commercial associates in the West Indies and Europe to procure essential manufactured goods for the Continental Army. It was a hugely profitable arrangement, and by the early 1780s, Morris had become, in the words of the historian Thomas Doerflinger, "a one-man conglomerate, simultaneously overseeing . . . investments in tobacco shipments, military contracting, dry goods importations and land speculations." Morris's voracious appetite for investment opportunity and his vast financial resources made him one of the very few American merchants who could seriously back a trading venture to the Pacific. And in John Ledyard he believed he had found a worthy supercargo for such a venture.[1]

Ledyard had no business experience, but his book was a substantial testament to his knowledge of the Pacific, its peoples, and their trading habits—certainly as substantial as any American had yet produced. The book also provided ample proof of the economic potential of the North Pacific fur trade—although it is unlikely Morris even needed such proof.

Natives interact with some of Cook's men at a Nootka coastal village. Engraved from a drawing by John Webber. From James Cook, A *Voyage to the Pacific Ocean*, 2d ed. London, 1785. Courtesy of Strozier Library Special Collections, Florida State University.

The seamen who sailed with Cook, now scattered around the British Atlantic, carried with them stories of the region's riches. As Second Lieutenant James King recalled, "The rage with which our seamen were possessed to return" to the region "and buy another cargo of skins to make their fortunes at one time, was not far short of mutiny."[2]

With Morris's patronage, Ledyard would now be the supercargo for what he described to his cousin Isaac as "the greatest commercial enterprise ever undertaken in this country."[3] The hyperbole was not entirely misplaced. Rarely had the potential profits been so great, and even more rarely had American merchants ventured so far beyond the Atlantic basin.

For Ledyard, suddenly at the center of this bold scheme, the reversal was astonishing, and a calmer spirit might have wondered whether it was too good to be true. Indeed, it was. Ledyard's sudden rise to commercial success would be delayed by scandal and financial double-dealing. The chaos and confusion of the postrevolutionary economy would treat Ledyard the merchant adventurer little different than it had treated Ledyard the author. It would leave him, once again, broke and defeated.

Morris's interest in the northwest coast reflected a larger trend among American merchants. The formal end of the Revolutionary War had freed them from the constraints of a British mercantile policy that sharply limited where, with whom, and for what they could trade. To obtain much-valued Chinese tea, for example, merchants had been required to purchase the tea from agents of the British East India Company. Purchasing such goods directly from the Chinese or other Europeans was forbidden, although before the Revolution smugglers (who counted among their ranks Robert Morris himself) illegally carried tea from the Dutch West Indies, forged excise documents, and bribed customs officials to get the goods to American markets. Still, the process was cumbersome and not nearly as profitable as direct trade with China would have been.

With independence, the former colonists could, in theory anyway, disregard the various British navigation acts and admiralty courts and customs duties to freely tap the world's markets. And the mother lode of those markets was in China. Profits from the China trade could be staggering, and the British government had carefully controlled the distribution of those profits by protecting the monopoly of the government-chartered

East India Company. Now, American merchants could contemplate the profits to be fetched from tea, porcelain, spices, silks, and other luxury goods imported directly from Asia.[4]

Of course many hurdles remained. While Morris and other American merchants had profited from the wartime military stores trade, they remained, as they had been before the Revolution, cash poor. Limited amounts of specie circulated in the new United States, and most of the paper money in circulation had suffered staggering depreciation. Furthermore, mercantile credit was now even more scarce as British merchants began calling in their long-deferred prewar loans. All of this made the financing of any trading enterprise difficult and costly. But a long-distance commercial voyage to Asia carried additional and very unique costs. The problem was not so much the high cost of ships and maritime labor required for such a venture. There were plenty of ships left from the war effort and much idle maritime labor. The real expense was the outgoing cargo. Having little silver or gold, American merchants would have to find similarly valuable commodities to pay for Asian imports. Ledyard suggested one such commodity: furs. These were compact, easily transported, relatively inexpensive, and highly valued by the Chinese, but to obtain them a ship had to sail to the northwest coast, and this meant either rounding the treacherous Cape Horn or traversing the Atlantic, Indian, and Pacific oceans.

There was a less risky alternative. Ginseng root, a highly valued aphrodisiac and herbal remedy, grew in the foothills of the Appalachian Mountains from Georgia to Quebec. The American variety was particularly potent and valuable in China. Before the Revolution, merchants had sold the root in London for eventual sale by British East India Company representatives at Canton, and by 1770 American colonists were exporting some seventy-four thousand pounds annually. Much like furs, the modest root would more than compensate its carrying cost. It also had the advantage of being far more easily obtained. Still, the ginseng solution had serious drawbacks. As Morris and his associates would discover, in an American economy starved for cash, the frontiersmen and itinerant merchants who acquired the root, often from native collectors, were in no mood to accept as payment the promissory notes of eastern merchants. The only real alternative was payment in actual gold or silver specie, but what little of this the merchants had was needed to pay duties and buy foreign goods. With demand high and liquid funds scarce, the price of ginseng would invariably rise and, indeed, this is precisely what happened when Morris and some associates began acquiring the root for a China voyage.[5]

It is a testament to Morris's powers of persuasion and his shrewd financial mind that despite these many risks and high costs, he was able to mobilize enough capital and credit to make this hugely ambitious project a reality, at least for a time. In addition to employing Ledyard to help with preparations for the voyage, he formed a partnership with the New York firm Daniel Parker and Company, recently flush from wartime military contracts, including one to evacuate British troops from New York. The partnership proved to be fruitful. In July 1783, Parker traveled to Boston to seek additional investors for the China scheme, and by the end of the summer Boston shipbuilders were constructing a four-hundred-ton vessel to be called the *Empress of China*. The ship was a copy of the *Bellisarius*, thought by some to have been the fastest ship in the British navy. Parker also secured six additional ships from a growing fleet of decommissioned naval vessels. By the end of September 1783, Morris, Parker, and company had seven ships preparing for the China trade.[6]

Ledyard's role in the enterprise over the following four months is unclear. He spent some of the time in New London, perhaps to oversee the outfitting of the *Comte d'Artois*, a six-hundred-ton French-built merchant vessel Parker had acquired for the venture. Ledyard was also in Boston and New York, consulting with partners and capitalizing on his newly improved prospects. He seems to have spent some of his time leveraging expected future earnings. Nearly forty years later, the New York merchant Comfort Sands recalled that he "never . . . Received a Cent for the moneys that I had advanced" Ledyard during these months in the summer and fall of 1783.[7]

Initially Morris and Parker had a vague plan—Ledyard's advice notwithstanding—involving two simultaneous voyages. One of these would travel to China via the northwest coast, and the other, loaded with Appalachian ginseng, would sail directly for Canton. The dual-pronged approach would protect the partners from the possible collapse of fur prices, a serious risk since British merchants were also eagerly preparing to enter the lucrative Pacific fur trade. If the market became flooded with furs, the Americans would be able to balance their losses with ginseng. But unanswered questions remained. For example, which ship would sail where? One associate suggested that the swift *Empress of China* serve as the "Furrman" because it could reach the northwest coast before the competition. The five other, larger ships could then follow while another sailed directly to Canton loaded with ginseng. But perhaps the better approach was to send the swiftest ship directly to Canton and the largest ships to the northwest coast. If fur prices remained steady, doing so would mean much greater profits.[8]

As the partners struggled with these choices, time ran short and by December 1783 it was becoming clear to some of them that the two-pronged plan was impractical. The financing for six simultaneous voyages was proving difficult to obtain, and the longer the voyages were delayed the higher the likelihood the Canton markets would be flooded with animal pelts. The partners also discovered that their profits would be eroded by heavy import duties the Chinese had begun levying on all foreign ships trading in Canton.[9]

The logical course was to cut losses. Instead of attempting to outfit six vessels, the partners would outfit only one; and instead of the hazardous westerly route via Cape Horn to the northwest coast, that ship would take the longer but safer easterly route around the much calmer Cape of Good Hope and through the Indian Ocean to China. On February 22, 1784, after continued wrangling and financial bickering, the *Empress of China* left New York harbor carrying thirty tons of Appalachian ginseng. The cost of this single expedition was a staggering $120,000. According to one estimate, this was the equivalent of twenty-four thousand acres of prime farmland or almost one-third of the total capitalization of the Bank of North America (founded under Morris's leadership in 1781). A little over a year later the ship returned to New York loaded with tea, cinnamon, porcelain, and silk. For the remaining owners the profit was an extraordinary $30,000, or a 25 percent return on investment.[10]

For Ledyard, the turn of events was naturally discouraging. "Since I saw you last," he wrote his mother Abigail in June 1784, "I have passed thro' a great many difficulties & disappointments." For a time it seemed that "all the fortitude that ten years' misfortune had taught me could hardly support me."[11] His failure to finish college, his failure to enter the ministry, his failure to obtain an officer's commission, and his failure to profit from his book, he was saying, did little to prepare him for this greatest of disappointments. From a man of grandiose ambition, a man boasting of his role in America's greatest commercial enterprise, he had fallen to dejected failure once again. But Ledyard's principal assets—his experience, his intellect, his candor—had impressed Morris, and the financier continued to support the New Englander and his bold commercial plan. The two agreed that until the American business climate improved, Ledyard would be better able to find backing in the much wealthier European commercial centers, particularly in France, where Morris's Revolutionary War dealings had left him with a powerful network of associates. Equipped with letters of introduction and a small loan from Morris, Ledyard sailed in the summer of 1784 for the Spanish port at Cádiz. The journey revived his spirits, and although he remained cash poor his new connection to the American merchant community afforded him sufficient social capital to more than survive.

Ledyard was not the only party to the early American China trade to look to improve his lot in Europe. Parker, Morris's initial partner, also went there, although unlike Ledyard he was not so much looking for new business relations as fleeing old ones. Parker, it turns out, had defrauded his creditors and embezzled from his partners. When they began to realize he had been pocketing money promised to the shipwrights and provisioners who prepared the partners' vessels, they took legal action to recover the funds; but Parker disappeared, eventually turning up in Europe and leaving the reputations of his partners in tatters.[12]

The collapse of this first feeble foray into the northwest coast fur trade did not mark the American death of Ledyard's scheme. It remained appealing, especially among Boston and Salem merchants, who had limited access to Appalachian ginseng. By the fall of 1787, the *Columbia*, a Boston merchant vessel, was preparing to sail for the northwest coast. The journey would take three years and though it would be only modestly profitable, it would establish the standard route for a vigorous and profitable Massachusetts–China trade. So promising was the northwest coast trade that just a month after its return, the *Columbia* embarked once again, this time amidst a veritable stampede of westbound sailing ships. The northwest coast would now be a vital extension of the New England economy and a west coast purchase for a new American empire. "On her first voyage, the *Columbia* had solved the riddle of the China trade," the maritime historian Samuel Eliot Morison observed. "On her second, empire followed in the wake."[13]

◆ ◆ ◆

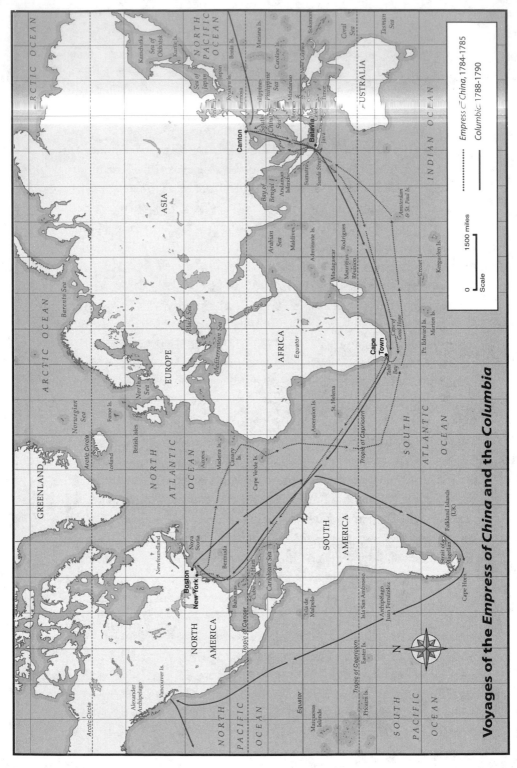

Voyages of the Empress of China and the Columbia

Empress of China, 1784–1785
Columbia, 1788–1790

0   1500 miles
Scale

By Mapcraft.

Eighteenth-century business was still, in many ways, medieval business. Information, goods, and capital all moved slowly, and merchants were as likely to spend their days idly fretting over the far-off and uncontrollable forces of nature as they were doing business. Much—if not most—of what they did was wait. They waited for the weather to change, they waited for the seasons to change, they waited for goods and news to arrive, and they waited for financing. That it took as influential a financier as Morris the better part of a year to launch America's first venture in the China trade is thus not at all surprising.

Given the slow pace of commerce, eighteenth-century merchants were as likely as the leisured, landowning gentry to spend their mornings studying, their days discoursing in coffeehouses or strolling the countryside, and their nights dining and dancing. It could be a very monotonous existence, especially for merchants living in countries whose languages they did not speak and whose local business practices they did not understand. For them, the comings and goings of ships' captains, government officials, and other notables provided welcome relief from a normally isolated existence. Nathaniel Cutting, an agent for Boston merchants who resided in the French port of Havre during the late 1780s and early 1790s, lived a life typical of these ex-patriot merchants. His days were spent promenading in the countryside or fawning over local women; his nights, in conversation. It was with great excitement that he confided to his diary the eventful evening when he met a mysterious English traveler. Such excitement did not come often to the isolated and homesick Cutting. The "eccentric genius" whom he met "at Table . . . has rambled over great part of the American states, and appears to have been acquainted with the principal Characters there. . . . He is now on one of his peregrinations, having a young Frenchman as his Companion.—and they pretend to have no fixed object in view;—but pass the high-road, or strike off at a tangent, just as fancy prompts them.—The Englishman, whose name I do not know, pretends to be enthusiastically fond of the American states, & the Disposition of its Inhabitants." A few meals was a small price to pay for the diversion brought by such amusing company. The merchants of Cádiz, most of whom were British, felt similarly when Ledyard arrived. The peripatetic American's tales of South Seas adventure were well worth the cost of room and board.[14]

Indeed, shortly after arriving in Cádiz, Ledyard could report happily to

Isaac that he was received with great politeness by the British proconsul and his merchant associates. How remarkable it was, he continued, to be enjoying one's self "am[ong] these gentry with only a half a Dollar and four [Spanish] Rials in my pocket." For all his trials, Ledyard had begun to enjoy the fruits of his accumulated experience. His odd career path and his expanding web of patrons had given him the capital needed to acquire a seat at the table of prominent gentlemen.[15]

Among the subjects Ledyard and his new British friends discussed was the American Revolution. To this particular group of local officials and merchants—the latter uncompensated for long-overdue American loans—the Revolution was something of a joke. And Ledyard seemed all too happy to entertain this sentiment. Addressing Isaac in the guise of one of these Britons, he condemned a Congress with no real power and ridiculed a group of former colonies wracked by petty politics. The governance of the new United States revealed so many "vulgar errors, as a people necessarily aiming at the most refined system of government could not commit without the imputation of perfect insanity." Back among the imperial Britons, Ledyard showed no particular interest in defending his country. Political conviction simply was not part of his makeup, but then again, "if the incongruity of my letter bespeaks a perturbation of the mind, it will not deceive you." The wine flowed in Cádiz, and it left Ledyard feeling "a suffusion of pleasure . . . round my heart, that the poorly unfortunate never, never felt." For the moment, anyway, the would-be American merchant was not among the poorly unfortunate.[16]

Sometime over the next year, Ledyard left Cádiz for Brest, on France's far northwest coast. From there he planned to ride "booted and spurred" south to the mercantile cities of Lorient and Nantes and then to Passy, where the American plenipotentiary in France, Benjamin Franklin, resided. Along the way he hoped to acquire investors, a vessel, and a crew for his great fur-trading venture. That that venture was much more than the fanciful dream of a few ambitious Americans quickly became clear to him when, in Lorient, he discovered a host of other schemes to reach what he came to call the "back of America." One involved a seven-hundred-ton vessel commissioned by Catherine the Great, and another a vessel owned by the Hudson's Bay Company. Still, there was enough interest in his own plan to assure him that by the following August, he would be guiding a Franco-American voyage to the northwest coast.[17]

◆ ◆ ◆

Finding no investors in Brest or Lorient, Ledyard moved on to Paris. With its wealth and growing American ex-patriot community, the capital city, he hoped, would do for him what the provinces could not: provide investors and patrons. The trip prompted Ledyard to write one of his most remarkable letters. Far from revealing some sort of calculating mercantile agent with little interest in the lofty preoccupations of his former life, the letter suggests a man too naïve and disconnected from reality to be animated by pure self-interest. It is a pose Ledyard assumes deliberately and, one must say, knowingly, but it clearly stems from the same sort of inner conflict that elicited his interest in Syphax. At the center of that conflict was simply the question of how he would make his way in the world. Would it be as a self-interested, calculating social climber or as a virtuous and noble servant of some greater human cause? The letter suggests no resolution of this question. But it does suggest a certain core sense that literary art might somehow afford a middle way. Much as had been the case on the *Resolution* and in his journal, so in his private correspondence Ledyard sought to display a taste for belles lettres, as if this might blunt the sharp edge of bare ambition. While his other correspondence displays occasional references to Shakespeare, John Bunyan, Joseph Addison, and others, none offers anything as sustained and inspired as this letter, whose allusions are to Miguel de Cervantes's *Don Quixote*. As was his fashion, Ledyard seems to have been most captivated not by the protagonist, but rather by a secondary character, Sancho Panza, Quixote's trusty squire. In an odd intertwining of Ledyard's quixotic reality and the fiction of Cervantes, Panza agrees to join Don Quixote in his quest for chivalrous distinction. In exchange, Quixote promises his squire the governorship of an island. The promise, in other words, is of greatness and power in exchange for blind loyalty.

Here was John Ledyard, the squire to the likes of Robert Morris or whoever would patronize his scheme, bumbling blindly into whatever fate would hand him. Like Panza, Ledyard rides forth not on a noble stallion but on a lame donkey. "Sancho Panza rode his ass like a patriarch," Cervantes's narrator explains, "longing to be the governor of the island his master had promised him."[18] Ledyard would do the same. Unaffected by the tempests surrounding the likes of Morris and Parker, indifferent to his rapidly shrinking wealth and to the insults that would inevitably find him, he would plod toward his final object, driven along by the encouraging words of his humble ass:

> Will you go to Paris said my ass: I fear I have not money said I:
> I will eat thistles said my ass: but what shall we do when there
> said I—tho I put the question wrong & so my ass was silent:
> I too shall be forced to eat thistles myself said I answering
> myself: and will you not also by continuing here rejoined my
> ass—and what is still more disconsonant to your feelings con-
> tinued the honest indignant animal—what is still worse will
> you not discover your nakedness to those who have respect
> only to the outward appearance and consequently ridicule ex-
> ternal poverty—at Paris you will be unknown. Thus saying
> my ass kneeled down and . . . I once more mounted.

It was this sort of resolve, Ledyard continued, that of a man indifferent to the humiliations of poverty and nakedness, that had been the engine for all great quests, including those of the likes of "Vasco da Gama and Columbus," builders of the Spanish Empire.[19]

In true Quixotic fashion, soon after arriving in Paris, Ledyard fell upon fleeting good fortune once again. He met the former American naval commander and Revolutionary War hero John Paul Jones.

The Scottish-born Jones, who was just four years older than Ledyard, had come to Paris in late 1783 to collect prize money owed American sailors and officers by their French allies. Jones had found his way into the fledgling American navy after a rocky career aboard a series of British merchant vessels, some of which plied the West African slave trade. As a sea captain, Jones had earned a reputation as a ruthless disciplinarian, freely flogging even the least wayward crewmen. When one of his carpenters died after a severe lashing, Jones was charged with murder and actually served time in jail. In 1773, Jones killed a member of his crew for what he believed to be mutinous behavior. With little hope of escaping conviction for this incident he fled to Virginia and, once the Revolutionary War broke out, found a new calling as a naval captain. In the September 1779 battle that launched him into the American pantheon, he nearly sacrificed his own ship, the *Bonhomme Richard* (named for Poor Richard, a former pseudonym of the American envoy to France and de facto navy minister, Franklin) to take the much larger British frigate *H. M. S. Serapis* off the Yorkshire coast.

While he waited for his money, Jones contemplated a return to commercial seafaring, and when Ledyard showed up with his plans for the northwest coast, the ever-daring Jones quickly seized on the idea. In the summer of 1785, he and Ledyard made plans to take two ships to the northwest coast, where they would establish a trading factory (literally, the residence of the factor, or middleman) staffed by a surgeon, a clerk, and twenty soldiers. Much as had been the case in the Morris plan, in this one Ledyard would be paid to represent others' interests. As the factor, he would set the terms of trade with local natives and manage the movement of goods to and from the factory. After six months, one of the ships would sail to China, loaded with furs. That ship would then return with additional trade goods, and six months later both ships would leave for New York, by way of China. Ledyard would remain to manage the factory until the ships returned to start the circuit again, an arrangement that would leave John at the remote outpost for up to seven years.

The experience he gained from the Cook voyage and his knowledge of American Indian customs presumably made Ledyard, in Jones's eyes, the ideal factor. And in Jones, Ledyard found a patron whose fame would lure investors. With the possible exception of Franklin, no American was more widely admired by the French. The king had personally received him and made him chevalier of the order of Military Merit. And when Jones appeared at the grandiose Paris Opera, he was greeted with enthusiastic applause.[20]

During the summer and fall of 1785, Jones traveled back and forth between Paris and Lorient, organizing financing and procuring ships and crew. Meanwhile, Ledyard awaited his commercial fate in the cultural capital of the universe. Never had his social life been better and never had he lived so comfortably for so long. With Jones's help, Ledyard became a fixture in the American ex-patriot community of Paris, circulating from one dinner to the next in the company of Thomas Jefferson (who arrived in France in August 1784 and would replace Franklin the following spring as American minister there), the Marquis de Lafayette, two sons of the venerable Fitzhugh family of Virginia, and assorted other American and French notables. It was, unquestionably, a gentleman's life, and it was a life that gave Ledyard time to reflect on himself and the extraordinary place that was Paris on the eve of the French Revolution.

The time in Paris also allowed Ledyard to make writing a part of his daily life once again—although in a way very different from his days aboard the *Resolution*. Now, writing had become a private, solitary kind of affair. As he explained to Isaac, he had acquired the habit of writing with quill in one hand, glass of wine in the other, and sitting "naked two or three hours before I sleep & in the same unconstrained situation I think & occasionally write my friends." What better proof could there be that "I write without disguise"? This characteristic disdain for artifice shaped a dense eleven-page Paris journal Ledyard appended to one of his letters to Isaac. It also revealed the continued animating philosophy of his life, a philosophy that left him appalled by the outlandish Parisian excesses he was beginning to notice.[21]

It is hard to imagine a place more unlike the Connecticut of Ledyard's youth than Paris under the old regime. Densely populated, flooded with agitated artisans, impoverished apprentices, hack writers, and dissipated aristocrats, governed not by local magistrates or town councils but largely by an immensely powerful and pervasive police force (of which Ledyard most ardently approved), Paris was about as foreign a place as a New Englander could find without leaving the European world. Like any provincial fending off the seductions of a chaotic capital city, Ledyard was at once repulsed and captivated by what he saw. The reaction was especially evident in his response to one of Paris's great edifices, the grand Palais-Royal.[22]

The Palais had been inherited by the duc de Chartes from his father, Louis XIV's brother, the duc de Orléans. Seeking to make the most of this part of his patrimony, the entrepreneurial duke undertook a revolutionary building experiment. He would transform the Palais and its gardens from a place of pleasant pastoral relief to a kind of city within a city.

As an act of entrepreneurship, the plan was pure genius. Here, in the heart of Paris, aspiring lawyers, merchants, and minor gentry could enjoy the fruits of their prosperity sheltered from the ordinary urban bedlam outside and free from the scrutiny of city authorities. In the arcades surrounding the Palais gardens, these Parisians could shop and be entertained at one of the many jewelers, silk merchants, tailors, museums, bookstores, and private clubs the duke counted among his tenants. In the Palais gardens themselves, visitors enjoyed additional high and low entertainment, ranging from theatrical performances and magic shows to the freakish displays of a hugely fat man and a wax figure purported to be the preserved body of a two-hundred-year-old woman.[23]

By the time Ledyard began frequenting the Palais, the liberties afforded this peculiar duchy within Paris had begun to yield its own kind of bedlam. The Palais had become a center of illicit commerce—commerce in hearsay, in forbidden pamphlets and books, and, of course, in sex. Though he spent much time at the Palais, the scene disgusted Ledyard. "The professed pride of the Ville de Paris," the Palais, he wrote, "is a vile cinque of pollution" populated by "bawds, pimps," their clients, and "those who by the glare of dress, equipage, or assumed titles hide their worst deformities." The latter were, no doubt, deformities of character. For the very "apartments of this . . . rich and elegant building are inhabited by coarse bred impudent abandoned and disgusting bawds . . . and impoverished young debauchees without pretension to family, fortune, or education." The debased sexual commerce of the place infected the most precious bonds of family. "I report for absolute fact," Ledyard concluded, "that the father, the mother, and the daughters are here for the sole and professed purpose of mutual prostitution."[24]

For all the venom it elicited from him, Ledyard could not resist the temptations of the Palais. One night after dining with Jefferson, he reported that he and the American envoy took a walk in the Palais gardens. After Jefferson retired for the evening, Ledyard continued strolling and heard someone calling his name. He was being propositioned by a prostitute and soon found himself entwined with this lady, "making a thousand protestations of eager desire and eternal passion." The encounter was of the most superficial and unsatisfying variety. For it occurred several feet from the woman's "little old four feet five inches husband . . . a true Parisian husband." In a moment of unintended emotional transparency Ledyard concluded that "it will not be her fault if I never see her again nor will [it] occasion her more than five minutes pain or pleasure whether I do or not."[25]

Ledyard's new friend Jefferson was also entranced by the Palais, though for very different reasons. To Jefferson, the remarkable thing about the building was not so much its illicit trade or its architectural beauty as its prospects as a model for real estate development. Less than six months after arriving in Paris, Jefferson reported to his friend the Richmond physician James Currie that if a similar palace were built in Richmond it would bring its owners great profit. Here there would be a carefully sheltered common, with no toiling slaves or laborers, ideally suited to the strolling sensibility of the genteel. Around the square would

Part caricature, part exposé, Philibert-Louis Debucourt's "The Palais Royal-gallery's Walk" depicts the full grotesque mix of prostitutes, fops, children, and pets who converged at the Palais Royal. The color engraving, from 1787, was made around the time Ledyard was frequenting the Palais and echoes his own strained ambivalence about this Parisian demimonde. Print Collection, Miriam and Ira Wallach Division of Art, Prints and Photographs, New York Public Library, Astor, Lenox, and Tilden Foundations.

be precisely the kinds of shops and accommodations that "would make it the resort of everyone for either business or pleasure, thus rendering it the best stand for persons of every object and of course entitling it to the highest rents." Jefferson was serious enough about a Virginia version of the Palais to earmark five hundred pounds for the project and to recruit a group of European artisans to build the building.[26]

Given this enthusiasm, one wonders whether Jefferson saw the same Palais Ledyard saw. Perhaps the Virginian simply thought the gaming and prostitution of the Parisian Palais would be unwelcome in a similar American structure; or perhaps he never actually saw the darker, carnivalesque side of the great palace, although that is certainly doubtful. At the very least, there is reason to believe Ledyard would have shared his own critical observations with the American statesman.

Ledyard had joined the circle of Americans who congregated around Jefferson's residence, some of whom in fact lived in the residence. The group included Jefferson's secretary, William Short, and the Connecticut-born David Humphreys, designated by Congress to negotiate foreign trade treaties. Ledyard became especially close to Humphreys, a noted poet and patriot. Though "devoutly fond of women, wine, and religion; provided they are each of good quality," he was, Ledyard wrote, "a sincere Yankee and so affectionately fond of his country, that to be in his society here is at least as good to me, as a dream of being home."[27] Others in the circle included Colonel David S. Franks and Thomas Barclay, also members of the new American diplomatic corps. Then there was the parade of prominent Americans who passed through the Jeffersons' house seeking passports, assistance with trade deals, and other favors.

To Ledyard, this ex-patriot circle was most agreeable. Not only did it provide him with a new circle of literate, aspiring young gentlemen against whom to judge himself, but it left him feeling positively flush. Compared to him, he wrote, "such a set of moniless rascals have never appeared since the epoch of Falstaff." More important, among even these "moniless rascals," Ledyard was well known. When Ledyard mocked Humphreys's poetry in Jefferson's presence, Humphreys rebuked him, reminding the audience that a man who returned from college cowering under a bearskin in a giant dugout canoe was unlikely to have sound literary judgment. In his journal, Ledyard noted proudly that Jefferson responded with a laugh and the astute observation that that trip "was no unworthy prelude to my subsequent voyages and that I had [displayed] a great consistency of character from that moment to this." In Ledyard's world, a man could hardly receive higher praise.[28]

Not surprisingly, Ledyard came to admire Jefferson. The tall, thin, and graceful American minister, eight years Ledyard's senior, struck him as unusually dignified and upstanding, an ideal representative for the young nation. Ledyard even came to feel that Jefferson was better suited to the job than the great Franklin, whom Ledyard had met when he first arrived in Paris. It was not so much that Franklin was a lesser man but rather that Jefferson simply seemed a more noble figure. Eschewing Franklin's showy Americanisms and his enthusiastic embrace of Parisian culture with all its tawdry intrigue, Jefferson presented a more restrained, more cerebral persona. In Ledyard's view, this distinguished him from all the European diplomats, the "lackeys of ministers and kings" who did little more than perpetuate "the pageantries of old sickly kingdoms." In Jefferson, America had a truly worthy minister: able, striking in appearance, and beholden to none.[29]

Ledyard was also clearly taken with Jefferson's intellect and seems to have absorbed the American's fascination with social and economic reform. In Ledyard's earlier writings there is little social commentary. Insofar as he looked objectively at human beings, it was to serve his ethnological and historical interests. But life in Paris seems to have taught Ledyard to think about the processes and forces that acted on human beings in the present. Most fundamentally, it taught him to think about exactly what it was that made human beings good or bad. The old Puritan morality, that a person was born either good or bad, had clearly lost whatever allure it may once have had for Ledyard. Now the question was, What social forces account for human morality and its absence?

The question was a crucial one for citizens of that novel entity the United States. If a society was to be governed by the governed themselves, it would have to find a way to ensure the goodwill and common sense of the citizenry. To anyone visiting a European city in the 1780s, this must have seemed like a hopeless challenge. Evidence of a morally corrupted populace was everywhere, from the petty criminals and beggars who filled the streets to the immoral bawds and their gentlemen clients who circulated through the Palais-Royal. For the forward-thinking, enlightened circle of which Ledyard was now a part, the source of these problems was institutional. It derived from human inventions that corrupted true human nature. The most pernicious of these were created precisely to counter antisocial, disorderly behavior: the law and the penal system. European states, these enlightened Americans had come to believe, had failed to grasp the great truth that arbitrary and inhumane punishment begets an arbitrary and inhumane populace. The evidence for this was everywhere in ancien régime France.

For the entire time Ledyard resided there the country was captivated by a series of sensational trials. One of these involved three men accused of robbing a farmer and his wife in a small rural village. With no real due process, the men were convicted and sentenced to death. But their execution would not come in some swift, humane form. It would come only after the condemned had been tortured on the wheel, after their limbs had been shattered and their backs broken. For reform-minded Parisians, the whole horrendous affair was a call to arms. The judicial system needed to be reformed; punishment needed to be made to fit the crime, and some form of due process needed to be instituted. As one reformer observed, the accused are brought before the court scarred by their inhumane incarceration. They appear "haggard, disfigured, white from hunger and fear," with faces "covered with hair like that of a wild beast." "Who is this being?" the writer asked. "None of his judges know—he is a shadow, a specter, appearing from the depths of a prison cell before judges whose power terrifies him. Of his interest, his character, his morals, who can know anything? Who even asks?" This, then, was a system that turned its charges into faceless beasts, making true justice impossible.[30]

Evidence of the failed penal system was everywhere for Ledyard to see. On a tour of the huge Bicetre Asylum, he saw several thousand insane, destitute, accused, and convicted prisoners randomly thrown together in the most appalling conditions and overseen by an indifferent militia. To Ledyard's reckoning, between ten and twenty prisoners perished per day, and those were perhaps the lucky ones. By far the sorriest lot were those prisoners convicted of capital offenses whose families could afford a sufficient defense to have the sentence commuted to incarceration. For the families, this was preferable to the humiliations of a public execution; but for the convicted, the fate was worse than execution. "Those offenders," noted Ledyard, "are let down in to a subterracous [sic] receptacle and it is said are never seen or heard of more. But the truth is that they are taken up after a certain time and assassinated and burned in secrecy."[31]

In addition to discussing France's social problems, Ledyard and his circle almost certainly reflected on the place of the new United States in an unfriendly world. Among the most pressing problems facing the country was the loss of British protection for seaborne trade, especially in the Mediterranean and along the West African coast. Until the Revolution, American trade in the Mediterranean had been made possible by the British government's purchase of passage from the so-called Barbary pirates plying the seas off North Africa. With American independence, the North African pirates were free to prey on American shipping, capturing ships, kidnapping and enslaving crew members, and otherwise disrupting what had been a major component of American trade. One of Jefferson's preoccupations during his mission was finding a solution to this looming scourge. In the short run, this meant forging diplomatic relations with the Barbary states of Algeria, Morocco, and Tunisia.[32]

In the long run, it meant bolder solutions. Not long after arriving in Paris in late 1784, Jefferson advocated a military solution to the Barbary problem, and as president he would send naval squadrons to attack Tripoli. But in the mid-1780s more idealistic solutions were in the air as well, and Ledyard and his dinner companions seem to have embraced them. Given the endless diplomatic imbroglios, the dangers of seafaring, and the caprice of foreign markets, would it not make sense for a republic to free itself entirely from foreign trade? "May America have no ships of war or any merchant ship that shall go off its own coast," Ledyard wondered, "but like the Chinese command the commerce of all nations that find it their interest to visit her and not suffer by those who do or do not?"[33]

It was, to be sure, on odd perspective for a man banking on empire in the distant Pacific Northwest. But perhaps Ledyard had come to see his own empire building in a new, Jeffersonian light. Instead of a beachhead for a network of transoceanic commerce, the northwest coast factory would be a western foothold for a new, continental empire. Such an empire, with ports on both coasts and a vast, productive, transcontinental hinterland, could attract foreign merchants to American ports and free American merchants from the hazards of oceanic commerce. Idealistic though it may have been, this Jeffersonian vision of a continental empire was born of very real geopolitical concerns.

Several years before arriving in Paris, Jefferson had written to fellow Virginian and Revolutionary War general George Rogers Clark about an alarming British proposal to explore North America from the Mississippi to the California coast. "They pretend it is only to promote knowledge," but, Jefferson added, "I am afraid they have thoughts of colonizing into that quarter." Jefferson even proposed that Clark lead an expedition to the region to preempt the British plan, but Congress had neither the will nor the means to support such an ambitious project. Something, Jefferson presumably concluded, needed to be done to counter this danger.[34]

Undoubtedly the prospect of giving up the far west to a colonial power like Britain was all the more disturbing if, as so many still hoped, there existed some sort of water route from the west coast to the Missouri or Mississippi river. If seized by a European power, such a navigable artery would facilitate foreign control of the far west and the lucrative China trade. Its existence had been suggested by a popular travel account that Jefferson had carefully studied, Jonathan Carver's *Travels in the Interior of North America,* published in 1778. Carver claimed that a series of great rivers descended from the center of the American continent, probably in the great "shining mountains," as he called the Rockies, in reference to "a number of crystal stones, of an amazing size, with which they are covered, and which, when the sun shines full upon them, sparkle so as to be seen at a very great distance." The headwaters of these rivers were "within a few leagues of each other." If one followed the Missouri to its farthest western point, one could relatively easily portage to the "River Oregon, or the River of the West, that falls into the Pacific Ocean."[35]

The possibility that the British or some other European power would discover this water passage had thus been a serious concern for Jefferson. After his arrival in Paris, that concern would grow. Jefferson discovered that the French navigator and Revolutionary War hero Jean François de Galaup, Count de Lapérouse, was preparing to lead an exploratory voyage to the North Pacific. The secretive naval voyage ostensibly had purely scientific purposes. But Jefferson believed Lapérouse's two ships were being outfitted with less benign intent, and he asked Jones to look into the matter. In a letter to John Jay, the American secretary of foreign affairs, Jefferson explained that his gravest fear was that the French had designs on the new frontier of European colonialism, the American northwest coast. "If they should desire a colony on the Western side of America," he

Jonathan Carver's "A New Map of North America," which began appearing with his
Travels in the Interior of North America in the second edition, of 1779. It represents the
vanguard of Anglo-American geographical knowledge at the time Ledyard and Jefferson
were planning Ledyard's journey across America. The path of the Columbia River,
indicated here as the "River of the West," is almost entirely conjectural, and the only
indication of the Rocky Mountains is a single small mountain called "Mountain of
Bright Stones." The map also suggests that the "River of the West" flowed into the
"Mantons R.," which ended near the headwaters of the Missouri. The "Mantons R."
appears to be the upper Missouri rather than a distinct river. The map pictured here is
from a London edition of 1781. Reproduced by permission of the Huntington Library,
San Marino, California.

warned, "I should not be quite satisfied that they would refuse one which
should offer itself on the Eastern side."[36]

It turns out that Jefferson's suspicions were partly correct. At almost
exactly the same time Jones and Ledyard were planning their voyage, the
French minister of ports and arsenals, Claret de Fleurieu, began exploring
the possibility of a French-sponsored northwest coast venture. Fleurieu
even went so far as to consult the Dutch-born merchant William Bolts,

who had long been planning a trading voyage to the region (including one in 1781 under the Austrian flag) and who had some influence on the French venture's final form. What Jones discovered was alarming: this was no pet project of a few inspired ministers. It was directly endorsed, designed, and underwritten by the French king Louis XVI himself. Among the other goals "worthy the attention of a great Prince," Jones explained to Jefferson, was very likely "to extend the Commerce of his Subjects by Establishing Factories at a Future Day, for the Fur Trade on the North West Coast of America."[37]

While the French prepared to stake their claims to the northwest coast, Ledyard's partnership with John Paul Jones collapsed. The reason for this latest failure is not entirely clear, but timing must have been a factor. As the two Americans pursued French ships and investors for their scheme, news of Lapérouse's departure was beginning to circulate. And it is hard to imagine any French merchants or sea captains embarking on an enterprise that would so clearly compete with the Crown's own plan. Even if some had been willing to do so, the timing would have been poor.

By 1785 at least one British vessel, the relatively small sixty-ton brig *Sea Otter,* had reached the northwest coast, and by the time Lapérouse sailed in August 1785 two other British ships, the *King George* and the *Queen Charlotte,* both under the command of veterans of Cook's voyages, had left from Britain bound for the northwest coast. The British were also beginning to outfit ships in India and China for the Pacific trade, and no fewer than seven expeditions arrived on the northwest coast during 1786, the year Jones's and Ledyard's ships would have arrived there. This stampede to the region would have given any sensible investor pause, as purchase prices for fur would no doubt rise while sale prices fell in a flooded Chinese market. For American merchants, the trade would not become profitable until the 1790s, when the French Revolution began taking its toll on French and British maritime resources.[38]

Ledyard's prospects in the fur trade had collapsed once and for all. But Jefferson's dinner table yielded enticing new paths for a man of his talents. By late fall of 1785, one of these had begun to take hold of him. It required little outside investment and promised great personal returns. It would also allow Ledyard to bank on the ethnographic and geographic knowledge he had acquired while sailing with Cook. He would become the first white American to explore the western expanse of North America.

CHAPTER VII

Becoming a Traveler in Thomas Jefferson's Paris

IN THE SPRING OF 1813, the Baltimore newspaper editor Paul Allen requested from Thomas Jefferson a biographical essay on the late Meriwether Lewis. The essay was to be included as a preface to the first published edition of the expedition journals of Lewis and Clark, a work that Allen was helping to prepare for publication. Jefferson agreed to Allen's request and produced a five-thousand-word essay. What is notable about the essay is that it is as much about Jefferson as it is about Lewis. Clearly the former president saw this as an opportunity not only to memorialize his friend (Lewis committed suicide in 1809 while traveling from St. Louis to Washington) but also as a way to explain his government's patronage of the greatest expedition in American history. That patronage, Jefferson emphasized, was not an opportunistic imperial gesture taken by a president emboldened by executive power. It was, rather, the culmination of a lengthy and difficult struggle to understand the American West. As early as 1783, Jefferson explained to his readers, he had recruited George Rogers Clark for a westward journey to the Pacific, but the funds for such an expedition were lacking, and Jefferson would soon be sent to Paris.

The quest for western reconnaissance had a more auspicious beginning in early 1786. For it was then, Jefferson recalled, that the American expatriot John Ledyard had begun "panting for some new enterprise," and, "being of a roaming disposition," he seemed the ideal man to undertake a western journey. "I then proposed to him to go by land to Kamchatka," Jefferson continued, "cross in some of the Russian vessels to Nootka Sound, fall down into the latitude of the Missouri, and penetrate to and thro' that to the U.S." Twenty years before Lewis and Clark concluded their famed expedition, Jefferson and this intrepid New Englander had begun planning a journey across America's western expanse.[1]

Possessing no real knowledge of the Cascade or Rocky mountains, Jefferson had a fairly truncated view of the West. Drawing on Carver and other speculative geographers, he believed that a single mountain range divided the continent and if a traveler could ascend one side to the headwaters of the Missouri, he could descend the lengthy easterly river with relative ease, perhaps in a dugout canoe. That, it seems, was the rationale for a west to east journey.

For Ledyard, the transformation from factor to traveler was easy and quick. He had learned of the collapse of the Jones venture sometime in the early fall of 1785, and by winter he was writing to Isaac of his new plan to cross America. It must have been at once jarring and exhilarating even for the peripatetic Ledyard. Here, with the endorsement of the likes of Jefferson, he would undertake the greatest physical challenge of his life, a challenge endorsed by some of the most luminous figures of his world. Writing to Isaac in early 1786, he confessed that he had—since the collapse of the northwest coast venture—been living in the most wretched imaginable state, "without anything but a clean shirt," when he was invited "from a gloomy garret to the splendid Tables of the first characters of this kingdom." The most important of those characters was the Marquis de Lafayette, whose military service during the Revolutionary War made him a hero on both sides of the Atlantic. Through Lafayette, Ledyard and Jefferson were able to brief both the French foreign minister and the minister of the navy. Lafayette also introduced their plan to Baron von Grimm, the French envoy of the Russian empress Catherine II. But of the great men who were coming to know John Ledyard and his scheme, it was Jefferson who would really make the project possible. He lent Ledyard money, coordinated the diplomatic preparation for the journey, and instructed Ledyard in the science of exploration. The men's relationship had clearly evolved beyond one of dinnertime companionship. Now, Jefferson was Ledyard's principal patron.[2]

Ledyard was never one to be driven merely by the need to put food on his plate and clothes on his back. The quest for some more distant fame and honor had long energized him, but with this new project it seemed to reach a higher pitch. "I am going my dear parent, to make another tour around the world, but it is by land," he explained to his mother. "If I effect it, I shall acquire, I hope, some honor, and some riches and I ask your blessing & your prayers for my prosperity." But to Isaac, he was more candid: "The Virginia Gentlemen here [in Paris] call me Oliver Cromwell, and say, that like him I shall be damned to Fame." The allusion is an interesting one since Cromwell was generally despised in revolutionary America. He was thought to be a despot on a par with Julius Caesar, destroyer of the Roman Republic. But Cromwell was also of relatively humble origins, and what he appeared to lack in refinement and wit he made up for with determination and zeal. "All Europe stood astonished to see a nation, so turbulent and unruly," wrote David Hume in his *History of England,* "now at last subdued and reduced to slavery by one who, a few years before, was no better than a private gentleman, . . . and who was little regarded even in that low sphere to which he had always been confined." Ledyard's Virginian friends, Jefferson and the Fitzhughs, saw in him a similar destiny: he would achieve fame through sheer determination, but the cost would be great. Instead of destroying republics, Ledyard would destroy himself. For Ledyard, the characterization was clearly somewhat flattering. He was well aware that his undertaking carried immense risk, but only in the face of such risk could he display the sheer will that was becoming his hallmark.[3]

In preparation for his voyage, Ledyard undertook a rigorous training regimen, regularly running several miles in the royal forest outside Paris and taking lengthy walks into the city. This vigorous life brought the comforting realization that he had now lived as long as his father. At age thirty-four, he wrote, "I am very well in health: a gracious providence, and the Indian corn I fed upon in my infancy, added to the robust scenes I have since passed through, have left me at the same age at which my father died 'healthy, active, vigorous, and strong.'" The latter phrase came from Captain John's epitaph and suggests that Ledyard well knew that however much he prepared for his journey, his destiny was uncertain.[4]

Ledyard had endured hardship during his time with Cook, and his life since then had been punctuated by moments of poverty and exhaustion. But he had never endured the physical and mental challenges he would soon face. He was about to travel thousands of miles alone, much of that in totally unfamiliar territory. And his survival would depend on Native peoples' natural goodwill, something his brief experiences in northeastern Indian country and among the Aleut taught him he could count on. But even with that goodwill, Ledyard had to know he faced extraordinary physical obstacles. In just those few days with the Aleuts and the Russians, he suffered from swollen feet and fainting spells. That he was prepared to endure months, even years, of such discomfort and suffering almost suggests that Ledyard felt the need to punish himself, perhaps atoning for the excesses of his Parisian days.

The self-denial and physical suffering Ledyard was about to face would not come only from the inevitable misfortunes and deprivations of solo travel in uncharted wilderness. It would also be completely intertwined with the highest rationale for the entire journey: the collection of geographical data. According to Nathaniel Cutting, the American merchant at Havre and an acquaintance of Jefferson's, the latter had devised for Ledyard an ingenious method of recording geographical coordinates. In place of the usual apparatus of journal keeping—the quill pen and notebook— Ledyard would "prick certain characters into his own skin with the juice of some herbs." Those characters—coordinates of important rivers and other landmarks—would be generated by an equally ingenious method. Instead of carrying ordinary navigational instruments, Ledyard would have the length of an English foot tattooed on his body. He would then be able to craft a stick of that length, fashion a primitive sundial, and, using some basic calculations, determine his latitude. The rationale for such crude scientific instruments was similar to that which Cook used to justify sending an unarmed envoy to meet with the Russians. Much like guns, so the reasoning went, unusual Western goods might endanger Ledyard's life. "It was natural to suppose," Cutting wrote, "that if [Ledyard] attempted to carry implements of any kind with him, he would soon be robb'd of them by the savages, and perhaps murder'd. . . . But it was probable they would readily admit a naked and unarm'd man to pass unmolested."[5]

The danger, Ledyard and Jefferson almost surely knew, was not simply that these peoples might kill Ledyard to obtain what he carried. There was also the possibility that his methods of data collection—if he were to use those employed by Cook and all other European explorers—might excite fear and anger. Writing in particular had a long history as a source of intra-ethnic misunderstanding. To take one example, in the mid-1780s, Grigorii Shelikov, founder of a Russian fur-trading factory on Kodiak Island off Alaska's southern coast, recalled the confusion his written notes produced in an Aleutian servant. Shelikov had sent the man with a note to another Russian on a distant part of the island. The note requested a specific amount of dried fruit, some of which the islander ate on his way back to Shelikov's camp. When Shelikov noted the missing fruit, the man "expressed the most extreme surprise, persuaded that the letter had seen him eat [the fruit]." It is likely that Ledyard himself had witnessed similar attributions of mystical power to writing by nonliterate peoples of the South Pacific or possibly North America. If so, the decision to forgo pen and paper was similar to the decision to forgo arms: it would make the European stranger's presence that much less unsettling.[6]

To extract knowledge that would be used to incorporate native peoples into some large imperial frame, Ledyard effectively had to become like them. He would carry no Western technology, and he would use his body as a medium of communications. The latter was of course something Ledyard was quite familiar with. The polite, gentlemanly circles in which he had spent the previous four years placed a high premium on comportment, clothing, and other aspects of physical presentation. But Ledyard's familiarity with bodily modes of communication went beyond simply the most common protocols of polite society.

As was the case with many of the men who sailed with Cook, Ledyard returned from the voyage with indelible marks on his hands. Although tattooing had been practiced in antiquity and the Middle Ages, it was largely forgotten among Europeans until the second half of the eighteenth century. Voyagers returning from the South Seas in the 1770s and 1780s adorned with Native Polynesian designs or European text and iconography imprinted through Polynesian technology revived the painful practice. What is significant about Ledyard's tattoos is that he possessed them before the practice had acquired its later class connotations. Among the first voyagers to the South Seas, a gentleman was as likely to have been "punctured" as was an ordinary seaman. Joseph Banks had been tattooed, as had William Bligh, future captain of the *Bounty*.

The best record of Polynesian tattooing among British seafarers actually comes from Bligh, who made a careful record of the appearance of the mutineers who expelled him from his ship one April morning in 1789. Most were tattooed. The young gentleman Fletcher Christian, master's mate and leader of the mutiny, had marks on his chest and buttocks; the midshipman Peter Heywood was heavily tattooed with, among other marks, the three-legged crest and Latin motto of his home province, the Isle of Man; the able-bodied seaman John Millward had a feathered Tahitian gorget on his chest; and the ship's youngest crew member, the fifteen-year-old sailor Thomas Ellison, bore on his right arm his name and the date he first saw Tahiti, October 25, 1788. The principal common denominator among the tattooed, then, was that they had been to Tahiti. Only at the end of the century did tattooing lose its exotic association and become a widespread emblem of the ordinary seafarer's trade.

Indeed, far from any plebeian associations, Ledyard's tattoos marked him as a distinct sort of gentleman. Shortly before beginning his round-the-world trek, he recalled a situation in a Normandy tavern. He was "busy in the kitchen" preparing a meal when the "Otaheite marks on my hands were discovered. The mistress and the maids asked . . . the history of so strange a sight. They were answered that I was a gentleman who had been round the *world*." Ledyard would wear his tattoos, in other words, as he would later wear his Siberian coat and boots: as displays of gentlemanly cosmopolitanism. To have traveled where Ledyard had still placed one in a very exclusive fraternity. Over the course of the next fifty years, the rush to the Pacific for furs, Chinese trade goods, and eventually whale oil would change that.

Unfortunately, Ledyard's chosen interpretation of his tattoos was not always accepted. From the Siberian city of Barnaul, he would write to Jefferson that among the ordinary residents of the city "the marks on my hands procures me and my countrymen the appellation of wild men" rather than of well-traveled cosmopolitans. For the educated provincial governor and his genteel circle, there was no such misunderstanding. These elites embraced Ledyard and freely toasted two of his countrymen, Ben Franklin and George Washington, whose stars, he recalled, "shine even in the Galaxy of Barnal."[7]

Ledyard's transformation from merchant to traveler, then, was akin to all the other transformations he had undergone during his life—from

lawyer's apprentice to student, from student to seaman, from seaman to
soldier, from soldier to gentleman author, from gentleman author to gentleman merchant. Ledyard donned professions as others donned costumes.

This ongoing process of self-reinvention was not born simply of a lack
of self-understanding or crude opportunism, although elements of both
are present in Ledyard. It was born of a fundamental sense that social
ascent demanded changes of costume—it demanded, for example, trading a marine's red coat for a naval officer's blue coat and white breeches;
it demanded abandoning the sailor's cropped jacket and trousers for the
gentleman's periwig, long coat, breeches, and stockings. To assume the
person of a "naked and unarm'd man" was perhaps an extreme expression
of this ethos, but it was the same ethos nonetheless. In John Ledyard's
world, one could be what one appeared to be.

Ledyard's preparations for the round-the-world journey were slow and
cumbersome. Nearly a year passed between the time he began planning
his excursion and his departure in December 1786. Part of the problem,
again, was money. While Jefferson had supported him in Paris, he was unable to extend Ledyard sufficient credit for the full journey in part because
Jefferson, the provincial American, had few contacts outside of Paris. His
word on a promissory note would be worth little in eastern Europe or
Russia. But the far more damning setback was the empress Catherine's
refusal to grant Ledyard permission to traverse her dominions. As she
pronounced to her French liaison Grimm, "Mr. Ledyard would do well to
take another route . . . I do not know those [Americans] at all and have had
nothing to do with them up to now."[8] In the face of this sort of rebuke, it
was becoming clear to Ledyard that Jefferson's suggested overland route
across the Russian Empire to North America would be very difficult.

Ledyard's hopes were revived by Sir James Hall, a young British geolo-
gist whom he had met in Paris and who secured for him passage aboard a
British merchant vessel bound for Nootka Sound. The problem was that
Ledyard, who was a deserter, would have to return to British territory and
undertake the voyage with British sponsorship. The risks of arrest for desertion were apparently small, but the political risks were not. Although
Jefferson never showed any particular concern about British sponsorship,
others in the American diplomatic corps were bothered by the new plan.
Colonel William Stephens Smith, a former officer in the Continental Army

whose honorable service had earned him the post of secretary to John Adams, then the American ambassador to Great Britain, strenuously urged Ledyard to undertake his scheme with the declared intent of giving the Americans first rights to his discoveries. "He came [to London]," Smith explained to his superior, John Jay, "with an intention of entering into the service of [Great Britain]." But, Smith continued, "I endeavour'd to convince him, that it was his duty as an American Citizen, to exercise his talents and industry for the immediate service of his own Country." Apparently Hall and perhaps some other British patrons (who now included the naturalist Joseph Banks) had attempted to secure from Ledyard a proprietary interest in his findings. But Smith was aware that if Ledyard were to discover some lucrative trade or even a Northwest Passage, such an arrangement would profoundly compromise American security.

Smith offered Jay the consolation that, although there was no way to guarantee the United States privileged access to Ledyard's discoveries, the traveler would at least depart "free and independent of the world, pursuing his plan unembarrassed by contract or obligation."[9] It was a peculiar assertion since Ledyard was never, even in this case, without some sort of contract or obligation. Before leaving London, he had compiled a short list of patrons who, in addition to Smith, included Banks, Dr. John Hunter, a Scottish dentist, and John Walsh, a member of Britain's Royal Society. Absent any binding legal grounds for laying claim to Ledyard's discoveries, Smith could only hope that his own modest investment and the vaguely defined and minimal trappings of citizenship would ensure Ledyard's loyalty. On a list of the journey's subscribers, Smith inscribed the following addendum: "wishing Mr Ledyard not to confine himself to the particular views of any gentlemen in England and that he should not be under the necessity of reporting to them the discoveries he may make in America [I] will make such advances of Cash as will enable him to move upon principles of economy free from those shackles which they appear disposed to confine him with."[10]

Had Ledyard been a shrewder political mind, he might have played this American anxiety to his advantage, perhaps extorting more financial support from his countrymen. But Ledyard lacked the instinct for this sort of horse trading. He would rely instead on the ideal that the universal human appetite for a good gentleman's company would sustain him long enough to reach North America. Once there, he believed, as a man of supremely good character, as a man unburdened by the material trappings of civilized society, the penniless traveler would find a universal human spirit of hospitality. As he observed to Jefferson, in the American wilderness "I shall not want money."[11]

That Ledyard so freely pursued patrons within a nation so recently at war with his own country suggests just how fluid and complex identity and legal status remained for a former subject of the British Crown. Ledyard was an American by birth, but there was no formal legal mechanism establishing his citizenship. He owned no land that would entitle him to franchise, and he possessed no formal passport or other legal document identifying him as an American citizen. Passports did exist, but they were not something one retained on one's person, as proof of citizenship and affording safe entry to one's distinctly defined nation of origin. Rather, they were ad hoc permissions granted by governments, their agents, or sometimes just powerful individuals for safe passage from one point to another. They were as likely to be used for travel within a country—especially in wartime—as for travel between countries. But they had little real legal importance as a guarantor of identity. The closest thing Ledyard would have to this was simply the testimony he carried in letters of introduction. Insofar as he had any formal identity, it rested on what his prominent friends said in these letters. In some sense, the absence of true legal identity was an advantage. Ledyard could freely circulate in polite circles, seeking patrons without much fear that his actions—soliciting funds from Britons, for instance—would cost him his citizenship. Because there was no large, impersonal state bureaucracy to enforce the terms of citizenship, Ledyard could effectively live as a citizen of the world.[12]

For all his anticipation as he embarked on this somewhat mad journey, Ledyard was worried. He never suggested that years on the northwest coast as a fur-trade factor would be particularly risky. Nor is there any indication that his mortality weighed heavily on him during his years as a soldier. But with this perilous trip ahead of him, he was beginning to fear that time was running out. "The villainous, unprofitable life I have led goads me [and] I would willingly crowd as much merit as possible into the autumn and winter of it," Ledyard wrote to Isaac in August 1786. Ledyard had already lived longer than his father, and for all his zeal he believed he had little to show for it. The time had come, he seemed to be saying, for extreme measures. Such was the lot of the damned. No length could be too great to overcome ill fortune, even—or perhaps especially—when it meant possible death.[13]

Careening between anticipation and dread as he set out on his journey, Ledyard struggled to find words for his mother, Abigail, and his sisters. To his mother, he wrote, "To have been able to live with [my sisters], to love them, to assist them, and protect them, would have been to me a delightful task," but life had dictated otherwise, and Ledyard was left to "leave them to their God and you." But he did so wearily, for his mother and sisters had been seduced by those evangelical preachers—those purveyors of false doctrine and uncontrolled enthusiasm whom the conservative Elnathan Whitman had so loathed—who seemed determined to prey on naïve and innocent New Englanders. What, though, could John do now? Would he be abandoning his responsibility to the true God by abandoning the women in his life to "poor mad fools or rogues"? In the end, he could only pray for the intervention of "the great and good being who delights in the cheerful praises of his creatures and who is not to be mocked by shriekings, quakings, groanings, grinnings, grimaces, and contortions of the body or mind. Bless us all."

Disturbed though he was, Ledyard seemed to blame himself for this situation. It was as if he needed to compensate his mother for abandoning her, as if he could not see that in a fashion she had abandoned him. Perhaps he bore a wayward child's sense of guilt for the opprobrium he brought upon his mother for his various failures. If so, he was unable to communicate those feelings without grandiloquence. "I steal a moment from the ministers of Kings to kneel before the woman who gave me existence, and kindly nursed me into Manhood, to present her my poor thanks," he wrote, but thanks could take no more material form than these written "assurances of gratitude, to you."[14]

With Sir James Hall's aid, Ledyard made his way to London and finally, in September 1786, boarded a Pacific-bound merchant vessel, but after British customs agents detained the ship Ledyard returned to Jefferson's initial plan of an overland journey. Still lacking permission to pass through Russian dominions, John nonetheless sailed in early December 1786 from London to Hamburg, intending to travel from there to St. Petersburg and then east across the full expanse of the Russian Empire. On this first leg of his journey, he did as he had always done in Europe: he gained entrée to the English-speaking ex-patriot community. In Hamburg the experience carried few of the pleasures it had in Spain and France. His dinner companions included an English physician and a "stiff rumped Calvanistical Chaplain and his mummy of a wife." After a dull dinner in the presence of these stern Germanic Britons, he compensated himself with a pleasing hour in the company of the charming wife of an ex-patriot English merchant.[15]

Ledyard's social spirits were revived by the discovery that another American, William Langborn, had recently passed through Hamburg. Langborn had been Lafayette's aide-de-camp during the Revolutionary War, a role that earned him a commission as major in the American army. He also came from a prominent Virginia family and would eventually amass a handsome estate of his own, but before settling into the life of a country gentleman Langborn had chosen to spend several years wandering around Europe. For Langborn, unlike Ledyard, travel was no vocation. It was a gentleman's pursuit, born purely of a quest for worldliness and learning. He nonetheless dressed simply and ambled across the European countryside, walking some forty or fifty miles per day. By walking, he could fully absorb his surroundings and avoid the many ill effects of carriage travel. As one contemporary traveler's guide explained, "Travelers in carriages are very liable to have their legs swelled; in order to prevent being thus incomoded, it will be advisable to . . . walk as often as opportunity permits it, which will favor circulation."[16]

After hearing that Langborn had been stranded in Copenhagen without his possessions, Ledyard moved on to help his countryman. He believed that his efforts on behalf of the major would be ample proof of his own honorable character and that the two might then travel together to St. Petersburg. But Langborn declined to join Ledyard, perhaps fearing that this American was in fact the textbook example of a bad traveling companion for a true gentleman. As the above-mentioned traveler's guide put it, "There are in all countries to be found some very dissolute countrymen of every traveler, whose company is by all means to be avoided; their chief effort will be to borrow money, to live, and riot at the expence of the unexperienced; to be introduced into respectable families, to whom foreigners of prudence are recommended; and to dishonour, and possibly plunder them also."[17]

Thus rebuffed, Ledyard made his way to Stockholm, expecting to then cross a frozen Gulf of Bothnia to Finland partly aboard a horse-drawn sledge and then to travel south and east to St. Petersburg. But it was an unusually warm winter and the gulf had not frozen. Ledyard persevered, traveling north aboard sledges and sleighs through Lapland, just below the Arctic Circle, and then descending through the Finnish interior to St. Petersburg. The twelve-hundred-mile adventure took some eight weeks and must have left Ledyard half-frozen and exhausted.

Exactly how Ledyard survived in such difficult and sparsely populated terrain is unknown. All he ever said about the trip was that it depended on the generosity of ordinary people. Peasants, small farmers, fur trappers, lumbermen: these were the sorts who seem to have kept the visiting American alive. "Though I have as yet reached only the first stage of my journey," he observed in a letter to Jefferson written after arriving in St. Petersburg, "I feel myself much indebted to the urbanity which I always thought more general than many think it to be."[10] Even among the woodsmen and natives of the harsh arctic North, human nature showed its best face.

CHAPTER VIII

Across the Russian Empire

LEDYARD ARRIVED IN St. Petersburg in March 1787. Although he would spend nearly three months in the Russian capital, he wrote little at all about Europe's newest city. The fact that St. Petersburg was less than eighty years old when he arrived there, or that it was constructed on inhospitable, windswept marshlands by tens of thousands of conscript laborers (many of whom died in the process), or that it grew from vast quantities of stone and marble brought from all over Europe and Russia seemed to impress him not at all. Neither did he show the least interest in the great baroque Winter Palace, completed in 1762, or the grand Nevsky Prospekt, with its fashionable residences and shops. He was simply too consumed with the frustrations of travel in Russian dominions.

There, unlike other places Ledyard had traveled, movement depended on the actions of a large, impersonal state bureaucracy. He would need formal permission from the government to traverse the Russian Empire—he had needed no such permission to travel back and forth across the Atlantic or around France and England. And, of course, he assumed his travels through the Pacific were facilitated by little more than the amicable diplomacy and common courtesies of polite society. That network of Anglo-American gentlemen who had helped him move from American city to American city, from European city to European city, from enterprise to enterprise also seemed to be totally lacking in Russia. Here Ledyard's social currency bought little. And after a month and a half in St. Petersburg, he confided to his American sponsor in London, Colonel Smith, "There is no country in Europe or Asia so difficult to pass through" and "I am too angry with the country to write anything of its political affairs."[1]

After much diplomatic wrangling, Ledyard eventually did acquire papers sufficient to commence his trek. But those papers proved all too powerless in February 1788, when Catherine expelled him from the country. Ledyard interpreted the act as one of sheer malice, perpetrated by a capricious and despotic ruler. He truly believed that his goals were pure, that his ambition was untainted by any selfish or crude economic or political motive, and that his own candor was incontestable. The possibility that a foreign power would come to question his motives, especially a power Ledyard regarded as backward and morally inferior, was simply impossible for him to grasp. But clearly he did not understand the diplomatic complexities his trip raised. For all his interest in empire building in the Pacific, he had a very limited understanding of the actual politics of empire in the region. Although he was one of the few people in the English-speaking world to actually set foot in Russian America, he had almost no sense about the larger significance of this small outpost. Perhaps he simply saw it for what, on the surface, it appeared to be: a few rude villages, with none of the obvious apparatus of a major element in a European power's imperial plan. On Unalaska, he saw no substantial harbor, no large oceangoing merchant vessels, no great fur-trading factories, no hustling, independent merchants. Instead, he saw a group of about thirty mud and grass huts, inhabited by a ragtag collection of Russian traders and their native Kamchatkan servants.

Unbeknownst to Ledyard, these humble Alaskan camps had become vital components in a larger Russian imperial project. Since the middle of the eighteenth century, Russian fur traders had been working their way east along the Aleutian chain and by 1784 had established a substantial factory—more substantial than that Ledyard had seen in Unalaska—on Kodiak Island, off Alaska's southern coast. The camp was populated by 130 Russians, provided a deepwater port, and would, by the early 1790s, become the focal point for Russian trade in the region. These developments had been prompted by the declining populations of sable and other fur-bearing mammals in Siberia. In retrospect, then, it seems obvious that the Russians would be reluctant to grant some foreign traveler—

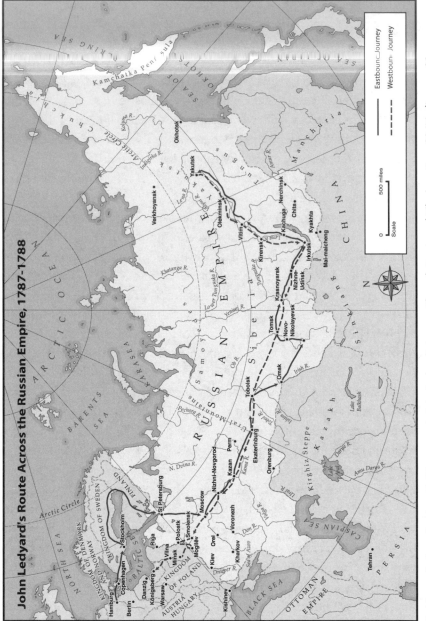

John Ledyard's Route Across the Russian Empire, 1787–1788

By Mapcraft, from Stephen D. Watrous, ed., *John Ledyard's Journey Through Russia and Siberia, 1787–1788* (Madison, 1966), 22.

particularly one with connections to Britain, a power beginning to en-
croach on Russia's North Pacific claims—permission to visit these lightly
defended outposts.

The reluctance seems even more obvious in light of recent geopolitical maneuvering in the North Pacific. Indeed, the European race to the
region had begun quickly and had elicited direct responses from major
powers as well as the brand new United States. It had been a mere six
years since Cook's final voyage had come to its end, and already Britain,
France, and even the United States had begun taking action to exploit the
newly surveyed territories of the North Pacific. None of this was lost on
Russian officials. In 1785, Catherine II sent an expedition led by Joseph
Billings, a member of Cook's last voyage, to survey and secure her far
northeastern possessions and in the years Ledyard was in Russia, officials
were secretly working to formalize Russian claims in Alaska.

Ledyard spent most of his time in St. Petersburg lobbying whatever official he could find for help obtaining a passport. He initially approached
the British embassy, but officials there claimed relations between Britain
and Russia were too strained for them to act on the American's behalf.
Ledyard dismissed the explanation as merely "polite language," disguis-
ing the "ill nature" of the legation's secretary. He then turned to another
British connection, an acquaintance of Joseph Banks's and someone
Banks likely suggested he contact, the German naturalist Peter Simon
Pallas. Pallas was a professor of zoology and botany at the St. Petersburg
Academy of Sciences and had himself led a natural history expedition to
Siberia between 1769 and 1774. He did what he could for Ledyard, but
ultimately that was not much. Though appointed by Catherine herself,
and the most prominent naturalist in her dominions, Pallas apparently
had few contacts within the government. The best he could do was to put
Ledyard in contact with officials in the French embassy. They then made
contact with a Russian official who in turn granted Ledyard a passport to
travel for scientific purposes. The Russian official also obtained equally
important papers from the postal service that allowed Ledyard to make
use of the Russian post roads at no cost.[2]

During his time in St. Petersburg, Ledyard had also met another
traveler, the Scottish physician William Brown. Together, the two men
traveled to Moscow and then east through the forested Ural Mountains

and across the vast swampy Baraba Steppe to the city of Barnaul, a trip of nearly two thousand five hundred miles. The journey lasted the better part of two months and took the travelers along Russian post roads, mostly in a crude covered coach, or *kibitka,* as it was called. The small horse-drawn coach would have been driven by a state-owned serf and resembled a small boat on wheels, with a fabric or animal hide canopy. It barely insulated the travelers from wind and rain as they endured day after day of monotonous journeying through desolate forest and boggy, subarctic plains. Fortunately they were traveling during the mildest season when temperatures would have reached the seventies during the day. Still, the trip would have been a grueling and bone-shaking one.

After several nights in Barnaul, sleeping "in my cloak on the floor, as I have done ever since I left Petersburg," Ledyard left his traveling companion and pressed eastward, another twelve hundred miles and several weeks, through the towns of Tomsk, Krasnoyarsk, Nizhne Udinsk, to Irkutsk, near the southwestern tip of Lake Baikal, the world's deepest freshwater body.[3]

At the end of this exhausting journey, more than four thousand miles long and two and a half months in duration, Ledyard found all the virtues a thriving commercial city could provide. "At this place," he wrote Smith, "I am in a circle as gay, rich, polite, and as scientific, as if at Petersburg[.] I drink my French and Spanish wines: and have . . . disciples of [the Swedish taxonomist] Linnaeus to accompany me in my philosophic walks."[4] Since 1661, Irkutsk had been the center of the Russian fur trade. Indigenous and Russian fur trappers came there to pay obligatory tribute to the tsars and to partake of a thriving China trade. Just a hundred and fifty miles northwest of the Mongolian border and the Chinese trading post of Mai-mai-cheng (literally, "buy-sell-city"), Russian furs, leather, ginseng, and manufactured goods found a ready market there, as did Chinese silk, cotton, tea, and medicinal rhubarb.

Lacking any real landed nobility, Irkutsk society closely resembled that of other frontier towns. There were protobourgeois merchant elites, often corrupt government officials as well as assorted petty traders, teamsters, and native servants. The absence of landed gentry meant there was no political counter to the merchant elite of the town, freeing them to buy off government officials and pursue their ambitions more or less as they wished. For Ledyard, son of another early-modern mercantile society, this would all have been quite familiar. But the lucrative and long-standing China trade had enriched the elite of Irkutsk in a way that Americans even in prosperous Philadelphia or Boston could barely match.

Here, in the center of the Eurasian hinterlands, was a city with imposing government buildings, a grand stone cathedral, hundreds of privately owned dwellings and shops, arcades for trade, taverns, public baths, a hospital, and an inoculation center from which the empress's agents directed the largest smallpox inoculation project anywhere in the world. The city's wealth supported a cultural infrastructure that dwarfed that of most American cities. There was a seminary, a public school, a library, a museum, and a theater for plays and musical performances. By the time Ledyard arrived, the erratic nature of the China trade and diminishing profits from a fur trade now centered in the North Pacific had stimulated the development of a considerable manufacturing sector that included a glassworks, a distillery, a saltworks, and a textile factory. The development was not unlike that in New England several decades later as merchants turned from trade to manufacturing.[5]

While at Irkutsk, Ledyard met Grigorii Shelikov, the fur-trading entrepreneur who founded Russia's principal American fur-trading factory at Kodiak Island. This was, at the time of its founding in 1784, the Russian Empire's easternmost outpost and represented a bold attempt to gain control of the North Pacific fur trade. With the support of a group of merchants based in Irkutsk, Shelikov brought a small amount of discipline and order to what had been a totally chaotic trade, governed by no rules and controlled by a collection of low-level fur traders, or *promyshlenniki*. Now, local native leaders had a single, relatively well-provisioned group of traders with whom to do business. Although the Shelikov group resorted to kidnapping and the murderous bombardment of villages to put down native Aleut resistance to enserfment, they were able to pay more for furs than lone traders. In 1799, four years after Shelikov's death, his company received a charter from the Russian government, establishing the Russian American Company. Much like the British Hudson's Bay and East India companies, Shelikov's company was now legally entitled to a trade monopoly in its huge North Pacific province.[6]

According to Ledyard, Shelikov was happy to share charts and maps of the American Pacific coast. He also offered Ledyard passage aboard one of his vessels leaving from the coastal town of Okhotsk for Kodiak the following summer. Little did the American know, however, that Shelikov had become suspicious of his interest in the North Pacific. Fearing that Ledyard was seeking intelligence for British or American competitors, Shelikov would use his clout to have the foreign traveler arrested and expelled from Russia.

From Irkutsk, Ledyard traveled north and east to the headwaters of the River Lena, the nearly three-thousand-mile-long easternmost river in Siberia. In early fall before much of the river froze, he was able to travel by water, huddled in a small open barge towed by horses trudging along the river's banks. From the town of Yakutsk, some fifteen hundred miles north of Irkutsk, he intended to travel east to Okhotsk and from there sail for America.

It was now late September, and snow and ice had begun to blanket this small fur-trading entrepôt and its surroundings. Local officials warned that any attempt to make the nearly five-hundred-mile final leg of this Russian journey before spring would mean certain death. Elsewhere in Siberia, winter cold would have eased movement by allowing one to travel along frozen rivers and iced-over roads aboard relatively smooth-riding horse-drawn sledges. But traveling from Yakutsk to Okhotsk in the winter months was a different matter. Cold winds, snow, and ice would be enveloping the region, especially the mountain passes Ledyard would have had to cross. And the massive caravans of hundreds of horses that carried goods back and forth during the brief summer window when the journey could be made safely had stopped for the year. Even had he come a month or so earlier, Ledyard would have faced a harrowing trip through the Verkhoyansk mountain range to the east. John D'Wolf, an American sea captain who traveled through the range twenty years later, recalled murderously steep mountains interrupted by vast swamps swarming with mosquitoes so bad that "our white horses became perfectly pink with blood."[7]

This delay could not be blamed on the government. "In the womb of this dread winter," Ledyard confided in the journal he had begun keeping, "there lurks the seeds of disappointment to my ardent desire of gaining the opposite continent."[8]

Ledyard would wait out the winter in this remote town, populated by assorted government exiles, Russian fur traders, Cossack officials, and

Ledyard sought to reach the port town of Okhotsk (pictured here) and then sail with Russian fur traders south around the Kamchatkan Peninsula and then north to a Russian fur trading camp in the eastern Aleutians. From Martin Sauer, *An Account of a Geographical and Astronomical Expedition to the Northern Parts of Russia* . . . London, 1802. Reproduced by permission of the Huntington Library, San Marino, California.

native Yakuti servants and herdsmen. And he would have much time to dine with local officials and write in his journal.

Not surprisingly, much that Ledyard wrote reflects his long preoccupation with the comparative character and nature of indigenous peoples. For example, he concluded that the indigenous people of the Yakutsk region had habits similar to those of other northern peoples. "Give a cake to [a] Swedish Finlander or northern Tartar [as he called all the native peoples of the Russian Empire], and he eats it leisurely: do the same to an Otaheitan, and Italian peasant or a Spanish fisherman and he will put the whole Cake into his mouth if he can." This lack of "voracity" Ledyard attributed to the northern climate. For the "atmosphere is constantly charged with snow," and there is "seldom a serene sky or detached cloud." Much like the population itself, "the motion of everything . . . is languid."[9] It was, on the surface, a strange juxtaposition: the languid, slow-eating northern Tartar versus the voracious Polynesian. After all, Ledyard had marveled at the ease of life produced by the plentiful Polynesian breadfruit, but for him, that ease did not produce languor or lassitude. On the contrary, it simply meant freedom from mundane labor, freedom that allowed men to live more nobly. Polynesia had powerful leaders because the patriarchs of the Tongan Islands and Tahiti and the Hawaiian Islands could spend their time fashioning themselves into dignified specimens of manhood. The native Yakuti lacked this particular luxury. For them, survival in a brutal climate had left little place for the cultivation of physical strength or grace or courage or any of the other attributes Ledyard had come to associate with indigenous nobility.

Though the Russia journal shares important qualities with Ledyard's earlier Pacific writings, particularly its interest in comparative ethnology, it also reflects important differences. Above all, it reveals very clearly the interests of Ledyard's patron, in this case Thomas Jefferson.

The connection between what Ledyard wrote and what was of interest to Jefferson is most apparent in Ledyard's comparison of the natural and human landscapes of the Russian Far East with those of North America. For Jefferson, that connection had to do with more than simply the quest for empirical proof of the unity of the human species. It also concerned the fate of human societies in America. According to one influential European view, the American climate had a degenerative effect on living things, leaving New World plants and animals physically stunted, and the native populations small in stature, immobile, and lacking in sexual ardor. The possibility that the American environment might somehow retard the development of the human—never mind the plant and animal—populations suggested that America might in fact be inhospitable to the highest achievements of humanity. Those achievements would, of course, include the creation of the world's first modern republic. For Jefferson, the argument and its implications were preposterous and damaging to the cause of the new nation. If European officials, already skeptical about the prospects of the Americans' bold political experiment, thought that it was also contrary to the dictates of nature, they would be little inclined to support Jefferson's mission. To counter so pernicious a line of thought, Jefferson spent much time and money disproving it, going so far as to request that a moose carcass be shipped from New Hampshire to Paris as proof that America had large hoofed animals. In his only published book, *Notes on the State of Virginia* (1785), Jefferson also wrote at length about the wooly mammoth, a creature he believed might still roam the unexplored north of America and Eurasia. But more important, he argued that mammoth bones found in North America came from the same species as those discovered in Siberia, suggesting that the largest of all quadrupeds lived in both the Old World and the New. The notion that the American climate could not sustain large animals was therefore patently false.[10]

During the course of his journey, Ledyard inquired about similar fossil evidence and was told that along Siberian riverbanks he would find "the same large bones that are found on the banks of the Ohio in America," further proof that Jefferson was correct. Similarly, Ledyard's copious observations of the native peoples of the Russian Far East boiled down to one basic conclusion: they and the American Indians differed little from each other. Ledyard saw the similarities in everything from footwear and clothing to burial customs, language, and architecture, further disproving the supposed distinctiveness of New World cultures. At one point he even took his own shot at the French naturalist Georges-Louis Leclerc de Buffon, the most widely read proponent of the American degeneration thesis. A man named Karamyschertt, director of the bank at Irkutsk, had suggested to Ledyard that native Kamchatkans had migrated from America, bringing with them their American inferiorities. But, Ledyard concluded, the Russian had been seduced by "the wild system of the French naturalist Buffon." In fact, Ledyard observed, the opposite was true: the Americans had migrated from Asia.[11]

After Ledyard had spent more than a month at Yakutsk, Captain Joseph Billings, former astronomer's assistant aboard the *Discovery* and the *Resolution* and now head of a Russian exploratory expedition, arrived there. Billings had joined the ranks of foreign officers in the Russian military—a group that in the spring of 1788 would come to include John Paul Jones, or, as the Russians knew him, Kontradmiral Pavel Ivanovich Jones.[12] Billings's commission was to survey the empire's north Pacific possessions, and after spending nearly two years charting the coasts of Alaska and the Cape of Chukotsk he had returned to Yakutsk for supplies.

Billings's mission was supposed to be secret, but it was known to Catherine's French envoy, Baron Grimm, who had suggested to Jefferson and Ledyard that Ledyard meet the expedition during one of its westward provisioning trips and then travel with Billings and his men on the final Russian leg of the journey. If Ledyard intended to join Billings's expedition, he did not say so in any of his correspondence, but the meeting at Yakutsk seems too fortunate an encounter to have been purely coincidental. And Shelikov, in a report about his visit with Ledyard, wrote that Ledyard had been planning to join the expedition. In any case, whether planned or not, the encounter with Billings was a fortunate one for Ledyard, since it would allow him to resume his journey sooner than expected and in the company of an old acquaintance. But before the travelers could depart, they had to retrieve most of Billings's more than one hundred tons of supplies which had been left in Irkutsk. After assembling a fleet of horse-drawn sledges, Billings thus proceeded south, accompanied by Ledyard and several other members of the expedition.[13]

This capital of the Russian fur trade was, it turns out, no place for an American traveler with uncertain motives. In mid-August 1786, Shelikov had sent a memorandum to Lieutenant-General I. V. Jacoby, the provincial governor at Irkutsk. The memo claimed that Ledyard's behavior had been suspicious and that his motives may not have been quite as benign as supposed. According to Shelikov, Ledyard had shown a suspiciously acute interest in the extent of Russian territories in America and had questioned Shelikov about the exact number of Russians residing there. Shelikov further claimed that Ledyard disputed Russian claims, saying that Cook had claimed the Cape of Chukotsk, on the western side of the Bering Strait, for England and that over ten thousand Europeans inhabited the California coast, north to Vancouver Island. "He conveyed this information," Shelikov recalled, "as if to alarm me, so I parried with the reply that people from other powers were not to be in these places without the permission of the Russian monarch."[14]

In November, Jacoby communicated Shelikov's concerns to one of Catherine's closest foreign policy advisors, Alexander Bezborodko, and further reported that although Ledyard's papers appeared to be in order, the traveler's motives were suspicious enough to warrant an interview. During the two men's discussion, Ledyard told Jacoby he was "traveling here and visiting this region to collect information pertaining to natural history," but this did little to allay official concerns. Jacoby did not feel justified in arresting Ledyard without the empress's permission, so he urged him to proceed to Yakutsk, a town with fewer merchants and officials who might reveal additional sensitive information to Ledyard. He also sent secret orders to the local commandant there to delay Ledyard's journey for as long as possible.[15]

What would have produced little concern a decade earlier was now clearly a matter for the highest offices of state. Before Cook's men returned with stories of the potential profits to be extracted from the North Pacific, the Russians faced very little competition in the region. But, as Ledyard's activities over the previous years demonstrate, the potential profits from the trade were exciting interest in the region across the Euro-American world. Two years earlier Catherine had requested advice from her foreign affairs advisors about securing formal claims to Russian America. They in turn reported that Russia had an "indisputable claim" to the American coast from 55° 21′ of latitude (roughly the southern tip of the present-day Alaskan mainland) north and to "all the islands situated near the mainland and peninsula [of] Alaska that were discovered by Bering and Cook." The justification for these claims, Catherine's advisors informed her, was not simply the presence of Russian commercial activity. That did not distinguish her claims from those of others. The real justification was, simply, the general law of discovery: "The first nation to discover an unknown land has the right to claim it." This had been the prevailing view since the discovery of America, according to these advisors, and there was no disputing the fact that Russian seafarers had far preceded Cook in charting the northern coasts of Eurasia and America. Her ministers urged Catherine to issue a formal declaration of ownership for these American territories and to send a Russian naval expedition to secure that ownership. The same intent led Catherine to send Billings in 1785 to inventory the far northeast reaches of her empire.[16]

Shelikov's interests and the government's interests sufficiently overlapped to prompt Catherine to take action against Ledyard. The fur trade was a source of income for both of them, and with its decline in Siberia and Kamchatka the American possessions were becoming ever more important. At the same time, in August 1787 Turkey declared war on Russia, drawing away military resources that might have been used to protect its American claims. That it took the better part of a year for the empress to act against Ledyard may have been in part because her advisors were unsure of this foreigner's actual identity. He was American born, but he traveled with British letters of introduction and was being assisted by the French embassy. It would have been one thing for the government to deny passage to a citizen of the new American Republic, a state with no particular diplomatic or military power. But it was altogether another to risk straining relations with France or Britain, the world's two superpowers.

Shelikov's influence seems ultimately to have prevailed over any earlier reluctance to stop Ledyard. By the time Ledyard returned to Irkutsk in early 1788, the empress had ordered that he be taken by military escort to Moscow and then expelled from Russia "with the admonition not to dare appear ever again anywhere within the limits of our Empire."[17]

Although Ledyard had had reason to complain about the difficulties of obtaining papers for travel in Russia, his five months' journey from St. Petersburg to Yakutsk had actually gone quite smoothly. So far as he knew, only the elements prevented his making further progress. And now, in the company of Billings and his men, his prospects of continuing once the weather permitted were excellent. This state-sponsored expedition had more than ample resources for carrying a supernumerary to the American coast. There was no reason—or at least none that Ledyard acknowledged—to think that his plans were in any jeopardy.

Reality confronted him in late February 1788 while he, Billings, and several of Billings's men were in Irkutsk, preparing to move supplies back to the Pacific coast. Martin Sauer, Billings's British secretary, recalled much confusion surrounding Ledyard's arrest. Local magistrates had received an order to arrest an Englishman, somebody other than Billings, and one of them came for Sauer. When the man explained the situation to Sauer, the Englishman immediately knew that of the two "Englishmen" who were in his party, it was more likely the arrest order had been issued for the other one, John Ledyard. Clearly the Russian authorities had determined that Ledyard was English or at least working for the English. Nevertheless, guards escorted Sauer to the governor's house, where he was greeted with news that Ledyard had been arrested. Billings assured Sauer that nothing could be done for their friend since the arrest had been ordered by the empress herself. With his fate sealed, "Ledyard took a friendly leave of me," Sauer recalled, "desired his remembrance to his friends, and with astonishing composure leaped into the kibitka, and drove off, with two guards, one on each side." Sauer had no idea why Ledyard had been arrested, though he speculated that his "haughty" behavior "certainly made him enemies."[18]

The "enemies" seem to have included Shelikov. The fur trader, whose company would come to control Russian America, viewed Ledyard as a threat. And it seems the Russian merchant was able to play on government fears of British encroachments in the North Pacific to prompt action.

Ledyard left little record of his immediate response to the arrest, but after several weeks traveling west with his Russian escorts, he returned to his journal. While briefly jailed in the city of Nizhni Novgorod, east of Moscow, he wrote of staying in a "vile, dark, dirty, gloomy, damp room" and of being seriously ill and emaciated. "I am treated in all respects (except that I am obliged to support myself with my own money) like a vile convict." It was a shocking assault on a member of that distinct class of human being that regards itself, by definition, as free to come and go as it pleases. So grave an insult could be countered only by an appeal to that same honorable character that had carried Ledyard so far in the world. He would neither succumb to passive, cowardly "resignation" nor debase his "honor, or sin against the genius of my noble country." For the Russians "may do wrong and treat me like a subject of this country, but by the spirits of my great ancestors, and the ignoble insult I have already felt, they shall not make me one in reality."[19]

From Nizhni Novgorod, Ledyard's escorts took him to Moscow, where he was interrogated by military officials. Then, after a little more than a week of additional travel with his two military escorts, he arrived at the Russian–Polish borderlands. The region was a thicket of disputed boundaries and ethnic mingling, in part because of the first of three late eighteenth-century partitionings of Poland. In the Treaty of St. Petersburg of 1772, Russia, Austria, and Prussia agreed to annex large swaths of Polish territory as a means of maintaining the fragile balance of power in central Europe. The result was, in part, an exodus: Polish Jews forced west, back into what territory Poland still claimed; Polish peasant refugees, fleeing civil war, often to the Ukraine, where they had been pushed by agents of Catherine the Great, ever determined to counter Russia's shortage of agricultural labor; Polish noblemen sent to Siberia; and other Poles drafted into the Russian army to fight the Turks. In the aftermath, observers found the Russian–Polish frontier a strangely lifeless kind of place, with villages deserted and fields lying fallow.[20]

Ledyard describes his own experience with this boundary zone in terms of the people he met—people who seemed somehow adapted to such a desolate landscape. At the town of Mogilëv, he was taken by his Russian escorts to a point on the Drut River, from which he crossed into

Horse-drawn sledges of the sort used to carry the expelled Ledyard from Russian dominions. From L'abbé Chappe d'Auteroche, *A Journey into Siberia*. London, 1770. Reproduced by permission of the Huntington Library, San Marino, California.

Poland and entered the small town of Tolochin, in present-day Belarus. Upon entering the town, Ledyard writes, he was led to the home of a local Jew, a fitting destination since such people would naturally inhabit the liminal territory at the edges of empires. "Not being permitted to enter the dominions of a [Russian] people more destitute of principle than themselves," he explained, "they hover about its boundaries here in great numbers." Of no consequence to Ledyard was the fact that this boundary was barely six years old, or that many of these people had been driven from their homes by the incessant civil war that plagued Poland. In Ledyard's mind, there was a natural convergence between the margins of empires and social marginality; it made sense, that is, to find living in a town like Tolochin a Jewish population banished from Russia but confined to a nation lost in civil and religious war.

After spending two nights in Tolochin, Ledyard moved on, heading toward the Prussian town of Königsburg (now Kaliningrad) on the Baltic Sea. Along the way, he saw dire poverty that rivaled anything he had seen before and that was perhaps aggravated by a smallpox epidemic. The disease raged around him, prompting the observation that "it is curious that I am so often exposed to the small pox without taking it."[21]

How strange it was to find among this depleted populace Jewish women of astonishing beauty: "The Jewish women have beautiful complexions. A fine skin and as happy a mixture of color as ever I saw; long black hair which among the demoiselles hangs down behind in one and sometimes two plaits, the rest is hid, . . . They have large full Jet black Eyes which like all others of that sort rather surprise than convince me into the idea of Beauty." The image was, unfortunately, tarnished by "a horrid clumsy, large coarse dirty hand" and "uniform filth, and now and then the itch." And finally, "I know nothing of their shapes; I regret it, but they are disguised under a vile Eastern Dress. The child of damned jealousy or damned superstition called into existence expressly to turn the eyes of man from viewing a work of nature as expressly formed to attract attention, admiration, Esteem and Love." Ledyard was undeterred, happily pursuing sex in these grim borderlands even though his liveryman "begged that I not . . . . [sic] the young woman I had with me in the Kabitka for if I did the horses would certainly be taken with sickness."[22]

Despairing and disgusted by Poland's contrasts, how delighted Ledyard was when on April 15, 1788, he finally crossed from the Polish borderlands of Russia into Prussia, the realm of one of Europe's most enlightened leaders. Here was an empire governed by no arbitrary despot inclined to deny the virtuous traveler his benign pursuit of geographic knowledge. Here was a Protestant realm, which much like the elite male New England in which he came of age, had drifted from Calvinism, not to thoughtless enthusiasms, but to rational religion, to philosophy, and to tolerance, the Enlightenment's highest ideal—or at least such was the reputation propagated by Voltaire and other admirers of the recently deceased Frederick II, king of Prussia.

For this American, the Prussian border taught just one very simple lesson: "If human imbecility will have kings to govern in god's name let them be men of genius." For on this day,

> I have within the space of three English miles leapt the great
> barrier of Asiatic and European manners; from servility, Indo-
> lence, filth, vanity, dishonesty, suspicion, jealousy, cowardice,
> knavery, reserve, ignorance, . . . and I know not what, to every

thing opposite to it, busy industry, frankness, neatness, well loaded tables[,] plain good manners, an obliging attention[,] firmness, intelligence, and, thank God, cheerfulness, and above [all] honesty, which I solemnly swear I have not looked full in the face since I first passed to the Eastward and Northward of the Baltic.[23]

Ledyard was relieved to be a free man once again, traveling in those Euro-American dominions where reason and gentlemanly civility seemed to prevail over crude animus. He would now make his way back to London in hopes of finding another way to his American object. And there, a loose fellowship of government officials and gentleman scientists would turn to him for his services as a gentleman traveler. It was, we can be certain, a great relief to be freed from the scrutiny of Russian authorities.

But that scrutiny had had some interesting results. It provoked Ledyard's most politically engaged writing. In ways the South Pacific had not, the Russian Empire compelled him to think about empire's impact on the wider non-European world. To him, the Russian Far East was a case study in the destructive effects of unchecked imperial power. It was also a stark expression of what had come to be Ledyard's guiding ideology: there was good empire, and there was bad. Russia claimed the latter.

CHAPTER IX

Despotism and Human Nature in Catherine II's Russia

FOR JOHN LEDYARD, the habit of ordinary Russians from the lowliest serf to the most elevated aristocrat of referring to their subordinates as slaves and to their superiors as masters was not merely rhetorical. These people were essentially enslaved and, as such, vivid exemplars of a culture of dependency that seemed to pervade every aspect of Russian life. It is true, Ledyard was himself something of a dependent, but the male, gentleman's republic of the Atlantic world had allowed him to sustain the illusion that he was a free man. It was perhaps the fragility of this status that explains Ledyard's hatred of Russia. Here, as he made his way across the vast empire of Catherine the Great, he found few advantages in his civility and worldliness. These bought him some friends, to be sure. But ultimately they could not influence a state and a government whose power, in its own dominions, was essentially unchecked.

Unlike the other societies with which Ledyard was familiar—pre-revolutionary New England and the new American Republic—here he found not even the slightest deference to the will of the people. There was, that is, no element of consent in the Russian state. The law, insofar as it existed, served the will of the state, and the state was described and governed according to no complex invention of mortals—the things the English and Americans called constitutions. For the state needed no worldly controls since it governed according to divine right, and similarly the people needed no protection from the state since it acted in the person of God. The only role of the people in this patrimonial political order was subservience, reverence, and loyalty. Such was the power of Russian monarchical despotism. Force, intimidation, and morally corrupting cruelty appeared to be the only rules of governance. At its core, in Ledyard's view, the Russian Empire was thus held together by the notion that individual human beings were worth little and that political unity came only with the sublimation of the individual to the will of the head of state.

Ledyard may not have been much of a revolutionary. But his experience across the Russian Empire, particularly the unsettling discovery that the rules of gentlemanly travel were not quite as universal as he had so long assumed, forced him to confront some of the fundamental political questions his nation's revolution had raised. He did not come out of the experience a strident republican, but there is no doubt he came out of it with a greater sympathy for the Revolution's core political innovation: government by consent.

If Ledyard had found much to admire about the societies of the South Pacific, in imperial Russia he found very little at all worthy of admiration. Among the indigenous populations there was little of that Syphaxian virtue he had found among the Tongan royalty and the Tahitians; and among the Euro-Russians, whatever civility they displayed, Ledyard concluded, was ultimately a veneer, obscuring fundamentally corrupt and dissipated natures. Evidence for the universality of human nature, so far as it existed at all, was shrouded beneath layers of social and cultural corruption of a sort Ledyard had never before witnessed—or at least never before witnessed on so vast a scale. But ultimately it was not the people themselves who were to blame. It was government, government that betrayed their trust and in doing so thwarted the good workings of human nature.

Since Ledyard wrote much while stalled in Yakutsk—as much as one-third of his remaining journal seems to have been written there—it is worth spending some time on this portion of the text. Aside from offering a striking portrait of the Russian Far East, this section shows Ledyard struggling to reconcile his universalist view of human nature with the reality of Russia's enormous diversity. Throughout his Russia trip, Ledyard struggled with this equation, looking constantly for proof that what distinguished the Russian Empire from the empires of the West—the

British or Spanish or French empires—was not so much its immense variety of peoples or its sheer size but rather its despotic government. That is, he struggled to reassure himself that size and ethnic diversity produced conflict and division only when coupled with despotism—a form of government that inhibited natural morality and, in turn, amplified superficial human difference.

Ledyard's was not a unique struggle. Perhaps the most prolific eighteenth-century Anglophone student of Russia, William Tooke, chaplain to the merchants of the British Russian Company at St. Petersburg, observed that precisely because of its extraordinary diversity Russia and its imperial domain constituted a novel and difficult political problem. Whereas European states had absorbed and diluted ethnic and linguistic difference, Russia appeared to have done no such thing. In his three-volume *View of the Russian Empire, During the Reign of Catherine the Second* (1800), Tooke explained that in all the countries of Europe "the dominant nation has in a manner swallowed up the conquered people; and the individuality of the latter has, in the course of some centuries, by insensible degrees, been almost entirely lost." In contrast, "in Russia dwell not only some, but a whole multitude of distinct nations; each of them having its own language, . . . retaining its religion and manners [and] bearing in their bodily structure, and in the features of their faces, the distinctive impression of their descent, which neither time nor commixture with other nations have been able entirely to efface." As if to make the empire's lack of ethnic and racial definition more tangible, Tooke further emphasized the difficulty of defining the empire in space. It was, in his view, a big, burly mess, lacking clear boundaries and at its farthest reaches dissolving into loosely defined frontiers populated by "various tribes of almost savage, nomadic, or, in one word, uncivilized nations." Russian government, that is, had done little to bring any unity or definition to the empire.[1]

For Ledyard, the ill-defined nature of the Russian Empire, the confused and confusing boundaries and borderlands, and especially an uncertain relationship between ethnicity, language, culture, religion, skin color, and status made for a cruel, corrupt mix.

In Yakutsk alone, Ledyard would have found exiled Russian nobility, Russian Orthodox priests, probably exiled Polish noblemen and military personnel, Greek merchants, French, Swedish, or German authorities employed by Catherine the Great, Kazakh slave traders, and indigenous

Yakut herdsmen and trappers. He also would have encountered native Kamchatkans, enslaved by Cossack fur traders through debt-peonage and transported westward to work as house servants or teamsters. In some ways, this collection of people resembled inhabitants of the frontiers of the British Empire. Race, consumer goods, language—all the social markers that defined people closer to the imperial center became fluid and confused as one moved to the empire's territorial fringes. In a certain sense, Ledyard seemed to find this state of affairs reassuring, indicating as it did the meaninglessness of superficial social and ethnic distinction. What was puzzling to him was that—much like what many observers found on the North American frontier—it did not produce any sort of natural virtue. Rather, despite the rampant violations of metropolitan social categories and ethnic norms, the Russian Far East seemed to retain much that Enlightenment critics from Rousseau to John Adams found repugnant about urbane, cosmopolitan Europe.[2]

As he traveled across Russian dominions, Ledyard had observed "a gentle gradation in which I passed from the height of civilized Society at Petersburg to incivilization in Siberia." That predictable gradation was revealed in a gradual shift in skin color from the "fair European to the Copper-coloured Tartar." This correlation between civility and fairness of skin color appeared to collapse in the rough world of the Russian frontier. There one found "the same variety of skin colour among the Tartars in Siberia as among the other Nations of the Earth." That is, in the Russian Far East, this correlation between lightness of skin color and levels of civility dissolved. These Tartars were not simply "copper-coloured" but widely varied in their complexions. Part of the reason for this, at least in the frontier towns limning the empire, was simply intermarriage. At Irkutsk, Ledyard observed "4 children descended of a Tartar & Russian Parents were alternately fair & dark complexioned." And at Yakutsk, the local governor "shewed me . . . a Man descended of a Yakutee Father & Russian Mother & the son of this man. I remark that the colour of the first descendant is as fair as that of the second, & that this colour is as fair as the Russian mother." After just one generation, children of mixed-race parents lost their Yakut complexion. No familiar physical trait, that is, distinguished aboriginals and mixed bloods from Euro-Russian colonials.[3]

Further complicating the ethnic and racial composition of Yakutsk was the presence of Cossack traders and military personnel. These descendents of runaway peasants and other Russians who had migrated to the country's southern frontier in the fifteenth century were employed by Russian monarchs to police the borderlands of the empire. By the eighteenth century, they occupied a distinct social position, neither peasant nor aristocrat; they floated through the interstices of the Russian social order, not unlike seamen or pirates in the Anglo-American Atlantic. Living on the geographic margins of the state, they enjoyed freedoms unknown to ordinary Russians, yet they generally embraced their own rigid military-style hierarchy.[4]

While most Cossacks were descended from ethnic Russians, Ledyard nonetheless associated them with the ethnic Tartars. The word *Tartar* was simply an eighteenth-century catchall for Turkic, North Asian, and others whose features and skin color suggested Asian lineage. Perhaps because their existence was generally limited to the fringes of the Russian Empire, Ledyard and other commentators associated the Cossacks with these non-Europeans even though they were in fact European Slavs. To accommodate this inconsistency, Ledyard divided the Tartars into three classes distinguished by the relative darkness of their complexions. The third and lightest of these were "fair complexioned Tartars which I believe include the Cossacs."

Ledyard's thinking here was consistent with the more general eighteenth-century racial map of the world. European commentators often associated the Cossacks with ancient Turkic conquerors of the great Nogai Steppe and the Caucasus Mountains. Voltaire, for instance, observed that "their life is entirely similar to that of the ancient Scythians and the Tartars on the shores of the Black Sea." Ledyard may also have been confused by the Cossacks' status in the Russian Far East. As Billings's secretary, Martin Sauer, wrote, Yakutsk "was the first town, in which I observed the officers from the highest to the lowest ranks form the poorer set of inhabitants; while the Cossack Sotniks [low-level officers] and the Pyat Debetniks [petty officers] were the most affluent." At Yakutsk, that is, the ordinary correlation between ethnicity and status appeared reversed. Far from being a marginal minority group, the Cossacks of Yakutsk had risen to prominence. Hence, Sauer continued, "a Cossack at Irkutsk is employed, by the governor and chief officers, in the most contemptible drudgery, such as cleaning the stable, scowering the kitchen, making fires, & c. At Yakutsk he is of more consequence, and finds employment as translator and emissary; . . . He lives in this part of the world like an independent chief, keeping Yakut laborers to assist his wife in all domestic drudgery, fishing, cutting wood, & c."[5]

Contributing to the absence of any clear correlation between skin color or ethnicity and social status was yet another factor. Much like the frontiers of the British Empire in North America, so the frontier of the Russian Empire appeared to have a leveling effect on its European inhabitants. That is, it appeared to erode the material distinctions between classes. "The Russ & [indigenous] Yakutee live together here in harmony & peace," Ledyard explained, "& without any difference as to national distinction, or of Superiority and Inferiority." Further, although the Russians had been at Yakutsk for more than a century and a half, "the Yakutee made no alteration in his manners or dress," yet "the Russians have conformed themselves to the dress of the Yakutee." Far from initiating any progressive civilizing process, in other words, Russian dominion seemed to have had a neutral effect on indigenous peoples and a reverse effect on Euro-Russians.

In the colonial world into which Ledyard had been born, the latter phenomenon took its most alarming form in Anglo-Americans who refused repatriation after being captured by Indians. As Benjamin Franklin explained, "When white persons of either sex have been taken prisoners young by the Indians, and lived a while among them, tho' ransomed by their Friends, and treated with all imaginable tenderness to prevail with them to stay among the English, yet in a Short time they become disgusted with our manner of life, and the care and pains that are necessary to support it, and take the first good Opportunity of escaping again into the Woods, from whence there is no reclaiming them." These former captives quickly tired of the restrictions and demands imposed by Anglo-American society and returned to the supposedly consensual and loosely ordered communities of their native captors. On the Russian frontier, however, little about the indigenous habits of Europeans could be explained by the libertarian ways of indigenous peoples. By the time of Ledyard's visit to Yakutsk, whatever remained of any sort of indigenous polity had largely been supplanted by the economic and social structures of serfdom.[6]

In some sense, if Ledyard's depiction of Yakutsk and its environs bears any comparison to the North American frontier, it is not to the often idealized societies of native peoples and their white converts, but to

Johnson Hall, the semifeudal upstate New York plantation of Sir William Johnson. This residence of the British superintendent of Indian affairs for the Northern Colonies constituted a strange amalgam of indigenous and European, a place where gentility, servitude, slavery, and hierarchy mingled with sweat lodges, native clothing, and indigenous religious practices. All of this cultural mingling occurred within a community whose ethnic bounds were bewildering in their complexity. In addition to the various native peoples who lived in and around Johnson Hall, there were Johnson's own métis (Indian–white parentage) children, sixteen black slaves, and more than fifty white laborers of indeterminate origin. Much as in Yakutsk, whatever ordinarily distinguished people of such widely varying lineages was muted at best. Johnson, for instance, had his slaves wear modified Iroquois clothing, and he referred to his mustee (African–Indian parentage) servant as Pontiac, the name of an Ottawa warrior. For some European visitors, the whole scene was disappointing. Far from a primitive world of native peoples and natural civility, they encountered fluid ethnic mingling and uncertain identities. As one recalled, Johnson "had Indian chiefs dine with him several times. Their attire was the same as white people, and for the most part they conversed in English. This disappointed me, because I wished to sit at table with genuine Indians in blankets and leggings and talking nothing but their gibberish through an interpreter."[7]

To a certain extent, then, Ledyard's experience at the fringes of the Russian Empire simply echoed the realities of early modern frontiers more generally. To travel from the imperial center to the edges of empire was not to experience a steady dissipation of the trappings of civilization, but rather to witness a mix of indigenous and European that produced unfamiliar social hierarchies and unfamiliar markers of status. As might be expected, for Ledyard, this state of affairs did not disprove the pieties of eighteenth-century ethnography—such as the idea that skin color and levels of civility were correlates. Rather, it produced an insistent struggle to understand the frontiers of empire in terms of familiar categories of peoples. And this struggle, in turn, yielded the peculiar notion that in fact the Russian Empire was ultimately quite uniform.

The chief manifestation of this, in Ledyard's view, was an attachment to luxury. Everyone within the empire, whether Russian or Yakut, whether prominent or base, seemed seduced by the feminizing frivolities that in western Europe were widely presumed to be the domain of the upper classes—and equally the source of their moral degradation. To Ledyard, there was no sense within Russian dominions that consumption was the prerogative of the elite or that sumptuous pleasures somehow subverted human nature. Everyone, whatever their station, appeared eager and free to indulge the collection of carnal impulses that produced an appetite for luxury. "I have frequently observed in Russian villages—obscured and dirty, mean and poor," Ledyard wrote, "that the women of the peasantry paint their faces profusely both red and white. I have had occasion from this, and many other circumstances I shall mention to suppose that the Russians are a People, who have been very attached to luxury." It was one thing to wear makeup, altogether another to indulge in such a frivolity when one is otherwise craven and debased. Ledyard went on to assert that the Asian inhabitants of southern Siberia were equally inclined toward extravagance and indulgence. Whether "the Grand Signor [or] him who pitches his tent on the wild frontiers of Russia & China . . . they deviate less from the pursuit & enjoyment of sensual pleasure, than any other people."[8]

Even at the farthest reaches of empire this general taste for luxury was evident. The peoples of Yakutsk, Ledyard explained in a letter to Smith, "live in all the excess of Asiatic luxury joined also with such European excesses as have migrated hither." That is, the people of Yakutsk enjoyed both the material productions imported from the West and the sumptuous goods of the East. Ledyard's perceptions were not unique. A magazine article published in Philadelphia in 1792 explained to readers that "the luxury of [Russian women's] cloathing among the inferior class, would astonish. . . . All their cloathing is of silk or cotton, of the most brilliant colours, never of woollen or linen, although Russia has those commodities in great plenty."[9]

The market forces that afforded material distinctions in the Anglo-Atlantic world thus seemed not to apply in the Eurasian world. For what was exotic in Britain or America was commonplace in the Russian Empire. This did not change the social and moral impact of such goods. Instead of clouding the judgment of a remote class of aristocrats, they clouded the judgment of a vast, otherwise widely diverse population. For Ledyard the most striking consequence of this was a general societal inability to discipline consuming impulses and, in turn, a compulsion toward "thieving."

Ledyard was endlessly interested in what he perceived to be the dishonorable and dishonest ways of the peoples of the Russian Empire. At a birthday party in Yakutsk, he observed "a melange of character I have seen in no other society, but this peculiar difference[:] that there is no particle of honesty or honour in the mixture." "If Mercury was the God of theft among the Ancients," he declared, "the Russians ought to enroll him in their mythology." For even after lavishing him with the most extraordinary hospitality, tables filled with every conceivable food and drink, his Russian hosts seemed inclined nonetheless to steal from him: "I wish I could think them as honest as they are hospitable."[10]

In the end, the real problem with the Russian Empire was not so much the prevalence of luxury goods and the confused nature of the social and ethnic landscape; the real problem was government, government that left its people intoxicated by their basest impulses and provided no reward for moral virtue. Coursing through Ledyard's thinking here is a familiar Enlightenment problem: what is the origin of human morality and how can that morality be cultivated and elicited from ordinary people? For Jefferson, much like Rousseau, Adam Smith, and other "sentimentalists," as the historian Ruth Bloch has perceptively described them, the answer is ultimately empathy, compassion, and love. These emotions, rather than bare calculating self-interest, held people together and transformed random collections of subjects into communities of shared interest. In subverting human nature, despotism forced such natural sentiments to remain latent.[11]

Perhaps nothing better revealed the moral failings of despotic states than their legal systems. Russian laws, Ledyard explained, are "mostly penal laws" or "negative instructors; they inform people what they must not do and affix no reward to virtue." They seemed, that is, designed solely to protect the state from the people; and did little to protect the people from the state. This in turn left the people with no unifying moral code, a factor that contributed to the nebulousness of the Russian Empire itself. No single positive value brought unity or differentiated subjects of this empire from those of the Asian empires to the south. Obedience alone unified the peoples of the empire, much as it did, Ledyard assumed, the other peoples of the Orient. As he explained, "A citizen here fulfils his duty to the laws if like a base Asiatic he licks the feet of his superior in rank."[12]

Ledyard's thinking here is consistent with much eighteenth-century political thought, particularly the idea that Eastern empires tended to be governed by force rather than by law. Such polities may afford their people access to exotic goods and physical luxuries, but in doing so they foster a passive, feminine spirit that leaves their subjects idle, weak, and unable to resist the advances of potentates and power mongers. The latter are thus left free to usurp the institutions of government, transforming them from benevolent caretakers of the people into mechanisms for absolute power. As a wide range of writers warned, luxury was the handmaiden of despotism. "We do indeed import gorgeous silks, and luscious sweets from the [East] Indies," the English cleric and schoolmaster Vicesimus Knox observed, "but we import, at the same time, the *spirit of despotism,* which adds deformity to the purple robe [of the monarch], and bitterness to the honied beverage [of the commoner]." Such luxuries, so the reasoning went, leave consuming classes addicted to base, carnal pleasures, so much so that they eclipse any natural affection for fellow human beings. It is one thing when only the wealthiest classes suffer the moral lassitude produced by luxury. It is altogether another when entire societies fall prey to the stultifying effects of short-term pleasures.[13]

Denied their sociable and affectionate nature by luxury and force, the people of imperial Russia had never grasped "that sweet truth that virtue is its own reward." "It is for this reason," Ledyard concluded, "that their peasantry, in particular are indubitably the most unprincipled in Christendom. I looked for certain virtues of the heart that are called natural. I find them not in the most remote & obscure villages in the empire but on the contrary I find the rankest vices to abound as much as in their capital." The prevalence of luxury, despotic government, the absence of any legal rights all combined to define the Russian Empire as the most unnatural of places. The goodness that inheres in human nature was not evident even at the empire's farthest limits.[14]

The iron grip of despotism had produced not merely an empire of consumption and luxury, but ultimately an empire of slavery. And slavery destroyed human nature. As Franklin famously explained the equation, "The unhappy man, who has long been treated as a brute animal, too frequently sinks beneath the common standard of the human species. The galling chains, that bind his body, do also fetter his intellectual faculties, and impair the social affections of this heart. Accustomed to move like a mere machine, by the will of a master, reflection is suspended; he has not the power of choice; and reason and conscience have but little influence over his conduct, because he is chiefly governed by the passion of fear." And in his *Anecdotes of the Russian Empire* (1784), the English playwright and critic William Richardson explained how this state of affairs produced a moral vacuum:

> The guile, the baseness, and rugged ferocity attributed to slaves, and men overwhelmed with oppression, are chiefly owing to their oppressors. Exposed to the avarice and pride of some haughty superior, who is himself a slave, and who has not in his breast one sentiment of humanity, they have no other defense against oppression but deceit; and feel no other emotion from the treatment they receive, but hatred and deep revenge. It is thus, in accustoming the mind to vicious habits, more than merely depriving us of our property, and the security of our persons, that despotism is the bane of society. Those poor unhappy men, who are bought and sold, who are beaten, loaded with fetters, and valued no higher than a dog, treated with unabating rigour, become inhuman; insulted with unremitting contempt, become base; and for ever afraid of rapacious injustice, they grow deceitful.

It was the universally servile condition of Russians, declared the French critic of European empire Abbé Guillaume Thomas François Raynal that thwarted the ambitions of even the enlightened Catherine the Great. "She is labouring to instill notions of liberty into a people stupefied by slavery," he explained, "but it is doubtful whether she will succeed in the present generation."[15]

Ledyard was thus echoing the most forward thinking of his day. Few European observers saw in any corner of the Russian Empire fertile ground for government by consent. The faculties that would allow human beings to govern themselves in a benevolent and consensual fashion had been beaten down for too long. While the effects of such oppression on individual morality produced conditions very different from what Rousseau and others may have expected at the fringes of the European world, the effects on material life and national identity were similar. If on the North American frontier such theory was confirmed by the effects of natural hardship on social, national, and ethnic difference, on the Russian frontier one found something similar. Everyone's character appeared uniform. But instead of being uniformly natural, it was uniformly inclined toward luxury and immorality. The point is especially important given the basically cosmopolitan character of Far Eastern portions of the Russian Empire. Having for more than a century been a repository for convicts, political exiles, prisoners of war, and foreign-born bureaucrats, the region had come to be populated by peoples of a host of castes and nationalities. For Ledyard and so many other observers, whatever their caste or nationality, these subjects of the Russian empress all appeared equally infected by the corrupting influences of oriental luxury and despotism.[16]

The Russian Orthodox Church, which Ledyard barely mentions, appeared to have done little to temper the psychological effects of despotic government. Perhaps Ledyard's near silence about the church reflects his assimilation of some republican views concerning the perniciousness of state-sponsored churches. According to this thinking, the primary function of these institutions was to sustain themselves rather than cultivate the moral character of adherents. The retention of a Catholic-style clerical hierarchy and the worship of icons in Russia thus produced obedient Christians but not moral followers of Jesus—so the thinking would have gone.

What was needed in Russia, Ledyard declared, was something of a Reformation. Only the introduction of a new, tolerant theology that recognized the primacy of innate morality over clerical authority could bring an end to the empire's moral lassitude. In one of his few overtures to formal Christianity, Ledyard referred to three moderate Anglican preachers, products of a late seventeenth- and early eighteenth-century revolution in British religious thought. "[Thomas] Sherlock! [John] Tillotson! [Laurence] Sterne!" he exclaimed, "what a Revolution would your sermons produce among [the Russian] people." These Latitudinarian divines, driven by an interest in theologically grounded religious toleration, shared a conviction that human nature was fundamentally good and that generosity, charity, and general good treatment of others were pleasurable and therefore right. Hence, were they to preach in Russia, the governing order would crumble. The cruelty and avarice that secured that order would decline in the face of an overwhelming spirit of benevolence. This development would also bring new definition to the Russian Empire by erecting a sharp moral barrier to oriental despotism. It would also, that is, establish the empire as an extension of Enlightened European dominion rather than a vague dissipation of the same.[17]

Ledyard was able to write little in his journal during his westward journey out of the Russian Empire. But when he arrived at the Russian–Polish borderlands in late March 1788, he resumed his analysis of the empire he was leaving. He now found himself, he explained, on "the uncertain boundary of a Queen on the one hand, whose rapacity of Empire is boundless, and on the other by a [Polish] people who I strongly suspect of all the Vices of indolence and vanity." In some sense, that is, the western boundary of the Russian Empire—much like its eastern counterpart—was no boundary at all. It merely distinguished the formal claims of Russia's female ruler from the informal. For, in the end, the passive and corrupt peoples of Poland were de facto part of the Russian Empire. In their very lack of morals and civility, they had, like the other peoples of the empire, given themselves over to despotism.[18]

Ledyard's assessment of Russia's western boundary points to an additional factor in the eighteenth-century Anglo-American view of the Russian Empire: its female ruler. For Ledyard, her boundless "rapacity of Empire" was merely another side of the "unprincely malice [that] made a prisoner" of him just as he was about to reach North America.[19] That "unprincely malice," Ledyard implies, was a sort of female capriciousness —a capriciousness that did to the sovereign what the sovereign's government did to her subjects: it eroded any sense of compassion and reason that might have been manifest in a more controlled and morally grounded ruler. Hence, Ledyard was banished from Russia not because he posed a security risk or because he had violated the law, but because the empress was incapable of making a dispassionate assessment of his purpose; pure jealousy and crude animosity animated her policy. The view was widely echoed in an American press that had begun to take an interest in the daring traveler. The *American Magazine* of October 1788 explained that Ledyard was arrested because of the "jealousy of the Russian Court"; the *New York Magazine; or, Literary Repository* of September 1791 explained that he was expelled "without any reason given"; and *The Time Piece and Literary Companion* of July 1797 recounted that "Ledyard, the celebrated traveler, after having traversed the continent of Europe and Asia, on foot, and experienced the tyranny of the late Russian *She Bear,* Catherine, by whom he was *sledged* out of the Russian dominions, got out of her clutches on condition of not returning on penalty of being hanged."[20]

Some European commentators expressed similar views. A contemporary French diplomat complained that Catherine the Great "offers the strange and inconsistent mingling of courage and weakness, of firmness and irresolution. Passing from one extreme to the other, she presents a thousand different surfaces to the attentive observer who wishes to know in vain her real point of view . . . and who finishes in his incertitude by placing her among the ranks of first comedienne."[21] To compare Catherine to an actress on a stage was to suggest that the moral failings of the Russian Empire were reflected in the monarch herself. Much like her subjects, she seemed so conditioned to performance that defied conscience as to have lost any real conscience at all. The moral failings of the Russian Empire, that is, extended from top to bottom; from the monarch to the lowliest Yakut servant.

Catherine the Great's supposed capriciousness is consistent with another distinguishing quality of her empire: its simple nebulousness. In its very form, that is, the empire seemed to mirror the irrationality and incivility of its ruler and people. Indeed, at some level, the Russian–Polish border was, for Ledyard, merely a small-scale expression of a problem that defined the empress's entire dominion. Nothing about it suggested any kind of real coherence. It was at once rational and irrational; savage and civilized; European and Asian; luxuriant and base; tightly bound in its mechanisms of discipline and yet completely undisciplined. The cohesive parts of a national body politic that some commentators imposed on the British Empire seemed simply not to apply to the Russian Empire. There was little, that is, that suggested the sort of defining order Thomas Pownall, a former governor of colonial Massachusetts, attributed to empire in his *Principles of Polity, being the Grounds and Reasons of Civil Empire* (1752): "This modeling of the people into various orders and subordinations of orders, so that it be capable of receiving and communicating any political motion, and acting under that direction as one whole is what the Romans called by the peculiar word *Imperium*, to express which particular group of ideas, we have no word in English, but by adopting the word Empire. 'Tis by this system only that a people become a political body; 'tis the chain, the bond of union, by which very vague and independent particles cohere."[22]

Far from being modeled into any kind of coherent set of social orders, the peoples of the Russian Empire existed as a confusing amalgam of peoples and boundary lands with no real order, either geographical or social. The empire was to the body politic what a malformed body was to the body physical. And much like the malformed physical body, so the malformed body politic reflected the confused inner faculties of bodily government. Instead of the collective moral faculties of the people, it is the sovereign who dictates the form and character of the body politic. And if the sovereign is distorted or corrupt, so too the body politic. This would be especially so in despotic regimes, in which no laws, magistrates, or other governing institutions mediated between king and people and the inebriating influence of court culture reached far beyond the court itself. As the Abbé Raynal summarized the problem, "Europe has long entertained the project of a code of laws preparing for Russia. . . . But what are laws without magistrates? What are magistrates, whose sentence the despot may reverse according to his own caprice, and even punish them for passing it? Under such a government, no tie can subsist between the members and their head. If he is always formidable to them, they are no less so to him. The strength he exerts to oppress them, is no other than their own united strength turned against themselves."[23]

In the absence of any real system of law and law enforcement, in other words, universal slavery is inevitable. To protect herself from the unbridled will of her people, the sovereign enslaved them. In so doing, however, she also effectively enslaved herself to the blinding passion of fear.

At some level, Ledyard's perspective on the Russian Empire echoes more general criticisms of the Anglo-European ancien régime. Luxury, corruption, moral decay, a peasantry as debased as its leaders—all of these moral failings can be found in eighteenth-century social criticism of cosmopolitan Europe. Even so seemingly distinct a notion that the Russian Empire failed to preserve orderly and evident divisions of status can be found leveled against European societies. Consider, for example, the following lament for a lost English countryside by the Welsh squire Matthew Bramble, a character in Tobias Smollett's 1771 novel *Humphrey Clinker:*

The tide of luxury has swept all the inhabitants from the
open country—The poorest squire, as well as the richest peer,
must have his house in town, and make a figure with an

extraordinary number of domestics.—The gayest places of public entertainment are filled with fashionable figures; which, upon inquiry, will be found to be journeymen tailors, serving-men, and abigails, disguised like their betters. In short, there is no distinction or subordination left—The different depart-ments of life are jumbled together—The hod carrier, the low mechanic, the tapster, the publican, the shopkeeper, the petti-fogger, the citizen, and the courtier, *all tread upon the kibes of one another:* actuated by the demons of profligacy and licen-tiousness, they are seen every where rambling, riding, rolling, rushing, jostling, mixing, bouncing, cracking, and crashing in one vile ferment of stupidity and corruption.[24]

This could just as well have been Ledyard writing about the Russian Em-pire. What is important about what he wrote—little of which was pub-lished until the twentieth century—is thus not its originality. Ledyard expressed a broadly assimilated Anglo-American critique of a dissipated and corrupt old order.

What is significant about Ledyard's views is their convergence with his American identity. No American of his generation had penetrated the farthest fringes of the vast continental empire of Russia. And that empire presented the American observer with a comparative perspective on em-pire that raised vitally important issues for the young Republic. In Russia, unlike Britain, Americans could view a continental empire rather than an oceanic one. In Russia, they could view an empire dependent, much as a new American empire would be, on transcontinental trade and the assimilation of a large indigenous population. And most important, in the Russian Empire they could bear witness to what in fact, if not in theory, would be the most vexing problem for America's imperial republicans: if, as Pownall suggested, empire was a system for ordering people in clear gradations to achieve political ends, what of the uncertain geographical limits of empire where social status exists in alien forms? For more than one hundred years, Yakutsk had been a Russian colonial outpost and yet, as Ledyard observed, little about it suggested the march toward civi-lization that so many thinkers of the age assumed was an inevitable—if not always positive—consequence of colonization. Much like that of the North American backcountry, the social structure of the Russian imperial periphery was confused and jumbled; order itself seemed absent. Law, identity, money, birth, race—none of these seemed to produce any kind of identifiable social gradations.

But whatever similarities imperial Russia and frontier America may have had were unimportant to Ledyard. What ultimately mattered to him had little to do with the distinct social and cultural forms evident in both the Russian and American backcountry. It had to do, once again, with government. In reflecting this fact, Ledyard's observations of the Russian Empire represented a reassuring demonstration that despotism produced thieving, licentious, and immoral people, whether those people occupied the empire's farthest reaches or its imperial center; whether the most remote Yakuti hunter or the empress Catherine herself. An enlightened government, such as that of the United States, would thus produce a different kind of empire, an empire of fundamentally moral beings at even its farthest frontier reaches. Had Ledyard been more interested in the commonalities of imperial Russia and the new United States—their vast inland frontiers, their extraordinary ethnic and racial diversity, their large indigenous populations, their dependence on unfree labor—perhaps his Russian writings would be better known. Instead of simply a purveyor of familiar Enlightenment truisms he might have been more sensitive to the perils of American expansion. He might have recognized, for instance, that far from yielding a new enlightened order in the North American backcountry, the republican Revolution produced only more chaos of a considerably bloodier sort than anything Ledyard saw on the frontiers of the Russian Empire. And this might have left him less sanguine about the sentimentalist view of human nature. But in the end Ledyard was limited by what he thought he knew about society and government. Little of this prepared him for a world of independent citizens, citizens who defined themselves less by enlightened values than by convenient rubrics of whiteness.[25]

CHAPTER X

To Africa

LEDYARD RETURNED TO London sometime in the early spring of 1788. His American benefactor, William Smith, had left for the United States, but Ledyard was able to get news of his country from the New York merchant James Jarvis. He would have learned that his world was in flux. The United States, where John had not been for four years, was in the process of ratifying a highly controversial new federal constitution, and America's former French allies were mired in a constitutional crisis of their own. The latter would culminate in a show of force by the army as it surrounded the Parlement of Paris. But momentous as these events would prove to be, a reasonable argument can be made that neither would turn out to be as earthshaking as a development in Great Britain.

For the previous three years, an unlikely collection of Quakers, conscientious booksellers, Manchester businessmen, politicians, and evangelical Christians had begun campaigning for the abolition of slavery and the cessation of the Atlantic slave trade. It is hard to exaggerate the radicalism and novelty of this movement. Two years earlier the idea of halting the colonial slave trade, never mind of calling for the abolition of slavery itself, would have been unthinkable to most Britons. Now it was being debated in Parliament.

◆ ◆ ◆

Having received only modest public attention previously, suddenly in the winter of 1788 debating societies across London were discoursing on the morality of the slave trade, gentlemen's magazines were printing one opinion piece after another on the matter, and, perhaps most important of all, John Newton, a onetime slave trader and now one of England's most celebrated evangelical preachers (and the author of the famous hymn "Amazing Grace"), had finally, after some thirty years in the pulpit, spoken out against his former trade. In *Thoughts on the Atlantic Slave Trade*, a searing jeremiad that appeared in early 1788, Newton condemned the practice for what it did to both its African victims and its European practitioners. Indeed, for this evangelical Christian dedicated to the cause of saving souls, the soul-robbing cruelty of the slave trade was fundamentally abhorrent. In language very similar to that Ledyard used when describing Russian despotism, Newton condemned the trade for robbing "the heart of every gentle and humane disposition" and hardening it "like steel, against all impressions of sensibility."[1]

Ledyard never wrote anything about African slavery, but this was not because it was unfamiliar to him. Although he had no experience with the harsh slave regimes of Virginia, Carolina, or the Caribbean, he had plenty of experience with slavery in New England and the maritime Atlantic. His grandfather had owned four slaves—a girl called Jill and three men of varying ages—some of whom likely lived with him as house servants. In addition, Squire John periodically rented other slaves from their owners, including one who belonged to Pastor Whitman, in exchange for lumber and firewood. Ledyard would also have known slavery from his time at Dartmouth College, where Wheelock's slaves labored, and from his months in port towns such as Groton, New London, New York, Philadelphia, and London, where slaves commonly worked as stevedores. Similarly, he would have known slaves during his time in the merchant marine. African slaves often traveled with sea captains as personal servants or worked on vessels as sailors.[2]

Though Ledyard never showed any special aversion to the slavery he knew, his Siberia journal is filled with rhetoric that would have registered in antislavery circles. The argument that tyranny and bondage corrupt human beings and cloud their judgment, the foundation for his complaints about the Russian Empire, lay at the very heart of much antislavery sentiment.

For figures like Newton, it was not so much that slavery was inherently cruel, although they acknowledged that it was. What was really troublesome was the effect the institution had on society as a whole. Much like despotic government, slavery dulled the moral faculties of both its victims and its perpetrators. Although no abolitionist, Thomas Jefferson did write in his *Notes on the State of Virginia,* of "an unhappy influence on the manners of our people produced by the existence of slavery among us." The struggles between slave and master infected every aspect of daily life and perpetuated themselves like so many faulty genes. Children see the "unremitting despotism" of the master and the "degrading submissions of the slave" and "thus nursed, educated, and daily exercised in tyranny, cannot but be stamped by it with odious peculiarities. The man must be a prodigy who can retain his manners and morals undepraved by such circumstances."[3]

Why Ledyard never saw the parallel between the effects of despotism and the effects of transatlantic slavery is unclear. The question is all the more puzzling in light of the servitude or slavery he witnessed across Russian dominions.

Although the portions of eastern Russia in which Ledyard spent most of his time lacked the huge numbers of serfs present in western areas, he nonetheless would have had ample opportunity to see the workings of serfdom. By the time he visited Yakutsk, local chiefs, or *toyons,* exercised a degree of control over many in their designated districts similar to that of lords over their serfs: they could restrict their movement, extract tribute from them, and punish them as they saw fit.[4] Elsewhere in Siberia, Ledyard would have encountered so-called state peasants, effectively owned by the state rather than by a noble landlord. These peasants had far more freedom than ordinary serfs or African slaves, but their movements were still restricted, they were obliged to deliver tribute to state representatives, and they were at risk of arbitrary enserfment as the tsars doled out land and bodies to favored noblemen. Furthermore, many of them were exiles, forced to travel to Siberia to provide labor and population in Russia's far-flung colonial empire. The effects of such coercion and domination in Ledyard's mind were, as we have seen, almost identical to what others saw as the effects of slavery.[5]

Perhaps Ledyard failed to see the connection between Russian serfdom and transatlantic slavery because his conception of freedom was anachronistic. His forceful arguments about the corrupting effects of despotism disguised an underlying assumption that freedom was not possible for some. However crucial it was to the flowering of true human nature, for some that nature was simply too far buried to flower under even the most benevolent circumstances.

For ethnic "Tartars," for instance, liberty meant something very different from what it meant to freeborn gentlemen such as himself. These apparently nomadic peoples of the Russian Far East were wanderers not because they loved their liberty—not because they preferred the uncertainties of the hunter's life to the tyrannies of a corrupt imperial regime. Rather, they were nomadic because they cherished a certain freedom from work. "I believe their ideas both of peace and liberty [are] very different from ours, and . . . a Tartar if he has his dear Otium [leisure] would be as likely to call it liberty as Otium." Freedom for these people was thus not freedom from oppression. Rather, it was freedom to—simply put—relax. "There is much liberty in England," Ledyard explained, "but I think it would be less agreeable to a Tartar to live there than in Russian Siberia where there is less Liberty." Freedom, in other words, was in the eye of the beholder.[6]

When it came to his own detention in Russia, Ledyard sang a very different tune. Suddenly, freedom was life's dearest commodity. It was one thing, in other words, for already debased peasants and displaced native peoples to be bound to the land, to be treated unequally before the law, and to suffer under the yoke of another's economic obligations. It was altogether another for an educated white gentleman, a man free in the world and beholden to none (despite his actual and very prolific indebtedness) to be deprived of liberty. After being taken prisoner by the Russian state and confined by military escorts, Ledyard lashed out in his Russia diary, perhaps with the gentleman Banks or Jefferson in mind. He began with a line from Shakespeare's *King Lear*: "Take physic, pomp." Take medicine, your majesty. For you yourself, Lear discovers, must suffer the bitter pill in order to cure the ills of your subjects. "Lose your liberty but once for an hour ye who never lost it that ye may feel what I feel," Ledyard wrote. "It gives me altho' born in the freest country in the world, ideas of its exquisite beauties and of its immortal nature that I had never before. Methinks every man who is called to preside officially over the Liberty of a free people should once—it will be enough—actually be deprived unjustly of his liberty that he might be avaricious of it more than any earthly possessions."[7]

Perhaps then, Ledyard's seeming indifference to slavery was simply the result of a gentleman's double standard. On the one hand, he believed, all human beings were fundamentally the same. On the other, he upheld an elitist sense that true freedom was best enjoyed by those freeborn elite white men who, like himself, were able to understand just what the absence of freedom was.

As the British were debating the morality of slavery and digesting the newly publicized horrors of the transatlantic slave trade, a group of twelve scientifically minded men, all friends of Sir Joseph Banks, was turning its attention to Africa. Sometime in the mid-1780s, these prominent Britons began meeting for dinner several times a year at St Alban's Tavern off Pall Mall. They initially referred to themselves as the Saturday's Club, and their dinner chat centered no doubt on questions similar to those that would have arisen at Jefferson's dinner table. Does commerce corrupt? Will the rule of law ever completely supplant the rule of force in dictating the relations between nations? Can there be empire without slavery? Would Britain find new arenas for empire where rebellion and slavery could be avoided? As they contemplated such questions, the group—eight of whom were members of Parliament and one of whom, Banks, as president of the Royal Society, was, with the exception of the king himself, the nation's greatest patron of science—concluded that the most important new frontier of geographic knowledge lay not in the Pacific but on Europe's southern flank.

The interior of Africa was almost entirely unknown to Europeans. Fear of disease and the failure of European military incursions had long stifled colonial activity much beyond the continent's coasts. Given the scope of European imperialism, it was truly remarkable that so little was known about Africa. Most of the great rivers and lakes of North and South America had been fully explored, and much of Siberia and China was mapped. But Africa's three great rivers, the Congo, the Nile, and the Niger, remained only partially charted. Indeed, as of the late 1780s, no European was known to have laid eyes on the Niger.

In Africa's exploration and ultimate exploitation, the liberal-minded members of the Saturday's Club could find a worthy object for their philosophical curiosity. Here were lands and peoples little known to the wider world and ripe for study and exploration. Of course, as we have seen,

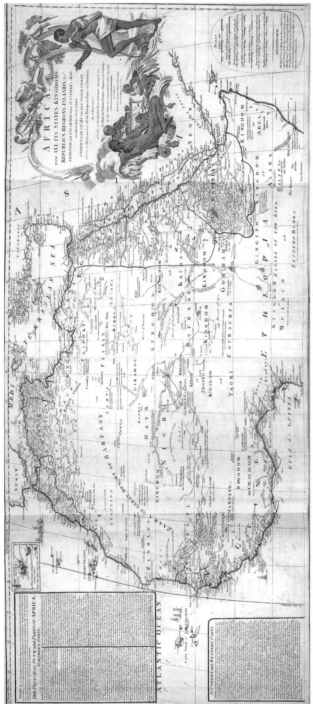

As this map from 1787 indicates, Ledyard's journey into Africa would be based on an absence of knowledge similar to that which existed about the North American West. The Niger River, which was Ledyard's object, existed in a conjectural fog (this cartographer had no sense of its southern branch or its mouth at the Gulf of Guinea) not all that different from that which enveloped Europeans' view of Africans themselves. Hence, the cannibalizing figures in the main cartouche echo so many archetypal European depictions of non-Europeans. Engraved by Thomas Kitchin for his *A General Atlas, Describing the Whole Universe.* London, 1794. Reproduced by permission of the Huntington Library, San Marino, California.

in the era of Captain Cook and Sir Joseph Banks, science and empire came together in a tangled web of personal ambition, enlightened virtue, and state interests. Such was the case with this early interest in Africa. Aside from satisfying an appetite for discovery, Africa offered solutions to the most vexing problems the British Empire faced. African raw materials for industrial Britain could compensate for the loss of natural resources from the American colonies; and African colonies would not be dependent for their labor supply on the cruel transoceanic shipment of enslaved human beings. According to the odd logic of the eighteenth-century imperial mind, the opening of Africa was a sensible course for a sensible nation. Here was a way to maintain the empire in a moral climate increasingly troubled by some of its sustaining institutions.[8]

On June 9, 1788, the members of the Saturday's Club thus resolved "to form themselves into an association for promoting the discovery of the inland parts of [Africa.]" The "African Association," as the group came to be called, would dedicate itself to generating useful knowledge about the little-known continent and to locating "persons who are to be sent on the discovery of the interior parts of Africa." This second undertaking would be the work of a subcommittee consisting of luminaries in British science and imperial politics. In addition to Banks and the Quaker MP and antislavery activist Henry Beaufoy, the group included Sir Francis Rawdon-Hastings, a veteran of the Battle of Bunker Hill, son of an Irish peer, and eventual governor-general of India; Richard Watson, the bishop of Llandaff, who for a time had occupied the first chair in chemistry at Cambridge; and finally, a Scottish lawyer named Andrew Stuart, who had served on the Board of Trade, which, among other things, helped shape the government's colonial policies.[9]

Through Banks, whom he had met while in London preparing for his failed journey across America, Ledyard became acquainted with this esteemed group, and shortly after returning to London in the spring of 1788 he offered them his services. In an account written after Ledyard's death, Beaufoy, the association's secretary, recalled his first encounter with the American traveler: "[Even before reading Banks's letter testifying to Ledyard's fitness for the expedition,] I was struck with the manliness of his person, the breadth of his chest, the openness of his countenance, and the inquietude of his eye." After all those years of working to perfect that gentlemanly art of manufactured persona, it would seem that Ledyard had succeeded spectacularly. He now appeared in every way the very embodiment of the gentleman traveler.

"I spread the map of Africa before him," Beaufoy continued, "and tracing a line from Cairo to Sennar, and from thence westward in the latitude and supposed direction of the Niger, I told him that was the route, by which I was anxious that Africa might, if possible, be explored. He said, he should think himself singularly fortunate to be entrusted with this adventure. I asked him when he would set out? 'Tomorrow morning,' was his answer."[10]

Ledyard's bold enthusiasm impressed Beaufoy and led him to the conclusion that this American was a distinct sort of gentleman—manly, powerful, physical, and rough hewn, yet refined and philosophical. Indeed, Beaufoy looked upon Ledyard much as the latter looked upon those Tongan chiefs or Syphax. He was a kind of noble savage, lacking a certain cultivation yet betraying a fundamental strength of character, a fundamental certainty in the righteousness of his acts that could be born only of some kind of natural, innate nobility. What in other men appeared cultivated, that is, was in Ledyard entirely natural. As Beaufoy explained,

> To those who have never seen Mr. Ledyard, it may not, perhaps, be uninterested to know, that his person, though scarcely exceeding the middle size, was remarkably expressive of activity and strength; and that his manners, though unpolished, were neither uncivil nor unpleasing. Little attentive to difference of rank, he seemed to consider all men as his equals, and as such he respected them. His genius though uncultivated and irregular, was original and comprehensive. Ardent in his wishes, yet calm in his deliberations; daring in his purposes, but guarded in his measures; impatient of control, yet capable of strong endurance; adventurous beyond the conception of ordinary men, yet wary and considerate and attentive to all precautions, he appeared to be formed by Nature for achievements of hardihood and peril.[11]

Beaufoy seems to have seen in Ledyard something of what Morris, Jones, Jefferson, and Banks had seen in him: a combination of bold derring-do and naïve idealism that made him the perfect agent for European designs on distant lands. Ledyard was sufficiently enlightened to communicate substantive information and engage whatever non-European peoples he might encounter; but he was also enough the rough-hewn semisavage to endure the physical hardships that awaited him. Between his weathered visage, his tattoos, and his quiet determination, that is, he seemed precisely the sort to journey into the unknown.

Ledyard had had the idea of exploring Africa well before his acquaintance with Banks and the African Association. Shortly after arriving at Yakutsk in September 1787, he had confided in his diary that once he traversed America he would turn his attention to Africa. The comment was an offhand one, and Ledyard did not elaborate, but judging from the rest of the diary it would appear that this interest in Africa grew out of his concern with the natural sources of human difference, particularly skin color.[12]

Ledyard's thinking on racial difference reflected the predominant Enlightenment view that environmental factors explained racial variations. Climate and topography had, over time, altered the appearance of some people, but this in no way altered the fact that all human beings had common ancestry. Summarizing his Russian findings on the matter for Jefferson, Ledyard proclaimed,

> Sr I am certain that all the people you call red people on the continent of America and on the continents of Europe and Asia as far south as the southern parts of China are all one people by whatever names distinguished and that the best general one would be *Tartar*.
>
> I suspect that *all* red people are of the same family, I am satisfied myself that the great general analogy in the customs of men can only be accounted for by supposing them all to compose one family: and by extending the idea and uniting customs, traditions and history I am satisfied that this common origin was such or nearly as related by Moses and commonly believed among the nations of the earth.

And most fundamentally, "Sr I am certain (the negroes excepted because I have not yet personally visited them) that the difference in the color of men is the effect of natural causes." A journey to Africa would, once and for all, confirm the environmental theory of race.[13]

Ledyard's interest was timely. The sudden surge of antislavery sentiment had elicited an equally sudden surge of new proslavery thought. One
strain of this thinking was the idea that people of African descent were
simply of a different species. And this species, judging from its generally
servile status in the world, was closer to animals on the chain of being.
Though not widely held at the time Ledyard wrote, the idea would be
trundled out again and again over the course of the next half century by
British and American defenders of human bondage. Ledyard's journey
could add overwhelming scientific evidence to disprove such theories.
By doing in Africa what he had done in Polynesia and the Russian Far
East—by identifying evidence of common human ancestry—Ledyard
could once and for all confirm his own theory of race and perhaps counter the advocates of so-called "poly-genesis."[14]

As he prepared to leave for Africa, Ledyard gathered his modest possessions to send to Isaac. Since most of these were clothes he had purchased
to survive the Siberian winter, they would not be needed in sub-Saharan
Africa. Perhaps Isaac would be able to use some of them, or perhaps
he and his friends would find ethnographic value in these curious Russian hats, coats, and boots. Ledyard also sent a coat he had had made in
London. It was obviously his most valued possession, the best evidence
of his trials, and a living token of remembrance for Isaac: "I traveled on
foot with it in Denmark, Sweden, Lapland, Finland and the Lord knows
where: in opulence and poverty, I have kept it, slept in it, eat in it, drank
in it, fought in it, negotiated in it; it has been through every scene my
constant and faithful servant from my departure to my return to London."
Isaac would perhaps "give it an asylum for I have none here." Ledyard's
only other possession of much value was his journal from Russia, and
this he left with Beaufoy.[15]

Before Ledyard's departure, the association commissioned a portrait
of him. The picture was painted by Carl Fredrik von Breda, a Swedish
painter who had come to London to study with Sir Joshua Reynolds, perhaps the greatest British portraitist of the age and certainly, through his
presidency of the Royal Academy of Arts, among the greatest patrons and
teachers of painting in late eighteenth-century Britain. Ledyard's portrait
hung in Somerset House (now the home of the Courtauld Institute of Art),
a recently completed government building that housed the Royal Academy

of Arts as well as the Royal Society and the Society of Antiquaries. There could be no better place for the portrait of a great traveler.

Ledyard briefly fantasized about employing the Connecticut-born Jonathan Trumbull to paint a family copy, but nothing came of this, and Von Breda took the original to Sweden, where it was subsequently lost.[16]

On June 30, 1788, Ledyard left London for Paris. From there he traveled to Marseilles, crossed the Mediterranean to Alexandria, and then sailed downriver to Cairo, where he arrived in mid-August. He carried with him funds from the African Association and the usual letters of introduction. Upon arriving in Cairo he planned to procure needed supplies and guides and then travel south to the city of Sennar (in what is now eastern Sudan) with one of the periodic trading caravans that made the trip. From Sennar he would travel west in search of the Niger. The whole scheme was foolhardy. Neither Ledyard nor the association had any idea what the traveler would find. While in Cairo, Ledyard had been told of a "Black King," who would receive him at the southernmost point in his journey, and he expected to proceed from this kingdom on his own. He also assumed that the headwaters of the Niger would be somewhere between twelve and twenty degrees of latitude but seemed totally unaware that much of Africa at this latitude is desert and arid plain.[17]

Ledyard spent between three and four months in Cairo, and as was his habit when stalled in distant lands he occupied himself with his pen and travel diary. Fragments of the diary from this time remain as a redacted version transcribed by Beaufoy and published in the proceedings of the African Association. They indicate that, in keeping with a practice he had begun in Russia, Ledyard traveled in local clothing, perhaps a turban and the loose-fitting pants and flowing robes common in North Africa, but beyond this they say very little about his personal experiences. They tell us little about how he occupied himself during those many days in Cairo; they say nothing about any ex-patriot friends or about how he filled his time in this teeming ancient city. Even more striking, they offer practically none of the kind of social and political commentary that fills the Russia journal. Aside from some remarks about the general Arab disdain for Christians, the only real echo of the earlier writings comes in an aside that Arabic has no word for "liberty," but it has words for slaves. The absence is striking, given the orientalist tendencies of Ledyard's writings on the

Russian Empire, particularly the insistence that the Orient was unified by its dependence on despotism.[18]

Most of what the association did reprint consisted of Ledyard's familiar ethnographic speculations. These claim that, like the Tahitians, the Arabs of North Africa tattooed themselves; that their tools were similar to those of South Pacific Islanders; that they spun cloth like the French peasantry; and that the women put their hair up in the Tartar manner. They also say that "it is a custom of the Arabs to spread a blanket when they would invite anyone to eat or rest with them. American Indians spread the beaver skins on such occasions." Here again we find Ledyard trolling the world for proof that all human beings had a common origin.[19]

The association also reprinted a section of the journal that describes Ledyard's interviews with slaves transported north from the lower reaches of the Nile. Bearing his mandate from the African Association, Ledyard asked these people, most of whom were women, about their homelands and learned that were he to travel there he would be treated respectfully, perhaps even royally. He was also impressed by the women's abundant beadwork. Perhaps he thought he could use similar beads as currency, much as he might have in American Indian country.

Ledyard says nothing about the effects of the slave trade on these Africans, nor does he reveal any particular sympathy for their condition. For Beaufoy and his readers, the omissions no doubt confirmed the view, widely held in liberal, antislavery circles, that domestic forms of slavery were less pernicious than forms dependent on large-scale export. Once the global trade in African slaves was abolished and slavery began to disappear in the colonized world, so they reasoned, forms present elsewhere would decline as well. But the fact that, according to Ledyard's account, some twenty thousand Africans were sold through the Cairo markets in a year had to give pause.[20]

A more familiar Ledyard appears in three letters he wrote to Jefferson from Egypt in the late summer and fall of 1788. These describe Alexandria as a scene "wretched and interesting beyond any other that I have seen." "Poverty, rapine, murder, tumult, blind bigotry, cruel persecution, pestilence," and "base and miserable architecture" left little evidence of the glorious past of this once charmed imperial capital. The much-vaunted Nile was "a mere mud puddle compared to the accounts we have of it," and Cairo "a wretched hole, and a nest of vagabonds." How sharply all

this departed from the popular image of the Near East—an image Ledyard so readily perpetuated in his condemnations of Russia's oriental-style
despotism. Here there was no luxury, no license, no craven eunuchs or
pashas among their harems.

"Sweet are the songs of Egypt on paper," he noted. "Who is not rav-
ished with gums, balms, dates, figgs, pomegranates, with the circassia [sic]
and sycamores without knowing" that in reality "ones eyes, ears, mouth,
nose is filled with dust, eternal hot fainting winds, lice, bugs, mosquitoes,
spiders, flies—pox, itch, leprosy, fevers, and almost universal blindness."[21]
It is hard to know what troubled Ledyard more: the unpleasantness of
Egypt in August or the naïvete of gentlemanly Europe. His third letter to
Jefferson (his last known letter), written the fifteenth of November 1788,
suggests the latter. For now, it is not so much Egypt that deserves reproach.
It is the learned West, and perhaps even the naïve Jefferson himself:

> I know your taste for ancient history I think: it does not com-
> port with what experience teaches me. There are besides yours
> many fine minds in the West in the same situation. . . . I
> should have wrote you the truth. And it is disagreeable to hear
> it when habit has accustomed one to hear falsehood. . . . Laugh
> at the eloquent loquacity of writers like Thucydides. The sub-
> lime poetry of Homer has nothing to do with historic *facts*. . . .
> I am certainly very angry with those who have written of other
> countries where I have traveled as well as of this, and of this
> particularly: they have all more or less deceived me: and they
> are the more blameable because I am (I suppose like others)
> inclinable by the common operations of the imagination to de-
> ceive myself in reading history, and therefore stand in double
> need of truth. In some cases it is perhaps difficult to determine
> which does the most mischief: the self love of the historian, or
> the curiosity of the reader: but both together have led us into
> errors that it is now too late to rectify.

Hindsight suggests foreboding in Ledyard's words. It was now, he explained to Jefferson, too late to correct the falsehoods propagated by historical literature, as if his own mission had somehow become hopeless.
Perhaps Ledyard had begun anticipating his end, and perhaps he was
blaming those self-proclaimed learned men, comfortably assured of their

bookish knowledge, and happy to send this American on a journey to nowhere.

Ledyard too was a man reared on the classics, a youthful admirer of Cato and the Numidian warrior Syphax, and a man who in his correspondence with his cousin Isaac used the pseudonym Josephus—the name of the Roman whose *Jewish War* describes the Roman suppression of the Jewish rebellion. Here he was, condemning the foundation of everything he knew to be true. The "elegant locquacity of writers like Thucidides," the geographies of Ptolemy and Leo Africanus, the "sublime poetry of Homer," the glimpses of Near Eastern manners, so popularly portrayed in contemporary works such as Montesquieu's *Persian Letters*—all were fiction."

Iconoclastic though these declarations were, they very much echoed the animating ethos of eighteenth-century science. Books amused, they educated the senses, they even offered moral lessons—but for understanding the affairs of humanity and the workings of nature they offered little more than ungrounded theory. The real target of the African Association was thus dogma. The notion was beautifully captured in a letter Banks wrote to Thomas Paine after the latter, a self-educated artisan, approached him about a design for a revolutionary new iron bridge. "I expect many improvements from your countrymen," he told the American Paine, because they "think with vigor, and are in a great measure free from those shackles of theory which are imposed on the minds of our people before they are capable of exerting their mental faculties to advantage." True innovation, in other words, would be the result not of careful study of stale knowledge, entombed in ancient texts, but rather of the workings of innate common sense applied to real experience in the real world.[23]

In July 1788, Ledyard had passed through Paris en route to Cairo. While there, he had visited his friend Jefferson, whom he had not seen in two years. Although the American minister criticized Ledyard "for being employed by an English Association," he was supportive of his countryman's latest endeavor and provided him with a letter of introduction to Stephen Cathalan, Jr., a merchant and local official at the Port of Marseilles. Ledyard would be sailing from there to Africa, and Jefferson believed Cathalan would be able to assist Ledyard should French authorities delay his departure. With this introduction in hand, Ledyard had continued on his journey to Marseilles. Once there, he showed what was becoming his trademark petulance when it became clear that his papers were not in order for a passage to North Africa. Cathalan intervened on Ledyard's behalf, but the American later complained to Jefferson that the delay was Cathalan's fault. When Cathalan heard of this, he explained to Jefferson, "I have done everything in my power for [Ledyard], and left all my business a full day to serve him."

The incident was a great embarrassment to Jefferson since Cathalan had been helping the Americans negotiate crucial Mediterranean trade contracts. But instead of dismissing Ledyard as a deranged fool, the American minister simply explained to Cathalan that the traveler was "a different kind of person," one whose abrasive conduct was owing only to "the enthusiasm of his temper, and his eagerness to pursue his enterprise."[24]

It was the following January before Jefferson heard from Ledyard again, and the letters he received had been sent months earlier. Exactly where Ledyard was in early 1789 Jefferson did not know. But he assumed that his countryman had plunged, with his usual enthusiasm, "into the terrae incognitae of Africa."

By late May 1789, news of Ledyard's death had begun to reach Jefferson in Paris. It was news Jefferson had anticipated but did not want to believe. Ledyard's final letter, written the previous November and also received by Jefferson months after it was written, seemed to contradict these reports. It indicated that Ledyard was several days from departure, suggesting that by the time of his alleged death in Cairo in January of the following year he would have been elsewhere.

Unfortunately, Tom Paine, Jefferson's contact at the Royal Society, knew differently. A month after the African Association began receiving word of Ledyard's demise, Paine, who had been in England to promote his iron bridge design, wrote Jefferson and confirmed the unfortunate Ledyard's fate. The news came directly from Banks. "We have lost poor Ledyard," the great scientist had written Paine; "he had agreed with certain Moors to conduct him to Sennar. The time for their departure was arrived when he found himself ill and took a large dose of emetic tartar, burst a blood vessel on the operation which carried him off in three days."[25]

On further inquiry, Paine discovered that what killed Ledyard was not negligence or accident. What killed him was not, as Ledyard might have expected, the misfortuncs incvitably visited upon a man who had dedicated his life to the fight against ignorance and parochialism. What killed him was the very spirit that drove him in the first place. Beaufoy and Banks told Paine that Ledyard's departure had been delayed, and this threw him "into a violent rage . . . which deranged something in his system."[26]

Epilogue

IT DID NOT TAKE LONG for news of Ledyard's death to reach the United States. By the middle of July 1789, the *Pennsylvania Packet* carried an obituary describing John as "strong and active, bold as a lion, and gentle as he was bold." His loss and the collapse of his projects to explore "either America or Africa," the author continued, "must be felt as a very general and public loss." In the same month, the Hartford pedagogue and lexicographer Noah Webster made laconic note of the event in his diary: "hear of the death of Mr John Ledyard." There is no indication that Webster ever met Ledyard or that the two ever corresponded; nor does Webster express any regret over Ledyard's passing. A famous countryman had died, and a scrupulous diary keeper had recorded for posterity the day he learned of this.[1]

In the three years after Ledyard's death, newspaper readers around the United States learned more of his remarkable exploits from Henry Beaufoy, whose lengthy obituary for a London newspaper was widely reprinted. The *Georgia Gazette*, the *Universal Asylum and Columbian Magazine*, the *Federal Gazette and Philadelphia Evening Post*, and the *Massachusetts Spy* were among those that carried Beaufoy's admiring portrait. From this British politician and antislavery activist, Americans learned of their countryman's "enterprising genius" and of his unusual capacity to overcome "accumulated misfortunes." "In the midst of poverty, covered with rags,

... worn with continual hard-ship, exhausted by disease, without friends, without credit, unknown and full of misery," Ledyard had emerged from his journey across Russia with new resolve. And he had set off once again, demonstrating to his employers that "he was a traveler of observation and reflection, endowed with a mind for discovery, and formed for achievements of hardihood and peril." Another obituary, originally appearing in Ledyard's hometown paper, the *Connecticut Courant,* spoke of his willingness to "scorn the allurements of ease and social life" and to carry himself to "barren wastes and the unknown retreats of uncultivated man, for the sake of shedding that new light upon science, for which, considering the immense difficulties and dangers he could not otherwise than expect to undergo, he could scarcely ever hope for an adequate return." The press was good to this penniless traveler.[2]

For Ledyard's family, the attention must have been bittersweet. Ledyard had attained the fame he sought, but it was mostly posthumous fame and it did little for the Ledyards' fortunes. The family also faced the painful question of how the most distinguished Ledyard since Colonel William would be memorialized. There was no body to bury and, besides his letters, Ledyard left the family little more than the clothes he had sent to Isaac. Perhaps some solace could be gained from the publication of his writings. A compilation of his letters and journals would be a fitting tribute to his labors and would leave the family with the comforting knowledge that the reading public would profit from the geographic discoveries of their remarkable relative.

To this end, Isaac wrote Beaufoy and Banks, pleading for the return of Ledyard's journals and any other property he may have had at the time of his death. His personal effects, he assured Banks, "though ever so inconsiderable" in themselves, "would be highly valued for his sake by his mother and sisters." The request could not have been more proper and just. But Banks's response was harsh. Ledyard's debts, it turned out, followed him to the grave. The Siberia journal, Banks informed Isaac, "was left in the hands of Mr. Beaufoy, a deposit as I understood to be returned to [Ledyard] in the event of his return to England and in case of his death to be retained by Mr. Beaufoy as testimony of gratitude" to the African Association for employing him. As for any papers from the Africa journey, they too were now "the property of [Ledyard's] employers." And any other possessions Ledyard might once have had were lost. Much like everything

Ledyard wrote, these final writings had effectively become someone else's property. Whether the Admiralty, the printer Nathaniel Patten, or the African Association—all came to control what issued from Ledyard's pen. For the family to secure the traveler's legacy through the written record of his journeys was thus no simple matter.[3]

Isaac nonetheless showed a doggedness similar to that of his cousin as he pursued publication of Ledyard's writings. By 1797, he had obtained a copy of the Siberia journal and had gained access to Ledyard's Africa writings, some of which the African Association had published in their *Proceedings* in 1790. Isaac also retained the editorial services of Philip Freneau, a prominent New York newspaper editor and poet and a relative of Isaac's by marriage. In this man of letters, John Ledyard had an editor worthy of Cook's Hawkesworth or Douglas. He also, it would appear, had an editor who was drawn to wanderers of Ledyard's type. A month after the British defeat at Yorktown, Freneau had published a brief story entitled "The Philosopher of the Forest." The main character was an orphaned child of the Swiss forests who had squandered his inheritance and stumbled through a lifetime of misfortune and misery. After aimlessly traveling the world in the company of a Neapolitan nobleman, the young man determined to take up the profession of traveler. He would become, like the wandering Jew who recommended this new vocation, a rootless, homeless being. Like a noble wandering savage, like Syphax himself, the wanderer discovered that freedom from obligation to family and nation afforded him great moral clarity. "I concluded by the advice of a trading Jew," announced Freneau's traveler, "to embrace the profession of traveling *pilgrim,* or religious and philosophical wanderer."[4]

Perhaps in John Ledyard Freneau had found his real Philosopher of the Forest. Here was a man who truly had made his way in the world as a kind of philosophical wanderer. Here was a man who appeared to have lived outside the confining institutions of family and nation, all for some higher philosophical purpose. Perhaps, too, Freneau was drawn to Ledyard as a refuge from his usual journalistic pursuits. As one of the nation's foremost partisan journalists and newspaper editors, he had spilled much ink during the 1790s attacking Alexander Hamilton and the other Federalist enemies of his Jeffersonian political allies.[5]

The editing advanced far enough for Freneau to publish announcements inviting subscriptions for the work. But by the late 1790s, Freneau had abandoned the project. With the Federalist John Adams in the presidency, there was no time for a diverting, nonpartisan literary enterprise.[6]

Sometime during the next few years, Major Samuel S. Forman, a brother of Isaac's sister-in-law, copied most of Ledyard's letters and other writings. The copy is interspersed with some narrative, suggesting that Forman had intended to take up where Freneau left off—publishing the materials as an edited and annotated collection of Ledyard's life and writings. But Forman never published his manuscript, depriving the public and the family of the published memorial John Ledyard deserved.[7]

It would be another three decades before the reading public gained access to Ledyard's full story. In 1828, the Unitarian pastor and eventual president of Harvard College Jared Sparks published the first complete life of Ledyard. Sparks assembled his story from the traveler's own writings and from extensive interviews with surviving acquaintances of Ledyard's. The resulting book, entitled *The Life of John Ledyard, the American Traveler,* offered readers a full portrait of Ledyard interspersed with lengthy selections from his journals and letters. As a memorial, it must have been pleasing to family members. For Sparks's was a deeply admiring though by no means idealized portrait. As the biographer of an adventurer and traveler, Sparks was exceptionally well equipped. He brought to his work a fascination with the sources of individual virtue and good character and an almost obsessive commitment to the documentary record. His substantial historical and biographical oeuvre (nearly all of which appeared in the two decades after the Ledyard book) reflects those predilections. He devoted two decades to assembling, editing, and publishing multivolume editions of the writings of George Washington and Benjamin Franklin. With a mandate from Congress and President John Quincy Adams, he also edited and published twelve volumes of diplomatic correspondence produced during the American Revolution. The cumbersome title of the volumes reads like a who's who of early American statesmen: *The Diplomatic Correspondence of the American Revolution. Being the Letters of Benjamin Franklin, Silas Deane, John Adams, John Jay, Arthur Lee, William Lee, Ralph Izard, Francis Dana, William Carmichael, Henry Laurens, John Laurens, M. Dumas, and others, concerning the Foreign Relations of the United States during the whole Revolution: together with Letters in Reply from the Secret Committee of Congress, and the Secretary of Foreign Affairs; also, the entire Correspondence of the French Ministers, Gerard and Luzerne, with Congress.* Sparks also wrote other biographies, many of which he assembled in a collection intended for young Americans entitled *The Library of American Biography*. Their subjects included the revolutionaries Ethan Allen and George Washington as well as explorers and missionaries such as René-Robert Cavelier Sieur de La Salle and Father Jacques Marquette. These portraits are testimonies to the great character of great men; they are meant to teach their readers that greatness comes not from the small-minded pursuit of profit or political power, but rather from a refusal to yield to such temptations and an insistent determination to pursue noble achievements, whether they be the forging of a nation or the exploration of unknown lands.

To this end, Sparks's biography of Ledyard gave readers a protagonist admirable for his fortitude and for an abiding refusal to be cowed by failure. Acknowledging that Ledyard ultimately accomplished little, Sparks concluded in the final paragraph of his book, "The acts of [Ledyard's] life demand notice less on account of their results, than of the spirit with which they were performed. . . . Such instances of decision, energy, perseverance, fortitude, and enterprise, have rarely been witnessed in the same individual; and, in the exercise of these high attributes of mind, [John Ledyard's] example cannot be too much admired or imitated."[8] Writing as he was amidst the explosion of market-driven individualism that enveloped Jacksonian America, Sparks no doubt saw in Ledyard a worthy role model for his increasingly materialistic, acquisitive countrymen.

Reviewers generally applauded Sparks's assessment. One of them urged his countrymen to better acquaint themselves with John Ledyard, for he was the progenitor of a very unique breed of men, a breed of men who selflessly served their nation and its imperial ambitions. "American history, condition, and habits," the reviewer wrote, "all argue a greater number of men qualified for penetrating into unknown regions, and enlarging the field of geographical knowledge, than have ever existed in any other empire." These included the likes of Lewis and Clark, Lieutenant Zebulon Pike, who was captured by the Spanish while exploring the southern Rockies in 1807, and Major Stephen H. Long, a Dartmouth graduate who led an expedition up the Missouri in 1819. But there were many others, less well known but equally courageous, "who now traverse the Rocky Mountains, and ply a lucrative commerce with the internal Mexican provinces; the solitary hunters who cross the path of the British traders and trappers in the north-west, and who, like the Indians, would surely and fearlessly pass alone, from the remotest northern lake to the extreme south-western limits, by the most rugged and unfrequented routes; the officers of the corps of engineers employed in surveys that give them character of adventurous explorers, rendering manifold service—all these might be cited as of a numerous order scarcely known in the more populous kingdoms of Europe." Here was a nation whose empire was not built by armies and navies. Instead, it was built by singular individuals who selflessly faced hardship and peril for the sake of commerce and knowledge. The American way of empire, the reviewer seemed to be saying, was somehow more noble and benign than the European. It was the work of heroic individuals such as John Ledyard, "the most curious, signal, and interesting example of that order or species," the American empire builder.[9]

Ledyard remained well known for decades after the publication of Sparks's book. In 1831, the Connecticut River Steamboat Company launched the *John Ledyard,* one of the first two steamboats to sail the Connecticut River. Historians of the American West, most notably Hubert Howe Bancroft, included Ledyard's exploits in their accounts of the nation's westward expansion, and throughout the century Ledyard appeared as a subject of short biographies and magazine portraits written for American boys. He remained particularly well known in his home state, where the Ledyards were sufficiently prominent to have a town named for them. After seceding from Groton, Ledyard, Connecticut, named for John's uncle William, was incorporated in 1836.[10]

In 1851, an essay celebrating John Ledyard appeared in the *Yale Literary Magazine.* It pointed to all of the traveler's familiar virtues: his perseverance, his zeal, his disdain for failure and misfortune. But the writer wrote as if these virtues were not somehow universally recognized, as if there had been some debate among Yale undergraduates about the true merits of John Ledyard. It would, in fact, appear that these nineteenth-century aristocratic sons had doubted the character of a man who, after all, had not fought for his nation's independence. "True," the author writes, Ledyard did not fight for his country, but that was because "his genius was of a more pacific turn. He chose to grapple with nature, and disclose her hidden resources to the world" instead of contending "with his fellow men on the field of sanguinary strife."

Much like Jared Sparks before him, this young writer urged his readers to recognize forms of patriotism and extraordinary character that may not appear in public life, but that are equally vital for countering "that selfish spirit, so prevalent in the world." Ledyard, unfortunately, was of that class of men "whose disregard for self the world has construed into shiftlessness. In fact, this was a gross mischaracterization, all too typical of the judgments of Americans whose "Yankee shrewdness and prover-bial tact for estimating profit and loss" had come at the cost of an ap-preciation for "true worth and merit wherever it is found." As other Yale undergraduates wrote on the final page of a copy of Sparks's *Life of John Ledyard* donated to the College Library by the class of 1830, "A noble man! Such men should be honored and remembered." "America has need to be proud of such men."[11]

Ledyard's fame diminished through the course of the nineteenth cen-tury. In part this simply reflected the age of the nation. By 1850, the country had plenty of exemplars of selfless industry and good character. All the famous explorers of the West; the Lewises and Clarks and the Pikes—but there were others. There was the New Yorker John Lloyd Stephens, whose travels through the Yucatan and Central America in the early 1840s uncov-ered for Americans a hitherto unknown Mayan civilization; and there were members of the great U.S. Exploring Expedition of 1838–42 that surveyed the Pacific. But perhaps the most important reason for Ledyard's declining popularity was simply the nature of fame in nineteenth-century America, particularly in the latter decades of the century. A man who ultimately accomplished little and who died penniless simply did not capture the imagination of a nation whose dominant figures were as outsized in their accomplishments as Andrew Carnegie and Theodore Roosevelt.

Ledyard lived on, though, mostly at Dartmouth College, where under-graduates appropriated him as symbol of their hardy manliness. In 1920, students created the Ledyard Canoe Club, and their first outing retraced Ledyard's trip down the Connecticut River. The club's building still stands on the banks of the Connecticut River, somewhere near the place where Ledyard made his dugout canoe. Next to the building, adjoining the spot where Ledyard is thought to have felled the tree for the canoe, there is a small stone monument. It was erected in 1909 and affixed to it is a plaque commemorating the college's first great adventurer and the man who "foresaw and foretold the riches of the Pacific Coast and advantages of commerce with the far east."[12]

Ledyard, the composers of this tribute recognized, was not simply an adventurer and traveler. He was also a colonizer and an empire builder. He wanted to find personal riches in the farthest known reaches of his world. That he did not says less about him or his character than it does about the ways in which his world worked. In the end, the project of creating empire was not the work of single-minded, heroic men. It was the product of that complex interplay of sociability, patronage, influence, and politics that constantly intruded on Ledyard's various projects. And for all his perseverance and literary ambition, Ledyard was ultimately unable to master these forces. When calculation and political acumen were called for, Ledyard failed miserably. But it was precisely this inability to reduce ambition to bare calculation that made Ledyard so appealing to his many admirers.

NOTES

ABBREVIATIONS

Add. MS	Additional Manuscripts, British Library, London, England
ADM	Admiralty Records, National Archives, Kew, England
BPL	Boston Public Library, Rare Books and Manuscripts Department
CC	*Connecticut Courant*
CHS	Connecticut Historical Society, Hartford, Connecticut
CSL	Connecticut State Library, Hartford, Connecticut
DCL	Rauner Special Collections Library, Dartmouth College Library
JCJC	*The Journals of Captain James Cook*, J. C. Beaglehole, ed. (Cambridge, England, 1961–67)
JLP	John Ledyard Papers, Photostat copy of Original Forman Transcript, Rauner Special Collections Library, Dartmouth College Library
MHS	Massachusetts Historical Society
MS Sparks	Jared Sparks, Miscellaneous Papers, Relating to John Ledyard, the American Traveler, Houghton Library, Harvard University
NMM	National Maritime Museum, London, England
N-YHS	New-York Historical Society
PBF	*The Papers of Benjamin Franklin*, ed. Leonard W. Labaree et al. (New Haven, 1959–)
PEW	Microfilm Edition of the Papers of Eleazar Wheelock, Together with the Early Archives of Dartmouth College and Moor's Indian Charity School (Hanover, 1971)
PTJ	*The Papers of Thomas Jefferson*, ed. Julian P. Boyd et al. (Princeton, 1950–)

SFL   Witaker Historical Collection, Southold Free Library, Southold,
             New York
WMQ   *William and Mary Quarterly*, 3d ser.

INTRODUCTION

1. Thomas Jefferson to the Reverend James Madison, July 19, 1788, *PTJ* 13:382.
2. On the founding generation's quest for fame, Douglass Adair, "Fame and the Founding Fathers," which appears as the first chapter in *Fame and the Founding Fathers: Essays by Douglass Adair,* ed. Trevor Colbourn (New York, 1974), 3–26, and, more recently, Joseph J. Ellis, *Founding Brothers: The Revolutionary Generation* (New York, 2000).
3. Robin Hallett, ed., *Records of the African Association, 1788–1831* (London, 1964), 61–62.
4. Scholarly work on the eighteenth-century cult of gentility and refinement has expanded exponentially over the past two decades. Some of the works on eighteenth-century America I have relied on are Richard L. Bushman, *The Refinement of America: Persons, Houses, Cities* (New York, 1992); David S. Shields, *Civil Tongues and Polite Letters in British America* (Chapel Hill, 1997); and Gordon S. Wood, *The Radicalism of the American Revolution* (New York, 1992). On the centrality of writing and print more particularly, see, for example, Michael Warner, *The Letters of the Republic: Publication and the Public Sphere in Eighteenth-Century America* (Cambridge, 1990), and Stuart Sherman, *Telling Time: Clocks, Diaries, and the English Diurnal Form, 1660–1785* (Chicago, 1996). On clothing, Linda Baumgarten, *What Clothes Reveal: The Language of Clothing in Colonial and Federal America* (Williamsburg, 2002). More generally on the languages of early modern elite male culture, also see Jay Fliegelman, *Declaring Independence: Jefferson, Natural Language, and the Culture of Performance* (Stanford, 1993); Joanne B. Freeman, *Affairs of Honor: National Politics in the New Republic* (New Haven, 2001); Andrew Trees, *The Founding Fathers and the Politics of Character* (Princeton, 2004), and Stephen Shapin, *A Social History of Truth: Civility and Science in Seventeenth-Century England* (Chicago, 1994).
5. On the broader culture of empire, see, for example, David Cannadine, *Ornamentalism: How the British Saw Their Empire* (New York, 2001); Linda Colley, *Britons: Forging a Nation 1707–1837* (New Haven, 1992); Eliga H. Gould, *The Persistence of Empire: British Political Culture in the Age of the American Revolution* (Chapel Hill, 2000); Eric Hinderaker, "The 'Four Indian Kings' and the Imaginative Construction of Empire," *WMQ* 53:3 (1996), 487–526; Kathleen Wilson, *The Sense of the People: Politics, Culture, and Imperialism in England 1715–1785* (Cambridge, 1995); David Armitage, *The Ideological Origins of the British Empire* (Cambridge, England, 2000); Peter Onuf, *Jefferson's Empire: The Language of American Nationhood* (Charlottesville, 2000), esp. chap. 2; David Shields, *Oracles of Empire: Poetry, Politics, and Commerce in British America, 1690–1750* (Chicago, 1990); Janet Sorensen, *The Grammar*

of Empire in Eighteenth-Century British Writing (Cambridge, England, 2000); and Todd Porterfield, *The Allure of Empire: Art in the Service of French Imperialism, 1798–1863* (Princeton, 1998). More particularly on empire and travel, Mary Louise Pratt, *Imperial Eyes: Travel Writing and Transculturation* (London, 1992), and Steve Clark, ed. *Travel Writing and Empire: Postcolonial Theory in Transit* (London, 1999). Also see the related discussions in Harry Liebersohn, *Aristocratic Encounters: European Travelers and North American Indians* (Cambridge, England, 1998); Barbara Maria Stafford, *Voyage Into Substance: Art, Science, and the Illustrated Travel Account, 1760–1840* (Cambridge, 1984); Dorinda Outram, "On Being Perseus: New Knowledge, Dislocation, and Enlightenment Exploration," in *Geography and Enlightenment,* ed. David N. Livingstone and Charles W. J. Withers, 281–94 (Chicago, 1999); Michael T. Bravo, "Precision and Curiosity in Scientific Travel: James Rennell and the Orientalist Geography of the New Imperial Age (1760–1830)," in *Voyages and Visions: Towards a Cultural History of Travel,* ed. Jas Elsner and Joan-Pau Rubiés, 162–83 (London, 1999); and Chloe Chard, "Crossing Boundaries and Exceeding Limits: Destabilization, Tourism, and the Sublime," in *Transports: Travel, Pleasure, and Imaginative Geography, 1600–1830,* ed. Chloe Chard and Helen Langdon, 117–49 (New Haven, 1996).

6. The best and most recent of these is James Zug, *American Traveler: The Life and Adventures of John Ledyard, the Man who Dreamed of Walking the World* (New York, 2005). Zug's book appeared after I completed the first draft of my own and while we agree on the broad outline of Ledyard's story, my own emphasis differs substantially from Zug's. If for him Ledyard is of interest for what makes him distinct, for me he is of interest for what makes him emblematic. The two other modern biographies are Kenneth Munford, *John Ledyard: An American Marco Polo* (Portland, 1939), and Helen Augur, *Passage to Glory: John Ledyard's America—The Life and Travels of the First Man to Envision America's Destiny in the Pacific* (Garden City, N.Y., 1946). The latter two works rely extensively on Sparks, but invented dialogue and undocumented facts make them significantly less reliable.

CHAPTER 1. A COLONIAL CHILDHOOD

1. On cousinage in Virginia, Allan Kulikoff, *Tobacco and Slaves: The Development of Southern Culture in the Chesapeake, 1680–1800* (Chapel Hill, 1986), 252–55; on New England, John J. Waters suggests the marriage of cousins was not uncommon, although he doesn't distinguish between first and second cousins: "Family, Inheritance, and Migration in Colonial New England: The Evidence from Guilford, Connecticut," *WMQ* 39:1 (January 1982), 66.

2. *The Diary of Samuel Sewall, 1674–1729* (New York, 1973), 1:349.

3. *Collections of the New London Historical Society,* vol. 1: *Diary of Joshua Hempstead of New London, Connecticut* (1901; reprint, New London, 1985), 548.

4. Charles M. Andrews, *The Colonial Period of American History: The Settlements, Volume 2* (New Haven, 1936), 163.

5. Captain John's house is listed in John Ledyard Probate Inventory, September 11, 1771, folio 9350, Hartford Probate District, Estate Papers, CSL.
6. Albert Edward Van Dusen, "The Trade of Revolutionary Connecticut" (Ph.D. diss., University of Pennsylvania, 1948), esp. chap. 10. Also, on the liquor trade, John J. McCusker and Russell R. Menard, *The Economy of British America, 1607–1789* (Chapel Hill, 1985), chap. 13.
7. *Diary of Joshua Hempstead*, 617.
8. *Boston Newsletter* (December 8, 1757), 1.
9. John Ledyard Probate Inventory, August 9, 1762, folio 3087, New London Probate District, Estate Papers, CSL. Toby L. Ditz, *Property and Kinship: Inheritance in Early Connecticut, 1750–1820* (Princeton, 1986), 125–27.
10. *CC*, September 22, 1766, 3; ibid., September 29, 1766, 2.
11. Ibid., December 3, 1764, 4, and ibid., December 15, 1766, 2.
12. *Public Records of the Colony of Connecticut*, ed. J. H. Trumbull (Hartford, 1873), 12:318–20.
13. Bruce Daniels, "Money-Value Definitions of Economic Classes in Colonial Connecticut, 1700–1776," *Histoires Sociale/Social History* 7:14 (1974), 346–52.
14. John Ledyard Account Book, 26, CHS; Franklin, *Autobiography*, ed. Leonard W. Labaree et al. (1964; 2d ed., New Haven, 2003), 168–69.
15. Edmund Morgan, *The Gentle Puritan: A Life of Ezra Stiles, 1727–1795* (1962; reprint, New York, 1984), 47–48, 386–87, 394–95, 398–400.
16. *The Character and Qualifications of Good Rulers, and the Happiness of their Administration* (London, 1745), 17, 40.
17. Ibid., 37–38.
18. *CC*, December 3, 1764, 1; Squire John quoted in Oscar Zeichner, *Connecticut's Years of Controversy 1750–1776* (Chapel Hill, 1949), 47; on Squire John's illness, John Ledyard to Jonathan Trumbull, November 6, 1764, CHS.
19. *CC*, May 26, 1766, 4.
20. Second Ecclesiastical Society Records, 1767–1920, vol. 1, Church Records, CSL; Edwin Pond Parker, *History of the Second Church in Hartford* (Hartford, 1892), 129–32, 140.
21. *CC*, Apr. 2, 1798, 1, quoted in Christopher Grasso, *A Speaking Aristocracy: Transforming Public Discourse in Eighteenth-Century Connecticut* (Chapel Hill, 1999), 439. On the law practice in eighteenth-century Connecticut, Charles Warren, *A History of the American Bar* (Boston, 1911), 128–34, 322–23; Grasso, *A Speaking Aristocracy*, chap. 3, esp. 162–68; Cornelia Hughes Dayton, *Women Before the Bar: Gender, Law, and Society in Connecticut, 1639–1789* (Chapel Hill, 1995), 46–53; Bruce H. Mann, *Neighbors and Strangers: Law and Community in Early Connecticut* (Chapel Hill, 1987), 93–100; and more generally, John Murrin, "The Legal Transformation: The Bench and Bar of Eighteenth-Century Massachusetts," in *Colonial America: Essays in Politics and Social Development*, 3d ed., ed. Stanley N. Katz and John M. Murrin, 540–72 (New York, 1983); and Daniel J. Boorstin, *The Americans: The Colonial Experience* (New York, 1958), 195–202. On legal studies, Warren, *History of the American*

Bar, chap. 8, and L. Kinvin Wroth and Hiller B. Zobel, eds., *The Legal Papers of John Adams* (Cambridge, Mass., 1965), 1:lii–lvii, 1–25. I am indebted to Sally Hadden for this reference.

22. *CC*, September 3, 1771, 3; Whitman, *A Sermon, Preached at Hartford on the Day of the Interment of John Ledyard, Esq: . . .* (Hartford, 1771), 6; *CC*, September 3, 1771, 3.

23. For Ledyard's inheritance, John Ledyard Will, September 11, 1771, folio 9350, Hartford Probate District, Estate Papers, CSL.

24. *CC*, September 17, 1771, 3.

25. James Axtell, "Dr. Wheelock's Little Red School," in *Natives and Newcomers: The Cultural Origins of North America* (New York, 2001), 174–88.

26. Leon Burr Richardson, *History of Dartmouth College* (Hanover, 1932), chap. 2.

27. JL to Aunt Elizabeth, March 13, 1772, N-YHS.

CHAPTER II. ON STAGE AT DARTMOUTH COLLEGE

1. Jared Sparks, *The Life of John Ledyard, the American Traveller* (1828; reprint, with introduction by James Zug, Mystic, Conn., 2005), 8; on John's arrival, James Wheelock to Richard Bartlett, November, 12, 1821, in MS Sparks, 2.

2. On John's dress, George Ticknor to Jared Sparks, August 7, 1824, MS Sparks, 69, and James Wheelock to Jared Sparks, January 29, 1822, MS Sparks, 22–23.

3. Fredric M. Litto, "Addison's *Cato* in the Colonies," *WMQ* 23:3 (July 1966), 431–49. For the Ames references, see ibid., 442–43. Also, Kenneth Silverman, *A Cultural History of the American Revolution: Painting, Music, Literature, and the Theatre in the Colonies and the United States from the Treaty of Paris to the Inauguration of George Washington, 1763–1789* (New York, 1987), 82–83.

4. James Wheelock to Sparks, January 29, 1822, MS Sparks, 22–23. On Washington and *Cato*, Garry Wills, *Cincinnatus: George Washington and the Enlightenment: Images of Power in Early America* (New York, 1984), 133–38.

5. Adams to William Tudor, August 4, 1776, Robert J. Taylor, ed., *The Papers of John Adams* (Cambridge, Mass., 1961), 2:126–27, quoted in Carl J. Richard, *The Founders and the Classics: Greece, Rome, and the American Enlightenment* (Cambridge, Mass., 1994), 61.

6. Axtell, *The School Upon a Hill: Education and Society in Colonial New England* (New Haven, 1974), 212, 226–27.

7. *A Continuation of the Narrative of the Indian Charity-School . . .* (Hartford, 1771), 23.

8. James Dow McCallum, ed. *The Letters of Eleazar Wheelock's Indians* (Hanover, 1932), 65; James Axtell, "Dr. Wheelock's Little Red School," reprinted in Axtell, *Natives and Newcomers: The Cultural Origins of North America* (New York, 2001), esp. 174–79.

9. Harold Blodgett, *Samson Occom* (Hanover, 1935), chap. 3. Commissioners for the Scottish Missionary Society, quoted in James Axtell, *The Invasion*

Within: The Contest of Cultures in Colonial North America (New York, 1985), 271.

10. Daniel J. Boorstin, *The Americans: The Colonial Experience* (New York, 1958), 182; Edmund Morgan, *The Gentle Puritan: A Life of Ezra Stiles, 1727–1795* (1962; reprint New York, 1984), 327. Also more generally on college education, Axtell, *The School Upon a Hill,* chap. 6.

11. Wheelock letter to the English Trustees, July 29, 1770, excerpted in James Dow McCallum, *Eleazar Wheelock: Founder of Dartmouth College* (Hanover, 1939), 177.

12. Edward C. Lathem, ed., *Jeremy Belknap's Journey to Dartmouth in 1774* (Hanover, 1950), 13, 15. The final two quotes on the dangers of luxury and excess are from the *Virginia Gazette,* June 1, 1769, reprinted in Jack P. Greene, *Colonies to Nation 1763–1789: A Documentary History of the American Revolution* (New York, 1975), 157.

13. Daybook, Moor's Indian Charity School and Dartmouth College, 1772–73, PEW. On Wheelock's slaves, Leon Burr Richardson, *History of Dartmouth College* (Hanover, 1932), 19.

14. Bernard Bailyn, *Voyagers to the West: Emigration from Britain to America on the Eve of the Revolution* (New York, 1986), 10; Colin G. Calloway, *The Western Abenakis of Vermont, 1600–1800: War, Migration, and the Survival of an Indian People* (Norman, Okla., 1990), chap. 10.

15. For example, sketch by Thomas Seymour of Ledyard's early life in MS Sparks, 44–45; [Mary Hempstead] to Jared Sparks, January 2, 1822, MS Sparks, 20–21.

16. *Collections of the Massachusetts Historical Society* (Boston, 1809), 10:117–18; Timothy Dwight, *Travels in New England and New York,* ed. Barbara Miller Solomon (Cambridge, Mass., 1969), 1:173; Bruce C. Daniels, *The Connecticut Town: Growth and Development, 1635–1790* (Middletown, Conn., 1979), 191. Daniel R. Mandell, "Shifting Boundaries of Race and Ethnicity: Indian-Black Intermarriage in Southern New England, 1760–1880," *Journal of American History* 85:2 (September 1998), 466–501; Donna Keith Baron, J. Edward Hood, and Holly V. Izard, "They Were Here All Along: The Native American Presence in Lower-Central New England in the Eighteenth and Nineteenth Centuries," *WMQ* 53:3 (July 1996), 561–86.

17. Dwight, *Travels in New England and New York,* 1:79.

18. *William Bartram: Travels and Other Writings,* ed. Thomas P. Slaughter (New York, 1996), 24–25.

19. James Merrell, *Into the American Woods: Negotiators on the Pennsylvania Frontier* (New York, 1999), esp. 54–56; Edward G. Gray, *New World Babel: Languages and Nations in Early America* (Princeton, 1999), chap. 2.

20. Merrell, *Into the American Woods,* 61–62.

21. James Wheelock to Jared Sparks, January 29, 1822, MS Sparks, 22–23; Eleazar Wheelock to Thomas Seymour, January 7, 1773, PEW.

22. Eleazar Wheelock to Thomas Seymour, April 26, 1773, PEW.

23. Francis Quarles to Eleazar Wheelock, September 30, 1774, PEW.

24. William Seymour to Jared Sparks, September 16 [no year], MS Sparks, 113–14. Also see ibid., 2–3, 21, 45, 181.

25. Eleazar Wheelock, "Some Minutes of Occurrences . . . ," October 13, 1773, Vault, PEW. Stephen Ambrose, *Undaunted Courage: Meriwether Lewis, Thomas Jefferson, and the Opening of the American West* (New York, 1996), 296. Also see Mike Volmar, "The Dugout Canoe Project," http://www .fruitlands.org/collections/Dugout_Canoe_Article.pdf.

26. Dwight, *Travels in New England and New York*, 2:223; Robert G. Albion, *Forests and Sea Power: The Timber Problem of the Royal Navy, 1652–1862* (Cambridge, Mass., 1926), chap. 6, esp. 273–74; William Cronon, *Changes in the Land: Indians, Colonists, and the Ecology of New England* (New York, 1983), 109–10; George Tichnor to Jared Sparks, August 11, 1824, MS Sparks, 67–68.

27. John Ledyard to Eleazar Wheelock, May 23, 1773, PEW.

28. Ralph Pomeroy to Eleazar Wheelock, May 19, 1773, PEW.

29. E. Brooks Holifield, *Theology in America: Christian Thought from the Age of the Puritans to the Civil War* (New Haven, 2003), 140; also see Mark Valeri, "The New Divinity and the American Revolution," *WMQ* 46.4 (October 1989), 741–69; and id., *Law and Providence in Joseph Bellamy's New England* (New York, 1994).

30. The quotes are from a letter quoted in Sparks, *The Life of John Ledyard*, 25. For other details about Ledyard's quest for the ministry, see ibid., 24–27.

31. Richard Buel, Jr., *Dear Liberty: Connecticut's Mobilization for the Revolutionary War* (Middletown, Conn., 1980), 6; James G. Lydon, "Fish and Flour and Gold: Southern Europe and the Colonial American Balance of Payments," *Business History Review* 39.2 (Summer 1965), 171–83; John J. McCusker and Russell R. Menard, *The Economy of British America, 1607–1789* (Chapel Hill, 1985), 108–11.

32. Sparks, *The Life of John Ledyard*, 39. On New England mariners' careers more generally, see Daniel Vickers with Vince Walsh, *Young Men and the Sea: Yankee Seafarers in the Age of Sail* (New Haven, 2005), chap. 4.

33. JL to Isaac Ledyard, January 15, 1773/74, JLP, 3; Sparks, *The Life of John Ledyard*, 38–39; JL to Isaac Ledyard, January 15, 1773/74, op. cit.

34. Ledyard discusses his arrest in a memorial presented to the Connecticut General Assembly requesting copyright for his first book. The memorial is reprinted in Hellmut Lehmann-Haupt, *The Book in America: A History of the Making, the Selling, and the Collecting of Books in the United States* (New York, 1939), 88–89.

35. Ibid.

CHAPTER III. SERVING CAPTAIN COOK WITH HONOR

1. On the history of the *Resolution*, J. C. Beaglehole, *The Life of Captain James Cook* (Stanford, 1974), 280–85. For comparative statistics on the size of

contemporary naval vessels, N. A. M. Rodger, *The Wooden World: An Anatomy of the Georgian Navy* (New York, 1996), appendix 1.

2. James Kenneth Munford, ed., *John Ledyard's Journal of Captain Cook's Last Voyage* (Corvallis, Ore., 1963), 91; *JCJC*, vol. 3, part 1, 448–49. The Englishmen learned the meaning of these notes from a Russian official in May 1779. Ibid., 384 n. 1 and 672 n. 3.

3. Munford, ed., *John Ledyard's Journal*, 91–99. Ledyard spent some of his time at the Russian camp making a vocabulary of the local Aleut tongue. For other vocabularies made during the expedition, see those of the *Resolution*'s surgeon, William Anderson, and his mate, David Samwell in *JCJC*, vol. 3, part 2, 956–57, 1146–47.

4. Paybook, The *Resolution*, ADM 34/651.

5. Beaglehole, *The Life of Captain James Cook*, 188. More generally on prostitutes and disease in a port city, Simon P. Newman, *Embodied History: The Lives of the Poor in Early Philadelphia* (Philadelphia, 2003), 32–36.

6. Munford, ed., *John Ledyard's Journal*, 107; *JCJC*, vol. 3, part 2, 1083.

7. Bound into the *Resolution*'s paybook is a list, compiled by the surgeon William Anderson, of men given "venereal cures on board his Majesty's sloop the Resolution" between July 1, 1776, and August 4, 1778, and Ledyard's name appears on the second page of the list. This indicates that his treatment came before the second visit to Hawaii in January 1779. ADM 34/651.

8. Quoted in Brian Lavery, *Nelson's Navy: The Ships, Men and Organization, 1793–1815* (London, 1989), 151.

9. Richard Hough, *Captain James Cook: A Biography* (New York, 1995), 274–80.

10. *JCJC*, vol. 3, part 1, 479–80.

11. Beaglehole, *Life of Captain James Cook*, 640–42.

12. Munford, ed., *John Ledyard's Journal*, 118.

13. Ibid., 135–36; on Hawaiians being paid for their labor, see Beaglehole, *Life of Captain James Cook*, 663.

14. Beaglehole, *Life of Captain James Cook*, 669–72; Rupert T. Gould, ed., "Bligh's Notes on Cook's Last Voyage," *Mariner's Mirror* 14:4 (October 1928), 380.

15. Munford, ed., *John Ledyard's Journal*, 229–31.

16. *JCJC*, vol. 3, part 2, 1457–80 (appendix 4, "The Ships' Companies").

17. Ibid., 1564.

18. Johnson quoted by Boswell in *Boswell's Tour of the Hebrides with Samuel Johnson*, ed. Frederick A. Pottle and Charles H. Bennett (New York, 1961), 104.

19. *JCJC*, vol. 3, part 1, lxxxviii.

20. Glyn Williams, *The Prize of all the Oceans: Commodore Anson's Daring Voyage and Triumphant Capture of the Spanish Treasure Galleon* (New York, 2000), 43–46, 135.

21. Beaglehole, *Life of Captain James Cook*, 704–05.

22. Cook and James King, *Captain Cook's Third and Last Voyage to the Pacific Ocean, in the Years 1776, 1777, 1778, 1779 and 1780. Faithfully Abridged from the Quarto Edition* (Philadelphia, 1793), vi; *Gentleman's Magazine* (April 1791), 319; Cook and James King, *Voyage to the Pacific Ocean. Undertaken by the Command of His Majesty, for Making Discoveries in the Northern Hemisphere* . . . 2d ed. (London, 1785), 1:lxxxvii.

23. Also see the nearly identical characterization in Midshipman George Gilbert's journal. Add. MS 38530, p. 94.

24. *JCJC*, vol. 1, 117, and ibid., n. 4.

25. On the cultural and social distinctiveness of the eighteenth-century seafarer, see, for example, Marcus Rediker, *Between the Devil and the Deep Blue Sea: Merchant Seamen, Pirates, and the Anglo-American Maritime World, 1700–1750* (Cambridge, England, 1987); Paul Gilje, *Liberty on the Waterfront: American Maritime Culture in the Age of Revolution* (Philadelphia, 2004); and Newman, *Embodied History*, chap. 5.

CHAPTER IV. SEEKING DISTINCTION WITH THE PEN ABOARD THE *RESOLUTION*

1. Burney, *A Chronological History of North-Eastern Voyages of Discovery; and of the Early Eastern Navigations of the Russians* (London, 1819), 280. On the broader social history of knowledge, though it deals with an earlier period, a relevant discussion can be found in Steven Shapin, *A Social History of Truth: Civility and Science in Seventeenth-Century England* (Chicago, 1994). Though I do not deal with the more specific matter of precise time-telling and its relation to the authority of narrative travel accounts, it speaks to a similar point. As the technology of time-telling improved, so the authoritativeness of time-bound travel narratives grew more dependent on chronological precision. See Stuart Sherman, *Telling Time: Clocks, Diaries, and English Diurnal Form* (Chicago, 1996), esp. chap. 5.

2. For another account of young, aspiring eighteenth-century men seeking to distinguish themselves through the use of the pen, see *The Autobiography of Benjamin Franklin*, ed. Leonard W. Labaree et al. (1964; 2d ed., New Haven, 2003), 89–91. On the culture of writing and publishing in eighteenth-century Britain, John Brewer, *The Pleasures of the Imagination: English Culture in the Eighteenth Century* (New York, 1997), chap. 3.

3. *JCJC*, vol. 3, part 1, clxxvi.

4. Add. MS 8955.

5. ADM 2/1332, p. 147.

6. *JCJC*, vol. 3, part 1, clxxii–clxxiii.

7. See, for instance, two accounts of Ledyard's excursion on Unalaska by the *Resolution* midshipmen John Watts and George Gilbert; Gilbert began the voyage as an ordinary seaman aboard the *Resolution* but was promoted to midshipman. Both accounts are dated October 11, 1778, the day Ledyard returned. Watts's account: "The Capt'n understanding from natives that

there were some Russians on this Island sent two days ago one of ye corporals of marines attended by one of [sic] natives to their settlement; PM the
corporal returned with 3 Russians." ADM 51/4559, p. 83. Gilbert's account:
"The Captain understanding from some natives that there were some Russians on this Island sent two days ago one of the corporals of marines, attended by one of the natives to their settlement. PM the corporal returned
with 3 Russians." ADM 51/4559, p. 200.

8. Herman Melville, *White Jacket: or, The World in a Man-of-War* (New York,
2002), 43.

9. Glyn Williams, *Voyages of Delusion: The Quest for the Northwest Passage*
(New Haven, 2002), 112.

10. Christopher Middleton, *A Rejoinder to Mr. Dobbs's Reply to Captain Middleton*
(London, 1745), 153.

11. For a full account of the Middleton voyage and its attendant controversy,
see Williams, *Voyages of Delusion*, chaps. 2–3.

12. Burney, *Chronological History of North-Eastern Voyages of Discovery*, 280–81.
As Beaglehole so wonderfully observes of Burney's aside, "Exciting and tan-
talizing glimpse! What would we not give for a single number of either of
those weekly sheets! What wealth of literary conjecture, even with Cook's
abstention, the fleeting vision opens up!" *JCJC*, vol. 3, part 1, xc. For later
examples of these papers, see the mid-nineteenth-century example, "The
Rocket," from the *H. M. S. Minotaur*, NMM MS54/967. Also see NMM
MS72/033 and MS57/008.

13. James Kenneth Munford, ed. *John Ledyard's Journal of Captain Cook's Last
Voyage* (Corvallis, Ore., 1963), 119.

14. On Hawkesworth and his terms, *JCJC*, vol. 1, ccxlii–ccliii. On the comparative value of Hawkesworth's earnings, John Lawrence Abbott, *John Hawkesworth: Eighteenth-Century Man of Letters* (Madison, 1982), 147. On lending
libraries and the popularity of Hawkesworth, Brewer, *Pleasures of the Imagination*, 180–81.

15. *JCJC*, vol. 1, ccxliii; Abbott, *John Hawkesworth*, chap. 7.

16. *JCJC*, vol. 2, cxliii–cxlviii.

17. *JCJC*, vol. 1, cclxxxiv; *JCJC*, vol. 2, clxix; *JCJC*, vol. 3, part 1, ccxxiv.

18. James King, *A Voyage to the Pacfic Ocean: Undertaken by the Command of
His Majesty, for Making Discoveries in the Northern Hemisphere . . .* , 2d ed.
(London, 1785), 3:414–15. Also see the unofficial published journal attrib-
uted to John Rickman, *Journal of Captain Cook's Last Voyage to the Pacific
Ocean* (1781; facsimile reprint ed., Amsterdam and New York, 1967),
382–83.

19. George Gilbert, midshipman aboard *Discovery*, recalled that the officers
made "a diligent search . . . amongst the sailors." Add. MS 38530.

20. *JCJC*, vol. 1, cclvi–cclvii.

21. *JCJC*, vol. 3, part 1, ccv–ccx.

22. Add. MS 38530.

23. *JCJC*, vol. 3, part 2, 1564–65.

24. Add. MS 38530, p. 165.

CHAPTER V. FOLLOWING THE REVOLUTION HOME

1. John Warner Barber, *Connecticut Historical Collections*, 2d ed. (1849; facsimile reprint ed., Storrs, Conn., 1999), 273–79; Frances Manwaring Caulkins, *History of New London . . .* (New London, Conn., 1895), 557–68; Cass Ledyard Shaw, *The Ledyard Family in America* (Kennebunk, Maine, 1993), 15–20; Richard Buel, Jr., *Dear Liberty: Connecticut's Mobilization for the Revolutionary War* (Middletown, Conn., 1980), 272–74. The *Connecticut Gazette* is excerpted in Barber, *Connecticut Historical Collections*, 275.

2. JL to Isaac Ledyard, January 15, 1782, N-YHS.

3. Shaw, *The Ledyard Family in America*, 10. On eastern Long Island, C. C. Goen, *Revivalism and Separatism in New England, 1740–1800* (New Haven, 1962), 184–85.

4. *Gentleman's Magazine* (June 1781), 279.

5. Two other unauthorized accounts appeared before Cook's official journal, but one of them was in German and was really more of a pamphlet than a complete journal. The other appeared after Ledyard had left Britain. Heinrich Zimmermann, *Heinrich Zimmermanns von Wissloch in der Pfalz, Reise um die Welt, mit Captain Cook* (Mannheim, 1781), and William Ellis, *An authentic Narrative of a Voyage performed by Captain Cook and Captain Clerke*, 2 vols. (London, 1782).

6. James Kenneth Munford, ed., *John Ledyard's Journal of Captain Cook's Last Voyage* (Corvallis, Ore., 1963), 217–18; F. W. Howay, "Authorship of the Anonymous Account of Captain Cook's Last Voyage," *Washington Historical Quarterly* 12 (1921), 51–58.

7. A classic account of this way of thinking is Daniel J. Boorstin, *The Lost World of Thomas Jefferson* (Chicago, 1948), esp. chap. 2.

8. Munford, ed., *John Ledyard's Journal*, 56.

9. Ibid., 74–75.

10. Ibid., 57.

11. Ibid., 13.

12. Ibid., 34.

13. Ibid., 28.

14. Ibid., 29.

15. Ibid., 132–33.

16. Jared Sparks, *The Life of John Ledyard, the American Traveller* (1828; reprint, with introduction by James Zug, Mystic, Conn., 2005), 26.

17. Munford, ed., *John Ledyard's Journal*, 137.

18. Quoted in ibid., 226, from Hiram Bingham, *A Residence of Twenty-one Years in the Sandwich Islands*, 3d ed. (Hartford, 1855), 33.

19. *JCJC*, vol. 3, part 1, ccix; the other twentieth-century Cook biographer quoted in Munford, ed., *John Ledyard's Journal*, 227, from Sir Joseph Carruthers,

Captain James Cook, R. N., One Hundred and Fifty Years After (New York, 1930), 65; Marshall Sahlins, *How "Natives" Think: About Captain Cook, for Example* (Chicago, 1995), 45.

20. Munford, ed., *John Ledyard's Journal*, 38.
21. John Rickman, *Journal of Captain Cook's Last Voyage to the Pacific Ocean* (1781; facsimile reprint ed., Amsterdam, 1967), 188; Munford, ed., *John Ledyard's Journal*, 63.
22. Munford, ed., *John Ledyard's Journal*, 102.
23. John Rickman, *Journal of Cook's Last Voyage*, 121, 166.
24. Munford, ed. *John Ledyard's Journal*, 99, 156.
25. Reprinted in Hellmut Lehmann-Haupt, *The Book in America: A History of the Making, the Selling, and the Collecting of Books in the United States* (New York, 1939), 91.
26. Quoted in Mark Rose, *Authors and Owners: The Invention of Copyright* (Cambridge, Mass., 1993), 7, from William Blackstone, *Commentaries on the Laws of England* (1766; facsimile reprint ed., Chicago, 1979), 2:2.
27. John M. Huffman, "'I, as a Republican Printer': Benjamin Franklin, Printing, and the Mission to France, 1776–1785," Honors Thesis, Florida State University, November 17, 2004, esp. 30–34.
28. Hellmut Lehmann-Haupt, *Book in America*, 48–52.
29. James Boswell, *Boswell's Life of Johnson* (London, 1960), 310.
30. The memorial is reprinted in Lehmann-Haupt, *Book in America*, 89.
31. John J. McCusker, *How Much Is that in Real Money? A Historical Commodity Price Index for Use as a Deflator of Money Values in the Economy of the United States* (Worcester, Mass., 2001), 34.
32. JL to Isaac Ledyard, January 15, 1783, JLP, 7.
33. JL to Isaac Ledyard, May 1783, JLP, 8–9.
34. Munford, ed., *John Ledyard's Journal*, 70.

CHAPTER VI. FROM AUTHOR TO FUR TRADER
1. Thomas M. Doerflinger, *A Vigorous Spirit of Enterprise: Merchants and Economic Development in Revolutionary Philadelphia* (Chapel Hill, 1986), 238.
2. James King, *Captain Cook's Third and Last Voyage to the Pacific Ocean . . .* (Philadelphia, 1793), 248.
3. JL to Isaac Ledyard [June–July 1783], JLP, 11–12.
4. Clarence L. Ver Steeg, "Financing and Outfitting the First United States Ship to China," *Pacific Historical Review* 22 (February 1953), 1–12; Jonathan Goldstein, *Philadelphia and the China Trade, 1682–1846: Commercial, Cultural, and Attitudinal Effects* (University Park, Penn., 1978), esp. chap. 3.
5. Philip Chadwick Foster Smith, *The Empress of China* (Philadelphia, 1984), 35–42; Goldstein, *Philadelphia and the China Trade*, 21–22; *The Papers of Robert Morris, 1781–1784*, ed. Elizabeth M. Nuxoll and Mary A. Gallagher (Pittsburgh, 1995), appendix 1, 862.

6. *Papers of Robert Morris*, 8:859–60; Smith, *Empress of China*, 23–30.
7. MS Sparks, 36.
8. Smith, *The Empress of China*, 29–30.
9. *Papers of Robert Morris*, 8:862–66; Smith, *The Empress of China*, 44–49.
10. Ver Steeg, "First U.S. Ship to China," 9; Goldstein, *Philadelphia and the China Trade*, 29–30.
11. JL to Abigail Hempstead Moore, June 8, 1784, BPL.
12. Smith, *Empress of China*, 115–21.
13. Morison, *The Maritime History of Massachusetts 1783–1860*, 2d. ed. (Boston, 1941), 51, and more generally on the Northwest trade, chap. 4.
14. Nathaniel Cutting Journals, May 26, 1787. MHS.
15. JL to Isaac Ledyard, August 16, 1784, JLP, 15–16.
16. JL to Isaac Ledyard, August 25, 1784, JLP, 20–21.
17. JLP, 22, 25, 31, 28, 32.
18. *Don Quixote*, trans. John Rutherford (New York, 2003), 62.
19. JL to Isaac Ledyard [July 1785], N-YHS.
20. Ledyard mentions the expected duration of the plan at the beginning of the Paris journal described below in note 21; John Paul Jones to Jefferson, September 5, 1785, in *PTJ* 8:492. On Jones, see Samuel Eliot Morison, *John Paul Jones: A Sailor's Biography* (Boston, 1959), esp. chap. 18. I have also found useful the sketch in H. W. Brands, *The First American: The Life and Times of Benjamin Franklin* (New York, 2000), 577–80. On Jones in France, Durrand Echeverria, *Mirage in the West: A History of the French Image of American Society to 1815* (Princeton, 1957), 45.
21. "Descriptions of Paris," 5, N-YHS. The original journal is in the New-York Historical Society and is entitled "Descriptions of Paris, in the Handwriting of John Ledyard." An edited version that includes a section no longer with the original is in the bound JLP, 44–58. Unless otherwise indicated, subsequent page references are to the original.
22. On the Paris police, Daniel Roche, *France in the Enlightenment* (Cambridge, Mass., 1998), 653–54.
23. Darrin M. McMahon, "The Birthplace of the Revolution: Public Space and Political Community in the Palais-Royal of Louis-Philippe-Joseph D'Orleans, 1781–1789," *French History* 10:1 (1996), 16–17 and *passim*.
24. JL, "Descriptions of Paris," 1.
25. Ibid., 3.
26. Thomas Jefferson to James Currie, January 14, 1785. *PTJ* 7:605.
27. *John Ledyard's Journey through Russia and Siberia, 1787–1788*, ed. Stephen D. Watrous (Madison, 1966), 95.
28. JL, "Descriptions of Paris," 3, 6.
29. Ibid., 4.
30. Quoted in Sarah Maza, *Private Lives, Public Affairs: The Causes Celebres of Prerevolutionary France* (Berkeley, 1993), 239–40. On judicial reform in France in the 1780s, ibid., chap. 5.

31. JL, "Descriptions of Paris," 7.

32. Robert J. Allison, *The Crescent Obscured: The United States and the Muslim World, 1776–1815* (Oxford, 1995), chap. 1.

33. JL, "Descriptions of Paris," 9; Merrill Jensen, *The New Nation: A History of the United States During the Confederation, 1781–1789* (New York, 1950), 211–13.

34. Thomas Jefferson to George Rogers Clark, December 4, 1783, *PTJ* 6:371.

35. *Jonathan Carver's Travels Through America, 1766–1768*, ed. Norman Gelb (New York, 1993), 98–99, 60. John Logan Allen, "Imagining the West: The View from Monticello," in *Thomas Jefferson and the Changing West: From Conquest to Conservation* (Albuquerque and St. Louis, 1997), 3–23, and Alan Taylor, "Jefferson's Pacific: The Science of Distant Empire, 1768–1811," in *Across the Continent: Jefferson, Lewis and Clark, and the Making of America*, ed. Douglas Seefeldt et al., 16–44 (Charlottesville, 2005).

36. Thomas Jefferson to John Jay, August 14, 1785, *PTJ* 8:373–74. Also see Jefferson to John Paul Jones, August 3, 1785, ibid., 339.

37. John Paul Jones to Thomas Jefferson, October 5, 1785, *PTJ* 8:588. Also see Robin Inglis, "Lapérouse 1786: A French Naval Visit to Alaska," in *Enlightenment and Exploration in the North Pacific, 1741–1805*, ed. Stephen Haycox, James K. Barnett, and Caedmon A. Liburd, 51–53 (Seattle, 1997); and James R. Gibson, *Otter Skins, Boston Ships, and China Goods: The Maritime Fur Trade of the Northwest Coast, 1785–1841* (Seattle and Montreal, 1992), 23.

38. Gibson, *Otter Skins, Boston Ships, and China Goods*, chap. 2; Morison, *Maritime History of Massachusetts*, chap. 4.

CHAPTER VII. BECOMING A TRAVELER IN THOMAS JEFFERSON'S PARIS

1. *Letters of the Lewis and Clark Expedition with Related Documents, 1783–1854*, 2d ed., ed. Donald Jackson (Urbana, 1978), 2:588.

2. Stephen D. Watrous, ed., *John Ledyard's Journey Through Russia and Siberia, 1787–1788* (Madison, 1966), 94–95, 38 n. 7.

3. Copy of JL to Abigail Hempstead Moore, April 8, 1786, SFL. The original letter is lost. Stephen D. Watrous, ed. *John Ledyard's Journey*, 96; David Hume, *The History of England* (London, 1789), 7:225.

4. Watrous, ed., *John Ledyard's Journey*, 96.

5. Ibid., 258.

6. *The Voyage of Gregory Shelekhof* (1795; reprint, Washington, D.C., 1941), 19–20.

7. Watrous, ed. *John Ledyard's Journey*, 105–06, 128. On tattooing, Nicholas Thomas, *Cook: The Extraordinary Voyages of Captain James Cook* (New York, 2003), 78–80, and Simon P. Newman, *Embodied History: The Lives of the Poor in Early Philadelphia* (Philadelphia, 2003), 113–22. On the tattoos among the *Bounty* mutineers, Greg Dening, *Mr. Bligh's Bad Language: Passion, Power and Theatre on the Bounty* (Cambridge, England, 1992), 35–36.

8. Watrous, ed., *John Ledyard's Journey*, 39–40.

9. Ibid., 112.

10. Ibid., 118.

11. Ibid., 115.

12. Jeremy Black, *The British Abroad: The Grand Tour in the Eighteenth Century* (Stroud, 2003), chap. 7 and *passim;* John Torpey, *The Invention of the Passport: Surveillance, Citizenship, and the State* (Cambridge, England, 2000).

13. Watrous, ed., *John Ledyard's Journey,* 105.

14. JL to Abigail Hempstead Moore, April 8, 1786, SFL.

15. Watrous, ed., *John Ledyard's Journey,* 120.

16. Count Leopold Berchtold, *An Essay to direct and extend the Inquiries of Patriotic Travellers . . .* (London, 1789), 1:56. On Langborn, see the reprinted affidavit, "Langborn, Taliaferro, Throckmorton, Dixon" in *WMQ* 19:2 (October 1910), 104–07.

17. Berchtold, *An Essay to direct and extend the Inquiries of Patriotic Travellers,* 48–49.

18. Watrous, ed., *John Ledyard's Journey,* 122.

CHAPTER VIII. ACROSS THE RUSSIAN EMPIRE

1. Stephen D. Watrous, ed., *John Ledyard's Journey Through Russia and Siberia, 1787 1788, The Journal and Selected Letters* (Madison, 1966), 126.

2. Ibid., 41, 141; Basil Dmytryshyn et al., eds., *Russian Penetration of the North Pacific Ocean: A Documentary Record, 1700–1797* (Portland, 1988), 340.

3. Watrous, ed., *John Ledyard's Journey,* 146.

4. Ibid., 129.

5. W. Bruce Lincoln, *The Conquest of a Continent: Siberia and the Russians* (New York, 1994), 143–50.

6. A concise treatment of Shelikov's activities is Alan Taylor, *American Colonies* (New York, 2001), 452. Also see Lydia Black, *Russians in Alaska, 1732–1867* (Fairbanks, Alaska, 2004).

7. Captain John D'Wolf, *A Voyage to the North Pacific and a Journey Through Siberia . . . (1804–1808)* (Cambridge, Mass., 1861), 95. On traveling the Lena, see ibid., 106.

8. Watrous, ed. *John Ledyard's Journey,* 168.

9. Ibid., 170, 168.

10. Thomas Jefferson, *Notes on the State of Virginia,* ed. William Peden (Chapel Hill, 1954), 43–47, 53–54. Also, Gilbert Chinard, "Eighteenth-Century Theories of America as a Human Habitat," *Proceedings of the American Philosophical Society* 91:1 (February 1947), 27–57.

11. Watrous, ed., *John Ledyard's Journey,* 155, 156.

12. Samuel Eliot Morison, *John Paul Jones: A Sailor's Biography* (Boston, 1959), chap. 20.

13. Martin Sauer, *An Account of a Geographical and Astronomical Expedition to the Northern Parts of Russia, . . .* (London, 1802), 99–100. While Ledyard was still in Paris there was apparently some discussion about his joining the

"secret" expedition. Watrous, ed., *John Ledyard's Journey*, 39–40. Shelikov's report is in Dmytryshyn et al., eds., *Russian Penetration of the North Pacific Ocean*, 338.

14. Ibid., 337.

15. Jacobi's report is translated and reprinted in ibid., 340–43.

16. Ibid., 321.

17. Quoted in Nikolai M. Bolkhovitinov, *The Beginnings of Russian-American Relations, 1775–1815*, trans. Elena Levin (Cambridge, Mass., 1975), 161. On the reasons for Ledyard's expulsion more generally, ibid., 157–62.

18. Sauer, *An Account of a Geographical and Astronomical Expedition . . .* , 100–101.

19. Watrous, ed., *John Ledyard's Journey*, 200–201.

20. See, for instance, Marshall, *Travels Through Germany, Russia, and Poland*, 183–86. On the partitioning of Poland, see Norman Davis, *God's Playground: A History of Poland*, vol. 1: *Origins to 1795* (New York, 1982), chap. 18.

21. Watrous, ed., *John Ledyard's Journey*, 202, 204.

22. Ibid., 209–10, 231–32.

23. Ibid., 227–28. On Frederick II, Peter Gay, *The Enlightenment: The Rise of Modern Paganism* (New York, 1966), 348–49.

CHAPTER IX. DESPOTISM AND HUMAN NATURE IN CATHERINE II'S
RUSSIA

1. William Tooke, *View of the Russian Empire, During the Reign of Catherine the Second* (London, 1800), 1:260–61, 11.

2. On Yakutsk, the Yakuts, and the Russian fur trade, James Forsyth, *A History of the Peoples of Siberia: Russia's North Asian Colony 1581–1990* (Cambridge, England, 1992), *passim*; R. Bruce Lincoln, *The Conquest of a Continent: Siberia and the Russians* (New York, 1994), 62, 88, 114, and *passim*; James R. Gibson, *Feeding the Russian Fur Trade: Provisionment of the Okhotsk Seaboard and the Kamchatka Peninsula 1639–1856* (Madison, 1969); and id., *Imperial Russia in Frontier America: The Changing Geography of Supply of Russian America, 1784–1867* (New York, 1976). Mention of Greek merchants can be found in the memoir of an exiled Pole, *Memoirs and Travels of Mauritius Augustus Count de Benyowsky: Magnate of the Kingdoms of Hungary and Poland* (Dublin, 1790), 1:58.

3. Stephen D. Watrous, ed., *John Ledyard's Journey Through Russia and Siberia, 1787–1788* (Madison, 1966), 178, 177.

4. Philip Longworth, *The Cossacks* (London, 1969). There remains considerable uncertainty about the origins of the Cossacks. See Shane O'Rourke, *Warriors and Peasants: The Don Cossacks in Late Imperial Russia* (London, 2000), 21–24.

5. Watrous, ed., *John Ledyard's Journey*, 153; Voltaire, *Essai sur les moeurs* in *Oeuvres Complètes de Voltaire* (Paris, 1835), 3:583, translated and quoted in Larry Wolff, *Inventing Eastern Europe: The Map of Civilization on the Mind*

of the Enlightenment (Stanford, 1994), 298; Sauer, *Account of a Geographical and Astronomical Expedition*, 26, 65.

6. Watrous, ed., *John Ledyard's Journey*, 175; Franklin to Peter Collinson, May 9, 1753, *PBF* 4:482.

7. Quoted in William B. Hart, "Black 'Go-Betweens' and the Mutability of 'Race,' Status, and Identity on New York's Pre-Revolutionary Frontier," in *Contact Points: American Frontiers from the Mohawk Valley to the Mississippi, 1750–1830*, ed. Andrew R. L. Cayton and Fredrika J. Teute, 93 (Chapel Hill, 1998). On the cultural and ethnic landscape around Johnson Hall, ibid., esp. 101–11, and Timothy J. Shannon, "Dressing for Success on the Mohawk Frontier: Hendrick, William Johnson, and the Indian Fashion," *WMQ* 53:1 (1996), 13–42.

8. Watrous, ed., *John Ledyard's Journey*, 145.

9. Ibid., 137; *Universal Asylum and Columbian Magazine* 9 (1792), 25. Other similar reactions can be found in *Memoirs and Travels of Mauritius Augustus Count de Benyowsky*, 1:149; Capt. John Dundas Cochrane, *A Pedestrian Journey through Russia and Siberian Tartary, to the Frontiers of China, the Frozen Sea, and Kamchatka* (Edinburgh, 1829), 2:80; Marshall, *Travels Through Germany, Russia, and Poland*, 140–41. More generally on eighteenth-century views of the Orient and its allegedly corrupting influences, Edward Said, *Orientalism* (New York, 1978), esp. 118–19, and Alain Grosrichard, *The Sultan's Court: European Fantasies of the East*, trans. Liz Heron (London, 1998).

10. Watrous, ed., *John Ledyard's Journey*, 188, 164–65.

11. Bloch, "Utopianism, Sentimentalism, and Liberal Culture in America," *Intellectual History Newsletter* 24 (2002), 47–59.

12. Watrous, ed., *John Ledyard's Journey*, 181–82.

13. Vicesimus Knox, *The Spirit of Despotism* (Morristown, N.J., 1799), 13. On fears of luxury in revolutionary America, Edmund S. Morgan, "The Puritan Ethic and the American Revolution," *WMQ* 24:1 (January 1967), 3–43, and Gordon S. Wood, *The Creation of the American Republic, 1776–1787* (Chapel Hill, 1969), esp. 107–14; and, by T. H. Breen in his "Narrative of Commercial Life: Consumption, Ideology, and Community on the Eve of the American Revolution," *WMQ* 50:3 (July 1993), 471–501.

14. Watrous, ed., *John Ledyard's Journey*, 182.

15. Benjamin Franklin, "An Address to the Public: From the Pennsylvania Society for Promoting the Abolition of Slavery . . ." (1782), in J. A. Leo Lemay, ed., *Benjamin Franklin: Writings* (New York, 1987), 1155; Richardson, *Anecdotes of the Russian Empire . . .* (1784; facsimile reprint, London, 1968), 241; Abbé Raynal, *A Philosophical and Political History of the Settlements and Trade of the Europeans in the West Indies* (1781; reprint, Glasgow, 1812), 1:422.

16. On the exile system, Forsyth, *A History of the Peoples of Siberia*, 43–44. Also see the following articles by Alan Wood: "The Siberian Exile System in Tsarist Russia," *History Today* 30 (September, 1980), 19–24; "Crime and Punishment in Imperial Russia," in *Civil Rights in Imperial Russia*, ed. Olga Crisp

and Linda Edmondson, 215–33 (Oxford, 1989); and "Sex and Violence in Siberia: Aspects of the Tsarist Exile System," in *Siberia: Two Historical Perspectives*, ed. John M. Stewart and Alan Wood, 23–42 (London, 1984).

17. Watrous, ed., *John Ledyard's Journey*, 182. On moderate Anglicanism, Gerald R. Cragg, *Reason and Authority in the Eighteenth Century* (Cambridge, England, 1964), chap. 2, and Frans de Bruyn, "Latitudinarianism and Its Importance as a Precursor of Sensibility," *Journal of English and Germanic Philology* 80 (1981): 349–68. The connection between latitudinarian theology, the eighteenth-century cult of sensibility, and Ledyard's own writings is implied in Donald Davie, "John Ledyard: The American Traveler and His Sentimental Journeys," *Eighteenth-Century Studies* 4:1 (Fall 1970), 57–70.

18. Watrous, ed., *John Ledyard's Journey*, 203.

19. Ibid., 252.

20. *American Magazine*, vol. 1 (October 1788), 808; *New York Magazine; or, Literary Repository*, vol. 2 (September 1791), 491–96; *The Time Piece and Literary Companion*, vol. 1:53 (July 1797), 216.

21. Quoted in Brenda Mehan-Waters, "Catherine the Great and the Problem of Female Rule," *Russian Review* 34:3 (July 1975), 294.

22. Thomas Pownall, *Principles of Polity, being the Grounds and Reasons of Civil Empire* (London, 1752), 93–4.

23. Abbé Raynal, *A Philosophical and Political History*, 421.

24. Tobias Smollett, *Humphrey Clinker* (New York, 1967), 118–19.

25. On the interplay of race and citizenship in the American backcountry, Eric Hinderaker, *Elusive Empires: Constructing Colonialism in the Ohio Valley, 1673–1800* (Cambridge, England, 1997), chaps. 5–6. See also the related discussions in John Mack Faragher, "'More Motley than Mackinaw': From Ethnic Mixing to Ethnic Cleansing on the Frontier of the Lower Missouri, 1783–1833," in *Contact Points: American Frontiers from the Mohawk Valley to the Mississippi, 1750–1830*, ed. Cayton and Teute, 304–26; Daniel K. Richter, *Facing East from Indian Country: A Native History of Early America* (Cambridge, Mass., 2001), chap. 6.

CHAPTER X. TO AFRICA

1. John Newton, *Thoughts on the Atlantic Slave Trade*, 2d ed. (London, 1788), 14. Also, on the rise of British abolitionism, see Adam Hochschild's *Bury the Chains: Prophets and Rebels in the Fight to Free an Empire's Slaves* (Boston, 2005), and Seymour Drescher, *The Mighty Experiment: Free Labor versus Slavery in British Emancipation* (New York, 2002).

2. On slaves owned by Squire John, John Ledyard Probate Inventory, September 11, 1771, folio 9350, Hartford Probate District, Estate Papers, CSL; on use of Whitman's slave, John Ledyard Account Book, p. 26, CHS. On maritime slavery, W. Jeffrey Bolster, *Black Jacks: African American Seamen in the Age of Sail* (Cambridge, Mass., 1997), chap. 1. More generally, Philip D. Morgan, "British Encounters with Africans and African Americans, circa 1600–

1780," in *Strangers within the Realm: Cultural Margins of the First British Empire,* ed. Bernard Bailyn and Philip D. Morgan, 157–219 (Chapel Hill, 1991).

3. Thomas Jefferson, *Notes on the State of Virginia,* ed. William Peden (New York, 1972), 162.

4. James Forsyth, *A History of the Peoples of Siberia: Russia's North Asian Colony, 1581–1990* (Cambridge, England, 1992), 163–64.

5. Stephen D. Watrous, ed., *John Ledyard's Journey Through Russia and Siberia, 1787–1788, The Journal and Selected Letters* (Madison, 1966), 63–65; Peter Kolchin, *Unfree Labor: American Slavery and Russian Serfdom* (Cambridge, Mass., 1987), 39 and introduction.

6. Watrous, ed., *John Ledyard's Journey,* 176.

7. Ibid., 197.

8. For a helpful discussion of the intersection of British antislavery thought and conceptions of empire, Christopher L. Brown, "From Slaves to Subjects: Envisioning an Empire without Slavery, 1772–1834," in *Black Experience and the Empire,* ed. Philip D. Morgan and Shawn Hawkins, 111–40 (Oxford, 2004). Also, Philip D. Curtin, *The Image of Africa: British Ideas and Action, 1780–1850* (Madison, 1964), part I.

9. Robin Hallett, *The Penetration of Africa: European Exploration in North and West Afrcia to 1815* (New York, 1965), 193–98; Robin Hallett, ed., *Records of the African Association, 1788–1831* (London, 1964), esp. chap. 1.

10. Hallett, ed., *Records of the African Association,* 54–55.

11. Ibid., 62.

12. Watrous, ed. *John Ledyard's Journey,* 167.

13. Ibid., 254–55.

14. Drescher, *The Mighty Experiment,* chap. 5, esp. 80–81.

15. Watrous, ed., *John Ledyard's Journey,* 247.

16. Ibid., 248–49, 250 n. 16.

17. JL to Jefferson, November 15, 1788, *PTJ* 14:182.

18. *Proceedings of the Association for Promoting the Discovery of the Interior Parts of Africa* (London, 1790), 33.

19. Ibid., 30–32.

20. Hallett, ed., *Records of the African Association,* 60. David Brion Davis, *Slavery and Human Progress* (New York, 1984), 301–04.

21. JL to Jefferson, August 15, 1788, *PTJ* 13:517; JL to Jefferson, September 10, 1788, *PTJ* 13:595–96.

22. JL to Jefferson, November 15, 1788, *PTJ* 14:181.

23. Excerpted in Thomas Paine to Jefferson, June 17, 1789, *PTJ* 15:193–94.

24. JL to Jefferson, September 10, 1788, *PTJ* 13:595; Stephen Cathalan, Jr., to Jefferson, November 17, 1788, *PTJ* 14:184–85; Jefferson to Stephen Cathalan, Jr., November 25, 1788, *PTJ,* ibid., 286.

25. Jefferson to William Short, February 28, 1789, *PTJ* 14:597; Jefferson to Benjamin Vaughan, May 17, 1789, *PTJ* 15:134; Jefferson to Thomas Paine, May 19

and 21, 1789, ibid., 137; Thomas Paine to Jefferson, June 17, 1789, ibid.,
193–94.

26. Thomas Paine to Jefferson, June 18, 1789, *PTJ* 15:198.

EPILOGUE: MEMORIES OF THE TRAVELER

1. *The Pennsylvania Packet, and Daily Advertiser* (July 16, 1789), 2; *The Berkshire Chronicle*, vol. 2 (August 10, 1789), *The Autobiographies of Noah Webster: From the Letters and Essays, Memoir, and Diary*, ed. Richard M. Rollins (Columbia, S.C., 1989), 268.

2. *The Federal Gazette and Philadelphia Evening Post* (October 1, 1790), 2; *American Mercury*, vol. 7 (October 4, 1790), 2; *Connecticut Gazette*, vol. 27 (October 8, 1790), 1; *Gazette of the United States*, vol. 2 (October 9, 1790), 621; *Herald of Freedom*, vol. 5 (October 12, 1790), 33; *Salem Gazette* (October 12, 1790), 2; *Newport Herald*, vol. 4 (October 14, 1790), 2; *Supplement to the Georgia Gazette* (November 11, 1790), 1; *Universal Asylum and Columbian Magazine*, vol. 6 (June, 1791), 393–96; *New York Magazine; or, Literary Repository*, vol. 2 (September 1791), 491–96; *Lady's Magazine*, vol. 1 (1791), 393–95; *Massachusetts Magazine*, vol. 4 (February 1792), 94–95. This is only a partial selection of periodicals in which Beaufoy's obituary appeared. For a more complete list, see the Readex, online database, *Archive of Americana: Early American Newspapers, Series I, 1690–1876*. Among the papers in which the *Connecticut Courant* obituary appeared are *Daily Advertiser*, vol. 6 (October 8, 1790), 2, and *Burlington Advertiser, or Agricultural and Political Intelligencer*, vol. 1 (October 19, 1790).

3. Isaac Ledyard to Joseph Banks, January 29, 1790, DCL. A copy of Banks's reply is included with the original letter.

4. *The Prose of Philip Freneau*, ed. Philip M. Marsh (New Brunswick, 1955), 199.

5. On Freneau's politics, Stanley Elkins and Eric McKitrick, *The Age of Federalism: The Early American Republic, 1788–1800* (New York, 1993), 239–40.

6. For example, *Time Piece, and Literary Companion*, vol. 1 (July 28, 1797), 240, and *City Gazette and Daily Advertiser*, vol. 15 (August 23, 1797), 3.

7. The publication history of Ledyard's papers is expertly recounted in Stephen D. Watrous, ed., *John Ledyard's Journey Through Russia and Siberia, 1787–1788: The Journal and Selected Letters* (Madison, 1966), introduction and chap. 4.

8. Jared Sparks, *The Life of John Ledyard, the American Traveler* (1828; reprint, with introduction by James Zug, Mystic, Conn., 2005), 214.

9. *American Quarterly Review*, vol. 3 (March, 1828), 90–91. Also, *Southern Review*, vol. 2 (November, 1828), 383–409; *Christian Spectator*, vol. 2 (June, 1828), 317–28; *The Spirit of the Pilgrims*, vol. 1 (September 1828), 486–92; *North American Review*, vol. 27 (October 1828), 360–72. The publication of Sparks's book also prompted magazines to publish glowing synopses of Ledyard's life. See, for instance, "John Ledyard," in *The Friend; A Religious and Literary Journal*, vol. 1 (March 8, 1828), 165, and ibid. (March 15, 1828),

169–70; and "The American Traveller," in *New York Telescope*, vol. 4 (April, 12, 1828), 183.

10. See, for example, *The Works of Hubert Howe Bancroft*, vol. 28: *History of the Northwest Coast* (San Francisco, 1884), 2:2; *The Works of Hubert Howe Bancroft*, vol. 33: *History of Alaska* (San Francisco, 1886), 212 n. 38; and "Restive Lads," *Ohio Farmer* (July 29, 1871), 475. On the steamboat, *New-Hampshire Sentinel*, vol. 33 (June 24, 1831), 3.

11. "John Ledyard," *The Yale Literary Magazine: Conducted by the Students of Yale University* (June 1851), 318; the Yale copy of Sparks is in the Newberry Library, Chicago.

12. www.dartmouth.edu/~doc/shrines/johnledyard/.

INDEX

Rivington, James, 96
Roberts, Henry, 57, 70
Roberts, Thomas, 60
Robertson, William, *Charles V,* 76
Roosevelt, Theodore, 192
Rousseau, Jean-Jacques, 88, 91, 156, 161
Rowlandson, Thomas, *81*
Russia: diversity in, 155–59, 164; and fur
   trade, 139–41, 147; governance of, 153–
   55, 161–63, 166–67, 169; incoherence of,
   166–67; Ledyard's journey across, 1–2,
   124–52, *138;* Ledyard's opinion of, 152–
   56, 160–64, 168–69; luxury as characteristic of, 159–60; Pacific designs of,
   77, 137, 139, 147; and Poland, 149; serfdom in, 158, 172; slavery in, 162–63,
   167; travel permission in, 136–37, 139,
   146–48. *See also* Russians
Russian America, 137, 147, 148
Russian American Company, 141
Russian Orthodox Church, 164
Russians: dependency of, 153; Indians
   compared to native, 145; Ledyard's
   meeting with, in Unalaska, 47–51;
   moral corruption of, 160–66, 169

sacrifice, 89
Sahlins, Marshall, 93
sailors. *See* seamen
Samwell, David, 53
Sancho Panza, Ledyard compared to,
   111–12
Sands, Comfort, 105
Sandwick, Earl of, 53, 77, 81
Saturday's Club, 174, 176
Sauer, Martin, 148, 157
science, 183
scientific data: gathered from voyages,
   4–5, 72; Ledyard's method of gathering,
   1–2, 127
Scottish Missionary Society, 28
scurvy, 65
seamen, 64, 67–68, 128–29
Sea Otter (ship), 123
serfdom, Russian, 158, 172. *See also*
   slavery: Russian
Sewall, Samuel, 10
sex: in Hawaiian islands, 53–54, 92;

Ledyard and, 53, 115, 151; in Palais-Royal,
   Paris, 115
Seymour, Thomas (Ledyard's uncle),
   18–20, 34–35
Seymour, William (Ledyard's cousin),
   35–36, 84
Shakespeare, William, 111
Shelikov, Grigorii, 128, 141–42, 146–49
Sherlock, Thomas, 164
Short, William, 117
Siberia, 140–42, 145
skin color, human difference and, 156–58,
   178
slavery: abolition of, 170–71; domestic
   versus global, 181; effects of, 162–63,
   171–72; Ledyard and, 171–72, 181; racial
   theories and, 179; Russian, 162–63, 167
smallpox, 12, 141, 150–51
Smith, Adam, 88, 161
Smith, Samuel Stanhope, 88
Smith, William Stephens, 130–31, 137,
   139–40, 170
Smollett, Tobias, *Humphrey Clinker,* 167
sodomy, 92
Spain, Pacific designs of, 77
Sparks, Jared, 7, 23, 31, 36, 40, 92–93, 98,
   189–90
Stamp Tax, 18, 26
Stephens, John Lloyd, 192
Sterne, Laurence, 164
Stewart, George, 60
St. Petersburg, Russia, 136, 139
St. Petersburg, Treaty of (1772), 149
Stuart, Andrew, 176
subscriptions, prepublication, 96

Tahitians: government of, 89–90; religion
   of, 88–89; tattooing by, 129; venereal
   disease among, 53
Tartars, 156–57, 173
tattooing, 1, 127–29
tea, Chinese, 100, 103
Thoughts on the Atlantic Slave Trade
   (Newton), 171
Tillotson, John, 164
*Time Piece and Literary Companion,
   The,* 165
Tongan Islanders, 90–91